TIME AND ITS END:
A Comparative Existential Interpretation of Time and Eschatology

Howard A. Slaatte

University Press of America™

Library of Congress Catalog Card Number: 80-7814

To my father and mother

FOREWORD

"That religion will conquer," said philosopher Alfred North Whitehead, "which can render clear to popular understanding some eternal greatness incarnate in the passage of temporal fact." "Religion," said theologian Harris Franklin Rall, "is the life of the Eternal in the midst of time." If these statements taken together are equated with neither total immanence nor an exclusive transcendence, they may serve to characterize the dialectic of time, eternity and the end set forth in this work with the support of what is basic to the thought of Nicholas Berdyaev. Berdyaev gives us some of the most poignant clues to the understanding of time and its end from the standpoint of man's concrete existence in the workaday world.

This book is an attempt to crystallize and apply that dialectic and show in comparison, especially with other existential views of the problem, how Berdyaev helps make it vital to a philosophy of existence, the meaning of human destiny and the interpretation of the Christian revelation. Without endeavoring to congeal Berdyaev's over-all philosophy, the undertaking is confined to the central problem of time and its end. As a comparative approach it offsets the views of Kierkegaard and Barth in the main body of the work even as it seeks to disclose and correct the weaknesses of several other thinkers, notably Bultmann and Cullmann, in the later chapters.

In general, the project stands on the border between philosophy and theology and communicates with both. In so doing it reckons seriously with a persistent philosophical problem in relation to what is deemed to be a necessary theological answer. Thus, the movement of thought is largely from philosophy to theology, the meeting point being one of a balanced existential perspective. Part II increasingly elaborates the theological answer in the light of New Testament eschatology and its implications. Included in both Parts I and II are historical backgrounds of the basic issues at stake, together with delineations and appraisaals of various thinkers in view of Berdyaev's dialectics. These are meant to show the developments in the philosophies which have dealt with the problem of time; to vivify the issues involved with respect for their contexts; to abbreviate the systems of thought under surveillance; and to anticipate matters essential to the unfolding of the thesis as related to Berdyaev and as pertinent to much in contemporary thought.

An apologia for the writer's style and approach seems apropos. The editorial "we" is employed freely. Softening the writer's role as an "I specialist," it also means he is engaged as more than a spectator. Even objective observations deserve appraisal. To exist is to choose, take sides or make commitments, as Kierkegaard intimated, and a neutral reason is artificial, as Berdyaev suggested. In Chapters IV and V Berdyaev is poised between Kierkegaard and Barth mainly to sharpen certain aspects of the argument so as to give reply to the one and anticipate the discussion with the other. In Chapter VI modern teleologists are given systematic treatment to show how Berdyaev addresses himself to their interests without capitulating to their limitations, a matter relevant to contemporary eschatologies. Also, Berdyaev's *Essai de Métaphysique Eschatologique* is given priority to its English translation, though the latter, entitled *The Beginning and End,* has influenced the documentation in some places. Much the same applies to Karl Barth's *Die Kirchliche Dogmatik.*

Much of the material is akin to lectures delivered in the graduate division of Temple University School of Theology. I am indebted to many. A special word of appreciation is extended to Dr. Carl Michalson of Drew University for counsel at certain points when the undertaking assumed the form of a Ph.D. thesis; and also to Dr. Evgueny Lambert and Dr. Nicolas Zernov of Oxford for enhancing my understanding of Berdyaev at points, especially relative to the spirit of Russian philosophy and theology. What I owe to my family cannot be measured, especially to my good wife Mildred who typed the manuscript. In addition, the personnel of many libraries during the past decade, especially at Drew University, Temple University, University of Michigan, University of Chicago, New York Public, Union Seminary, Princeton Seminary, Garrett Biblical Institute; Hoyt in Saginaw, Dow in Midland and the Public in Alpena, Michigan; Bibliothèque Nationale and Sainte-Geneviève of the Sorbonne in Paris; University of Oslo; British Museum and Dr. Lincoln Libraries in London; Cambridge University Library;

the Bodleian, the Camera, Pusey House, Mansfield College, and other libraries of Oxford. I shall be happy to supply complete bibliographical data to readers who request it.

Also, may I extend my appreciation to the Bross Foundation of Lake Forest College, whose judges of their 1961 national prize contest placed the manuscript in the finals.

HOWARD A. SLAATTE

ACKNOWLEDGMENTS

The author gratefully acknowledges permissions to quote from the books named.

To E. P. Dutton & Co., Inc., New York for the quotations from the Everyman's Library Edition of *The Confessions of St. Augustine*, translated by E. B. Pusey, D.D.

To Harper and Brothers, New York, for the quotations from *Man, the Unknown*, by Alexis Carrel; from *The Beginning and the End* by Nicolas Berdyaev; and from *Apostolic Teaching* by C. H. Dodd.

To Longmans, Green and Co., Ltd., London, for the quotation from *Time and Eternity in Christian Thought* by F. H. Brabant.

To The Macmillan Co., New York, for the quotations from *Dream and Reality* by Nicolas Berdyaev, and from *The Meaning of Revelation* by Richard Niebuhr.

To Charles Scribner's Sons, New York, for the quotations from *Christianity* by Harris Franklin Hall; *Church Dogmatics* by Karl Barth; *Slavery and Freedom* by Nicolas Berdyaev; and *The Nature and Destiny of Man* by Reinhold Niebuhr.

To the Society for Promoting Christian Knowledge, London, for the quotation from *Theology of Crisis* by Ulrich Simon.

To Olin A. Lewis for the quotations from *The Creator and the Adversary* by Edwin Lewis, published by Abingdon Press, Nashville, Tenn.

To Geoffrey Bles Ltd. London, for the quotations from *The Meaning of History* by Nicolas Berdyaev.

To The Westminster Press, Philadelphia, for the quotation from *The Eternal Hope* by Emil Brunner.

CONTENTS

PART I

THE EXISTENTIAL MEANING OF TIME

Chapter I

EXISTENTIAL TIME AND ITS CONCRETE PROBLEM

Time is a problem which literally plagues our existence. The tick and chime of the clock, the calendar on the wall, the date-book on the desk, the metronome on the piano, the sundial in the garden, the season of the year, the schedule for the day—all serve to remind us of time.

Not only does time tend to enslave the average person to its imposing demands but it tends to baffle the most astute minds that seek to understand it. The problem of time is one of life's subtlest and profoundest, having been an enigma to Western philosophers and theologians for at least twenty-five centuries. Perhaps St. Augustine spoke for every generation of thinkers when he said, "What then is time? If no one asks me, I know: If I wish to explain it to one that asketh, I know not . . ."[1] He then added, ". . . or is it perchance that I know not how to express what I know?"[2] Augustine is to be credited for seeing time as indigenous to a person's concrete existence. He did not shrink from this tremendous problem, nor should we.

An Existential Problem and Perspective

Time must be reckoned with, for it is something which pervades every aspect of human thought and activity. It is this which makes it an "existential" problem, a matter of personal existence. Not limited to theories reserved for books, laboratories and classrooms, but a matter of Mr. Everyman's down-to-earth, concrete existence, time cannot be ignored if human existence, our very own in fact, is to be found meaningful. Time is a mystery that demands penetration. While ever so elusive conceptually, it is just as tenacious and real experientially. It can neither be sloughed off as imaginary nor be isolated like a chemical element. It sticks to one's selfhood like tartar to his

17

teeth. A matter of profoundly personal concern, we cannot step outside of time to analyze or inspect it. We are always involved in it like the dust on our shoes and the perspiration on our skin. It belongs to us in a way that eludes an objective pinning down. It is more like breathing in your own breath than whiffing your feet or sizing up your waistline. Time is a part of one's very self.

Time has a remarkable depth dimension that makes some days and nights, even moments, seem like little eternities, yet, too, a strange relativity that makes other minutes and hours, even days, like effervescent atoms. The watched pot almost characterizes the one, the soda glass the other. Under the pressures of routine and schedule, time seems to climb stealthily aboard like a pirate, only to steal treasures of thought and energy, on the one hand, and to steer a constraining course, on the other. Under intense emotional strain or misgiving, time sometimes proves itself a healing balm to the inner-torn self when memories of the past, reassurances of the present and hopes for the future qualify life's tempo and tension. Under the soothing hours of sleep or rest, time's pseudo measurements startle us almost into cursing the day the alarm clock was invented. But, once awake, we think perhaps it is for the best and march forth to face the day as a self-invested enterprise with problems to be met and overcome.

Not enough, then, to think of time as an abstract essence of some kind or even a cosmic force or stuff that shapes our lives and destinies without our concern. It is too close to us for that kind of intellectual comfort! Time involves us even as we involve time. This perspective means that, however related to the cosmic process, time is to be regarded as a fundamental constituent of a person's concrete existence. It belongs to his total situation as a thinking, feeling, choosing, imagining, fearing and yearning *self*. Unless otherwise specified, this will be what we shall mean by "time" throughout this essay. First and foremost, it is a problem of the self in his everyday existence.

Not alien to life as it is lived intensively in this world, but very much a part of it, time is not a mere theory or abstraction, then, but a problem and reality intrinsic to our personal existence in the workaday world. In this respect, we cannot extricate ourselves from time but must come firmly to grips with it, and do so from within our existence, not from without. What we call the existential perspective of time questions, therefore, the finality or adequacy of any abstract or arbitrary notion of time which leaves it merely an objective entity, whether conceived idealistically or empirically. To project time beyond a man's down-to-earth self and existence is a misleading rationalization. It fails to do justice to the particularity and meaning of personal life in the arena of daily toil and tragedy, conflict and choice. Time is not to be interpreted apart from the interpreter, the knowing *self* immersed in such an existence. To refuse to acknowledge this is to jeopardize the reality of time and its consequence to our personal existence, the only existence we can claim to know. Augustine was perhaps the first thinker to see this problem of understanding time from within one's own relationship with it, a matter as real today as in the fifth century. As Daniel Lamont has stated, "I am so wedded to Time that I cannot adopt the observer-attitude toward it."[3] Such is the existential problem and perspective. The self is steeped in its own problem of time. To ponder the subtlety of the present is to begin to confirm this. To know the throes of ethical, domestic and vocational decision is to be convinced of it.

These assertions are meant to describe the stark reality of time in relation to human existence and its perspective. As a perennial problem of knowledge and experience it belongs, consequently, to our own perspective as we attempt to penetrate some of its mysteries and their meaning to human life and destiny. There are other approaches to time which will be touched upon; however, only the existential approach takes this point of view seriously. It respects a person's situation and outlook, his universe of discourse and posing of the question. It sees the concrete knowing subject at the very heart of a time-imbued existence. This is exceedingly important to a position which takes seriously the meaning of persons.

"Truth is subjectivity," said Soren Kierkegaard, the titular father of existentialism. "Subjectivity is reality,"[4] he added. Nicholas Berdyaev, whose view of time and the end we shall keep before us, put it this way: "Personality is an existential center, which can be expressed neither in terms of society nor in terms of nature; it is solely the subject, not the object."[5] Only a *person*, a knowing subject who exists concretely with all the particularity and intensity of a whole self, can know reality, and this includes time. Existence always belongs to a knowing person. Such a person is a particular self, not an abstract or ideal Man in the form of an ideational universal such as meets us in the writings of many idealistic philosophers and poets, but *a man* who can say "me," i.e., any and every man with a name who has not run away from himself or explained away his selfhood. Alfred, Lord Tennyson broached this perspective of personal existence in these lines from *In Memoriam*, xliv;

> The baby new to earth and sky
> What time his tender palm is prest
> Against the circle of the breast,
> Has never thought that "this is I:"
> But as he grows he gathers much.
> And learns the use of "I," and "me,"
> And finds "I am not what I see,
> And other than the things I touch."

To enlarge this existential problem and perspective, may we take note of Berdyaev's statement, "I cannot be an object in relation to myself."[6] This connotes that what is real, including a relevant time, pertains to such a knower. It matters primarily "in here," not "out there." While this is not to deny objects, it says "existence cannot be an object of knowledge."[7] Cognition itself is a creative event within the subject who exists. This includes the cognition of time. Cognition is not to be objectified beyond the existing subject. Epistemologically, this lends pertinence to the dictum of Socrates: "Know thyself." The down-to-earth self is the crossroads of all relevant truth, ethical decision and temporal tension.

This perspective of existence challenges the classical idea of Plato that the thinking person must be a "spectator" removed objectively from what is observed. In his *Sophist* (I, 216, c) Plato depicts Socrates referring to some philosophers who "go from city to city surveying from a height the life beneath them . . ." They "visit the cities beholding from above life of those below." Actually, this is characteristic of the mere spectator and his aesthetic outlook on things. Similarly, we challenge Aristotle's more consistent refusal to relate the relevance of the object to the subject, to be touched upon in the next chapter. Likewise, the view of complete scientific detachment must be

20

called in question, for a person interested in the whole truth must be a positive participant in the struggle of existence and see things like time from *within*, especially where their meaning and relevance are sought. A monsignor cannot interpret marriage adequately when he knows nothing about it from within; nor can a sister-in-law counsel the raising of children when she has none herself; nor can a parent be at his best when he forgets that a child's problem is as big to the child as an adult's is to him. Spectators and participants, respectively, have a much different view of things. King Charles at Chester watched from the tower on the city wall as his men waged battle in the meadow below. The king's men and horses were living far more authentically than the king! Upon visiting the historic site in England one is reminded of how unrealistic, noncommittal and pedestrian much rational thought proves to be. It is not geared to the *concrete* existence of the individual, *whole* self.

In contrast to the objective, rational approach, existential thinkers like Kierkegaard and Berdyaev draw closer to truth by rubbing elbows with the world of experience from within, not just from without. They resort to no immunity here. For them, where a man stands affects what he sees and how he sees it. With Heidegger they see that to remove oneself from his concrete situation, his *Dasein* or "being there,"[8] is to obscure the truth. Almost any problem including that of time is involved here. Time, its cognition, interpretation and consequence, is related profoundly to the knowing subject's orientation. Time is a problem of far-reaching significance for existence and cannot be dealt with meaningfully from a position of remote neutrality. The thinker is steeped in his problem and his problem in him. Nicholas Berdyaev is right, "A neutral reason is fiction." The man of existence cannot project himself legitimately into a protected wall-tower of pure, neutral reason or naked objectivity. To objectify man from his *Dasein* is to reduce him to something less than man, as Heidegger has pointed out.[9] Such a practice may suit pompous protected kings but not the king's men!

Time, then, is not a matter of aesthetic neutrality, for it belongs to a concrete existence of much intensity and necessary commitments.[10] "To exist is to choose," said Kierkegaard. The setting is no wall-tower of cool detachment, but a field of heated struggle. Unless the tensions of time are given meaning on this level they have no meaning, for they cannot be relevant to men save as they are authentically involved.

The big question before us, then, is not "What legitimate theory of time may be held?" but, "What is the *meaning* of time?" And to ask this is to inquire, "What does time mean *to me*, the inquiring, personal subject and participant in concrete existence?" By "meaning" here we imply more than a mere objective explication, for it entails the personal dimension of relevance and consequence to *me*, my existence and destiny. Time is significant and consequential only from such a standpoint. It is the existential perspective taken by one who is removed or aloof from neither the question nor the problem behind it. Thus Berdyaev has shrewdly shown that man is not simply in time, but time is in man. Philosophically, time is not objective but subjective. But by "subjective" here we do not mean to limit reality to subjective ideas in a Berkeleyan manner,[11] rather to aver that the knowledge and relevance of time belong to the concrete self-in-existence. This involves the *whole* self, not just his power to reason. Bishop Berkeley's subjective idealism was in error at this point to the extent that he even equated time with its measure.[12] This Aristotelian notion could only continue to help enslave men to an artificial time by equating what is subjective with what is objectified, as though the calendar and clock yielded time or an equation thereof.

It is just as fallacious, or more so, to ontologize time so as to postulate it beyond the knower as something "out there" either in the natural process, the material order or in the ideational order of ultimate being. Berdyaev has rightly shown that here is one area in which the rationalists are prone to falsify time and, consequently, much of human existence. We might say that a man does not find himself swimming in a quasi-objective essence labeled "time"; rather, he finds time and related problems nettling his consciousness from within his experimental situation as a normal full-scoped person. Time confronts him from within his consciousness, not from without. Since centered in the knowing person who exists, time is more than a matter of rational speculation, more than an intuition, idea, concept or percept; it is far more than a logical deduction or inducement. Belonging to all experience or to a complex combination of experiences, time would be more apt to answer to all of these and much more. It belongs to any and all experience that contributes to a person's particularity or "being there." It involves the irrational factors of emotion, imagination, creativity, anxiety, anticipation and intuition just as much as the processes and products of reason, if not more so. Whatever factors contribute to the *self* and his *total* existence contribute to his experience and knowledge of time. To *exist* is to have actual or real being both spiritually and materially, morally and rationally. "Existence" is an emergence of selfhood the root meaning of which is "to cause to stand." Martin Heidegger suggests that it also includes the self-consciousness of "standing apart from." This implies the self's capacity to transcend things, as well as itself, to some extent. Time, then, is a product of the whole self in experience. Reason and its working sense data cannot yield it, for they are but parts of *a man*, who in turn, is either a *whole* self or no self.

Even physicist Martin Johnson is sensitive to this problem of time's relation to the whole knower of existence. Speaking *qua* physicist, he is reluctant to concede that time is subjective in this sense, while, speaking *qua* man and philosopher, he must assert, "On the other hand, we never quite evade the feeling that some personalities are less subject to the dominion of Time than other personalities."[13] Having in mind the poet, lover and worshipper, Johnson concedes, to the support of an existential position, that some people "realise Aeternitas within their own time." Recognizing this paradox Johnson speaks of time as something ". . . we must accept logically and supplement imaginatively."[14] This is quite existential. It reminds us of what Albert Einstein, author of the theory of relativity, would say to his neighbors. As his hand pointed from his head to his heart, he remarked, "Somehow what I think here does not always agree with how I feel in here." Time is just such a problem with that kind of relevance to life as confronted in this world. It pertains to what Rudolf Allers, Viennese psychologist, referred to when he said that human nature is the mystery with which science both begins and ends.[15] What is said here of science must also be said of philosophy and religion. A thinking self cannot escape his selfhood-in-its-situation. Thought, even of time, is attached to one's concrete existence as a person.

The existential view of time belongs also to what Nicholas

Berdyaev deemed "the philosopher's tragic situation."[16] The specific problems of thought with which a thinker deals are as much a part of himself, or his existence, as his personal anxieties and aspirations. To treat them otherwise is to retreat from the milieu of daily conflict and decision, the realm of realistic existence, to the pressbox of secondhand understanding and speculation. Time as a problem is much more real and intense to the signal-calling, ball-toting quarterback on the gridiron of struggle and crucial decision than it is to the cheering or jeering spectator in the grandstand. Detached appraisal is different from personal involvement, participation and commitment. Unless this point of view is given due consideration we are in danger of obscuring our problem by being obsessed with artificial concepts of time and ideas which fail to shed light on the meaning of human existence, history and destiny. Thus, in this undertaking, we are engulfed admittedly in the very problem we seek to understand. The chime of the tower clock, as we write or read, the noon whistle and the passing bus are irksome reminders. This demands all the more that *time* and *its end* be understood as consistently as possible from within our own time-imbued existence, not from without. Again, this makes time an existential matter, one which "must be interpreted perspectively from within itself," as Lamont puts it, since "it belongs to the subject side of existence." Lamont is right here. "No man can get outside it to observe it."[17]

The pursuit of the meaning of time must include the endeavor to uncover the meaning of our existence. Centering in the knowing and existing self, then, is to recognize man as a subject of everyday life and a maker of history as well as a creature and contributor to destiny—his own and that of the world. This is especially true of an approach which looks with profound respect to the basic views of Berdyaev on this matter. Such an existential perspective eventually turns our attention to a distinctive type of religious philosophy, one which does not stop with an empirical or rational theory but which finds concrete existence illuminated by a depth-dimension of eternity. The existential personalism of Nicholas Berdyaev is most provocative in this respect. The recognized Russian thinker, who was once aligned with Soviet Communism but was led to Christianity through philosophy and its unanswered questions, could say,

"The problem of time may very well be the fundamental problem of philosophy, especially the philosophy of existence."[18] Could there be a problem "closer to home" than this? It helps account for the eschatological motif in most of Berdyaev's writings; the classic problems of being and becoming are posed in terms of time and eternity rather than in abstract ontology.

Why do we look with special respect to Berdyaev? The basic answer is that as a religious existentialist he helps us communicate with both philosophy and theology. He is one thinker who has seen how the persistent problems of philosophy which go unanswered demand theological answers. Such is the problem of time. The counterpart to this is that insights derived from this communication can do much to help clarify the important eschatological issues in Christian theology. The outline of thought in our present undertaking reflects this concern; it moves from classical to modern insights in philosophy to theological and eschatological principles in the Bible.

Time is a basic problem of existence for at least three reasons: first, time is intrinsic to the activity, thought and decisions of the person; second, since the concrete knower is at the heart of existence, existence *per se* is a scene of considerable tragedy and trial, comedy and error, failure and opportunity, all profoundly related to time; third, since man is a creature confronted also by eternity, time and its supratemporal seat of meaning are essential to the meaning of human destiny and the end of time itself.

With these factors in mind, existence is seen to have both a temporal and religious orientation. Only the existing subject can ask: "What does time mean?" Only the person of such a realistic and intense situation can inquire: "What difference does time make to me, my life in this world and my very destiny?" To come at our problem with this in mind is not to rest content with a pseudo-objective or idealistic theory of time's essence, but to seek its consequence to the life problems of the average person. Impressive as a theory may be, if it speculatively ontologizes time beyond the man of down-to-earth existence, it serves only to falsify time and to leave its intrinsic problems meaningless to the existing self. Such a view remains irrelevant. Unless one's view of time enhances the meaning of his existence, it remains sterile of any consequence to his vocation and destiny.

25

Partly under inspiration from Berdyaev, the present study seeks to show how this issue pertains to most of the outstanding theories of time which have been crystallized in the history of thought. Other views will be dealt with comparatively in terms of what they may or may not contribute to an existential answer to the problems before us. The fundamental question behind this will be: What bearing does a certain view of time have on the existence of men in their specific, mundane situations? And, what significance does it have for the meaning of history, the destinies of men and the course of the world?

An Existential Purpose and Procedure

With the problem and perspective set forth, we may undertake the comparative study as one involving a thesis centered about two rudimentary questions in Parts I and II, respectively. (1) What is the existential meaning of time? (2) What is its eschatological dimension? The one pertains to the problem of human existence, the other to that of destiny, while each involves the other. Our over-all purpose is to show how principles derived from the biblical revelation illuminate the basic problems of time and its end. But this demands conversation between the philosophical and theological disciplines. We shall find this possible under our claim to a balanced existential view, one which makes for communication without submerging either the philosopher's role or the biblical truth.

Germane questions left unanswered by various philosophies will be seen to have important theological answers. Something more than a monologue in either camp will be needed. This means a dialectical dialogue, yet not one implying a rational synthesis but a reciprocal *diastasis* with mutual regard for the differences. This dialectic implies neither dichotomy nor fusion but legitimate tension among mutually relevant opposites. An improved view of time and history is needed in contemporary thought. We shall endeavor to articulate it through an adjusted existential view of time and its end. The contributions of Berdyaev will be set in bas relief against those of other existentialists, classical philosophers, teleologists and contemporary biblical eschatologists so as to help correct the deficiencies and extremisms of each.

The specified thesis is this: Nicholas Berdyaev proffers us *an existential view of time which, unlike other claims to the existential perspective, holds together eternity and time without jeopardizing the reality and role of either.* This implies such principles as the following: (a) The clue to this unity-in-duality is found in the Incarnate Christ. (b) Lending significance to time and its end, this also provides a realistic time base for eschatology. (c) It implies, too, that while time without eternity is meaningless, there is equal danger in positing an eternity **aloof from, or immune to, time, lest it be static, on the one hand,** or irrelevant to historical existence, on the other.

That the stated contention might be more of a guide for the build-up of the arguments in the following chapters it would be necessary to divulge some of the main points to be treated subsequently. 1. We shall look with special concern to Berdyaev, because his view of time unfolds the eschatological potential of existential time so as to allow it a dynamic eternal quality of special significance to the present moment as well as to the end of time. 2. This is handled in such a way as to preserve both the temporal and the eternal aspects of existential time and the end without negating the reality of either historic or cosmic time. 3. This enhances the relation of time to destiny, first by relating the "existential moment" and the "existential end" to a dynamic eternity which is not timeless, and second by relating them to a realistic, historic time which is neither illusory, restricted to the present, nor identified with chronological measurement.

In this respect, our project is a study while being more than a study; it is a thesis with a stage-by-stage, facet-by-facet development and defense of the two main strands of the central issue of time and its end as related to a meaning-giving eternity. Beginning with a background of existential insights into time within classical and modern philosophy, it builds up and unfolds what we see to be the solution to the basic issues at stake. The basic clues are proffered us by Berdyaev's eschatological existentialism and its relevance to the Christian view of existence and the end. The analyses and appraisals are treated in comparison with various outstanding existential and what we shall call pre-existential views, and in special comparison with certain modern teleological views of time and the end. The teleological

27

views will be shown defective and driven to make concessions which we deem pertinent to an eschatological interpretation of the cosmos.

Leading Christian "existentialists" besides Berdyaev to be given serious consideration include Augustine, Soren Kierkegaard, Karl Barth, Rudolf Bultmann, Emil Brunner and Paul Tillich. Barth will be considered principally because of his views on eternity. Those whom we describe as "pre-existentialists" will be considered for their partial or potential insights into time which are of existential character. Plato, Plotinus and Kant fall into this category. Contemporary theologians of existential leanings including Rudolf Bultmann, Paul Tillich and Reinhold Niebuhr will be treated comparatively together with others, while the emphasis upon their views will vary much in proportion to their concern for, and contributions to, eschatological matters discussed in the later chapters.

The criteria of appraisal also will be existential, since they include the following factors: 1. The relevance of a thinker's proposed ideas to the idea of time and the meaning of human existence. 2. The ability of an interpretation to illuminate subordinate problems within the main problem being considered. 3. The relation of an idea to the concrete knowing and existing person. 4. The consistency of an idea with the existential ideas proposed mainly by Berdyaev. 5. The congeniality of a principle to these revealed truths and principles of Christianity which illuminate our understanding of time in terms of existence and the meaning of the end.

The special consideration given to Berdyaev's position is not without foundation. Berdyaev not only saw the subtle character and existential setting of the problem of time but confronted it as one called to help resolve its perplexity. Few thinkers have reckoned with it with a greater sense of vocation than Berdyaev. He could say, "The conquest of the deadly flux of time has always been the chief concern of my life."[19]

Berdyaev has come to grips with this problem with a special regard for the matter of destiny, both personal and cultural as well as cosmic in scope. As his sister-in-law Madame Rapp said to me when I visited her in Berdyaev's home at Clermont near Paris in April of 1950, "He saw everything great and small in view of the end."[20] Both the present moment of existence and the ultimate end are of existential meaning to Berdyaev. This marks the eschatological quality and character of his view of existential time, which he applies to both philosophy and theology. We shall attempt to elucidate and appraise this in view of Berdyaev's retention of both the temporal and eternal aspects of the end. Here, too, the nature and character of eternity will be seen as being of profoundest significance to the meaning of time.

Our procedure will move beyond the background already referred to, taking us to a close examination of what is germane to "existential time," followed by a comparative study of the meaning of eternity and a comparative study of the meaning of the end. The eschatological principles of these critical studies will be related to the interpretation of history, destiny, progress, cosmic process and Apocalypse. The latter will be given special attention in terms of New Testament problems of eschatology. Comparatively, again, Berdyaev will be shown making powerful contributions to each of these areas and rendering rich meaning to human existence and destiny because of them. His chief clue will be seen in the Cardinal Event of Christian revelation, a faith factor which sheds Light on the problems and their answers in ways that can hardly be ignored wherever man is not heralded as his own saviour.

With the thesis and accompanying principles in mind, perhaps a more succinct formulation of the endeavor is in order. While the details of this "formula" must await subsequent explanation, a "map" of the undertaking put in biblio-philosophical terms might be rendered as follows: The present critical study seeks to demonstrate and support how Berdyaev, through his interpretation of the *ekstasis* (divine incursion in Christ), relates *chronos* (common historic time) and *kairos* (God-qualified time) to the *eschaton* (the divinely fulfilled end) in preference to *finis* (durational end) and *telos* (cosmological end), even as *chronos* and *kairos* are related, existentially, to each other. Suffice it to say here, this implies a dynamic time-eternity relationship through the *ekstasis* giving rise to a *kairos* which lends meaning to *chronos* and the *eschaton*, which, in turn, is related to, while above, *telos*. While this formulates that which charts our course, the details of our itinerary must await explication.

Thus, just as the problem and perspective are existential, so, to a marked degree, are the purpose and procedure. Enmeshed in the very problem we seek to probe, our situation is described by Blaise Pascal when he says, "You are embarked!"[21] So with the forthrightness of seamen hoisting sail we must concede that our purpose is to find the meaning of one of our own life's problems, one which almost frustrates the attempt. But embarked as we are, what better can we do than consider seriously the courses of others who have assumed a somewhat similar venture? Berdyaev becomes our chosen captain, for he has steered this way before, and creatively and daringly indeed. Yet even among existentially oriented observers the logs of observation vary and maps may be redrawn. This, too, belongs to our task.

But before we launch out into the gulf stream of this venture we might well peruse the background of what we mean by existential time. The philosophical shoreline might be scanned so that our pursuit toward new horizons on the sea of temporal existence might be better understood. It is to this background that we now must turn.

NOTES

1 *Confessions*, Bk. xi, 14:17, p. 262.
2 *Ibid.*, 32, p. 270f.
3 *Christ and the World of Thought*, p. 71. Cf. pp. 89, 69.
4 *Concluding Unscientific Postscript*, p. 306. In our use of the term "existentialism" we do not mean to be so technical in the use of the "ism" as to apply it strictly to Martin Heidegger's distinction between "existential" and "existentiel" as though the one were only the ontologized form of the other, i.e., the idea of the "Is" (Being) of "existence." Rather, we use the term as apropos to any position which keeps foremost the self in concrete existence-as-it-is-experienced and known.
5 "Christlicher Personalismus und marxistische Anthropologie," *Orient und Occident*, Heft 2 (new series). June, 1936 (pp. 28-44), p. 30.
6 *Spirit and Reality*, p. 4. Cf. pp. 8-10, 31.
7 *Truth and Revelation*, p. 11. Cf. *Solitude and Society*, p. 53.
8 Martin Heidegger, *Existence and Being*, p. 314 ff. Cf. pp. 335 f, 344, 355, 358 ff, 367 ff.
9 *Ibid.* Cf. footnote 16, below, esp. the reference to Berdyaev.
10 Influenced by Heidegger, the N.T. scholar Rudolf Bultmann has seen the profound significance of these matters and how a person's own *Fragestellung* (putting of the question), *Bergrifflichkeit* (mental presuppositions,

thought forms and universe of discourse) and *Weltanschauung* (outlook and intuitive perception of the world) are of marked consequence in the recognition and understanding of any truth. Cf. John Macquarrie, *An Existentialist Theology*, pp. 10-14.

11 *Essai de Métaphysique Eschatologique*, p. 232. Cf. George Berkeley, "Principles of Human Knowledge," *Landmarks in Philosophy*, eds. Edman and Schreiber. Bishop Berkeley, while repudiating abstract objective ideas in his empiricism, nevertheless equates the object with its perception or with the subject's concept. "To be is to be perceived." Cf. C. E. M. Joad, *Guide To Philosophy*, pp. 71, 113, 369 ff. While we see a latent existential factor here, it is hindered by Berkeley's subjective idealism, which equates the object with the subject's intellectual idea. Berdyaev is not such an idealist. He keeps the subject related *to* objects as well as to itself and other subjects without necessarily objectifying and ontologizing what is *related* to the knower. What belongs to existence is not an object of knowledge. While Berdyaev discounts self-subsistent things as the basis of *knowledge* he does not preclude everything save the knowing subject and its ideas, which is what subjective idealism connotes. Cf. Evgueny Lampert, *Modern Christian Revolutionaries*, p. 334. One's concepts are not to be equated with Being, as in Berkeley. Being is a predicate of the subject belonging, e.g., to the *verb*; it is not "what" but "that," while *depending* on the "what." Furthermore, knowledge is an integral spiritual act involving more than intellect, for it involves the entire self with all its sentient, intellectual, imaginative, volitional, intuitive and emotional capacities, including faith. Cf. *Solitude and Society*, pp. 5-12, 53, 128. As W. M. Dixon has said in his Gifford Lectures, *The Human Situation*, p. 64, "Life can be understood only by living . . . reason is an attribute but most obviously not the whole of us." (Cf. pp. 59, 69) For Berdyaev, even "revelation is an event within human existence . . ." Lampert, *loc. cit.*, p. 335. Knowledge for Berdyaev is not based on the identity of subject and object but is an intuitive creative relationship. Truth belongs to existence known via *gnosis*. Cf. Paul Archambault's treatment of Berdyaev's epistemology in "Le Drame de la liberté dans la philosophie de Berdiaeff," *Politique*, no. II, Feb.-Mar., 1937, pp. 123-143. Intuition is basic to the reasoning process; also it is what allows faith to speak to reason. The "heart" is the "integral whole" of the knower, says Berdyaev, the capacity of "evaluation." Cf. *Solitude and Society*, p. 128. Cf. Pascal: "The heart has its reasons, which reason does not know." *Pensées*, no. 277. Cf. 277-282. Both Berdyaev and Pascal suggest to us that reason is an instrument, not a final authority. Yet reason is not to be "offended," as Pascal suggests. *Pensées* no. 273. It has an important, but not an ultimate or all-inclusive, role of authority.

12 Leslie Paul, *The English Philosophers*, p. 138. Cf. footnote 11 above.

13 "Physics, Logic and the Imaginative Significance of Time," *Transformation Four*, p. 32 f.

14 *Ibid.*, pp. 36-38.

15 Allers, *The New Psychologies*, p. 8. Cf. Carl Gustave Jung, *Psychology and Religion*, p.11 f. Speaking of the subjective side of knowledge Jung says, "Psyche is existent, it is even existence itself." This has an element of truth but is too narrow. Is not a person's existence even that which surrounds, feeds and pertains to the *psyche* while centered therein in such a way that each factor is essential to the other?

16 *Solitude and Society*, p. 2 ff. Heidegger, *op. cit.*, in "What Is Metaphysics?" p. 355, poses the same problem when he says, ". . . every metaphysical question can only be put in such a way that the questioner as such is by

31

his questioning involved in the question." Berdyaev says, "The neutrality of reason . . . is a fiction." ("Le philosophe et l'existence," *Actualités scientifiques et industrielles*, IV, Paris, 1937, p. 47.) There is an inter-relation between the philosopher's situation and his philosophy. This includes his own tensions and aspirations, reasoning as well as faith; in short, his existential situation.

17 *Loc. cit.*, p. 69.

18 *Dream and Reality*, p. 30. The central idea here has been supported also by such thinkers as Bergson, Bosanquet and Eddington. Cf. R. W. Inge, *God and the Astronomers*, p. 71.

19 *Ibid.*, p. x. The writer has shared a similar yearning since a New Year's Eve when at the age of seven he wept in solitude over the awesomeness of time's passing.

20 My thanks are extended to Berdyaev's friend, Peter Pianoff of Paris, for this personal introduction and for conducting me to the little Orthodox Church where Berdyaev worshiped. Berdyaev had moved to Paris after a year in Berlin upon fleeing from Moscow when authorities moved to silence his criticism of the rising Soviet regime. He had earlier been deported to Siberia but upon his return he remained a fearless prophet.

21 *Pensées*, 233, p. 81. Cf. Pascal's "wager."

CHAPTER II

EXISTENTIAL TIME AND ITS PHILOSOPHICAL BACKGROUND

The philosophical background of existential time may be considered to better understand the problem before us and its possible solution. Basic to this will be the relation between time and the knower in the history of philosophy and some insights into time's relation to eternity and the present. Lest we be taken off course, however, the Aleutian chain of existential and pre-existential insights which constitutes this background must be but briefly explored and serve to direct us toward richer inlets of meaning. But even this background has a distinctive contour and color.

Like most metaphysical issues, the questions raised by the problem of time are implicit in those debated by the ancient Greek thinkers Parmenides and Heraclitus. Contrasted are the classical principles fundamental to all thought: *to hon*, the one, and *panta rei*, "all things flow." This means permanence versus change, unity versus multiplicity, likeness versus difference, being versus becoming, the one versus the many. Most thinkers have catered to the idea of time as change. Heraclitus in his *Cosmic Fragments* saw all things in flux. But it is frequently overlooked that his doctrine of the *Logos* represented a paradoxical unity and stability from within flux, i.e., the constancy of change was in itself a permanent principle. Even Aristotle misinterpreted Heraclitus at this point.[1]

Yet few thinkers have refused to identify time with change, while some monists like the Hindu mystics and Spinoza, the "windowless philosopher," as well as Hegel, the "System-builder," have sought to resolve the flux or stream of time within a permanent scheme of cosmic immanence in such a way as to either obscure or dissolve the very reality of time. Hume, at the other extreme, tried to identify time with the changes in sense perception. This amounts to a disjointed succession with no

33

duration, since he saw no causal nexus between instants; everything is contingent. This illustrates the fundamental philosophical debate to which the interpretation of time is by no means immune.

Now it is in order to ask: What are the existential elements in the philosophical interpretations of time which provide the historic background for a view of time akin to Berdyaev's insights and those of other existential thinkers? This demands that particular attention be given to outstanding thinkers in the history of philosophy who have wrestled with the problem and raised existential and pre-existential thoughts which deserve our consideration. Beginning with classical Greek thinkers in this chapter, we shall move up to Augustine before treating the views of Locke, Kant and Hegel, followed by Kierkegaard and, in the next chapter, Berdyaev.

Existential Elements in the Classical Views of Time

Plato, the distinguished headmaster of the Academy at Athens, was prone to reduce time and things temporal to an illusory "moving image" of eternal Being.[2] This is basically a metaphorical view which defines time as a product of the creation of a moving universe. "Time came into being along with the visible Heaven," wrote Plato in his *Timaeus*. Yet our universe is one which has an eternal Model, an "eternal Living Creature," as Plato referred to it.[3]

Here is an immanental dualism in which we see time as a unity within variation, while belonging to the realm of "Becoming" in contrast to the Model of pure eternal "Being." Thus Plato speaks of a "movable image of Eternity . . . an eternal image, moving according to number, even that which we have named Time."[4] Not only related to motion as well as to image and number, time to Plato is also the cyclical behavior pattern of the planets.[5] All time belongs to *Becoming,* and *Becoming* would ever emulate eternal and immutable *Being.*[6] Thus time as number is change, while as the image of eternity it has an element of permanence, which helps account for time's unity and reality. Somewhat paradoxical and akin to Heraclitus' permanence within change via the *Logos*, neither factor must be overlooked here. The fact that time belongs to Becoming implies that it has some degree of reality, since Becoming images forth eternal Being. Yet the temporal refraction of the eternal must be conceded, and this gives rise to Plato's stress on the illusory aspect of time. For Plato to leave time a mere image, reflection or copy of the eternal, was, in some respects, to leave it illusory and unreal, at least fairly inconsequential. This tendency comes strongly into appearance in the position taken by the existentialist Kierkegaard, as we shall see, and becomes a point at which we must encourage Berdyaev to take issue with him. This is not to say, however, that Plato equates time with evil, for it still "reflects" eternal Being, which he regards as pure good.

Aristotle, the distinguished student of Plato and systematizer of the scientific method, held to a more physical view of time. He associated time with physical motion. Despite his overlapping dualism of Being in Becoming, Aristotle left time unrelated to two matters deemed important to the existential perspective: (1) the meaning of eternity and (2) the role of the knowing subject.[7] Actually, for Aristotle, time meant little more than "the number of motions."[8] This left it a chronological measure, a notion common to subsequent Western civilization. Epicurus attributed time to the movement of objects. This also remained Aristotle's temptation, for he saw the successiveness and continuity of time in terms of spatial magnitude and the continuity of motion.[9]

Plato also saw time related to movement, but did not limit time to this extent. He saw time as belonging to the whole cosmic order of Becoming, whereas Aristotle limited it to the objective changes in nature. Yet all motion, said Aristotle, goes back to an Unmoved Mover, the infinite First Cause of time and finitude. Time is potentially infinite by number conceived *ad infinitum* but, as such, is never actual.[10] "No motion goes on to infinity," said Aristotle.[11] Time is continuous, successive and divisible while in no relationship with eternal Being. This leaves Aristotle with a linear, serial and historic view of time, though he also acknowledged cyclic or cosmic time, which he likened to a circle because of the ongoing repetitiousness of the cosmic process.

While Aristotle's concept of time is too physical, objective, and spatial to contribute directly to an existential view of time, we must take note of how he raises an important pre-existential question. He asks: Could there be any time were it not for the "soul?" [12] He then concedes, "If there cannot be some one to count, there cannot be anything that can be counted . . ." [13] Despite the concession, it is precisely this existential problem of the knowing subject's relation to time from which the distinguished Greek rationalist really withdraws lest he venture too far, it would seem, from his objective approach to time. Aristotle raises the crucial matter only to drop it abruptly as if it were too subtle for his objective ontology.

Aristotle also clings to the assumption that things exist whether or not we are aware of them; hence, even time is left independent of the knower while inseparable from motion and change, though not quite identical thereto. But it is this epistemological issue we find basic to time as an existential phenomenon. Later thinkers like Plotinus and Augustine, whom we shall consider, delve into this matter in such a way as to introduce and sharpen what belongs to the existential perspective of time.

Plato, we find, actually came closer to grips with this epistemological issue of time than did Aristotle. This he did by asserting that the mind perceives and imitates eternal "forms" from within the realm of time itself.[14] The subjective factor in Plato actually anticipates Plotinus and Augustine and, in a limited sense, Kierkegaard and Berdyaev. The knower can perceive the temporal image of the eternal. This much was indicated by Plato in his doctrine of "recollection" and the importance he attributed to memory.[15] It is also illustrated in Plato's parable of the cave with its place for man's intuitions of pre-existence. While time for Plato belongs strictly to the realm of becoming, it is only as perceived by the mind which would imitate the eternal model. As such, in contrast to Aristotle's physical version, time is indigenous to the knowing subject and is not just a matter of objective movement and cyclic necessity.[16] Here we perceive a latent existential principle in Plato's scheme which must not be overlooked. It contributes provocatively to the background of existential time, we believe, to the extent that it might be regarded as "pre-existential." Its existential pertinence lies at the point of distinguishing what is in time from what time is in. It is aligned with the principle introduced in the previous chapter that the knowing subject is the seat of time and the engenderer thereof. However, its deficiency from the existential point of view seems to lie in Plato's failure to relate the mind, the knowing subject, to the individual man, the "me," of concrete existence. It is treated as if it pertained to an objective, universal man, a weakness of most, if not all, idealists. But to fully appreciate this observation we must await subsequent discussions, especially on the knowledge of time in the next chapter.

Meanwhile, what did neo-Platonism do with what we regard as the pre-existential insights of Plato and Aristotle?

Existential Elements in the Neo-Platonic View of Time

Plotinus of Rome, the main contributor to neo-Platonic philosophy, moved beyond the metaphorical and physical ideas of time held by Plato and Aristotle, respectively, to a profounder metaphysical view. Actually, Plotinus did much more to illuminate the main pre-existential factor so far considered, viz., the intrinsic relation of time to the knower, even as he introduced other pre-existential elements of significance to our background and comparative study as a whole.

In his monistic scheme of cosmic emanation from oneness to manyness, time for Plotinus is neither measure, number, motion nor period. It is in no sense a quantity. In contrast to Aristotle, Plotinus held that what is conceived to be numerically infinite could not be numerical. This is another problem of the knower. Also, time must be to be numbered, he contended. Later we see Berdyaev adapting this principle in contrast to both Aristotle and Plato.

While accepting the basic ideas of horizontal, durational time and cyclic or cosmic time held by his predecessors, Plotinus raised the problem to a higher level. Time, he asserted with pre-existential insight, is the very medium in which every form of movement and activity occurs. Furthermore, he said, it is *in* the subject or the soul.[17] In fact, Plotinus even defines time as "the Life of the Soul in movement . . ."[18] While this is perhaps too closely identified with the soul of man immanent to the cosmic Soul, it relates time to the knowing subject much more closely than do the positions of Aristotle and Plato. The restless soul engenders time as it experiences and contemplates the sensible world. Time becomes a product of a kind of moral fall from pure contemplation into practical life.[19] Here we are reminded of the position taken by Paul Tillich today wherein man is held to have fallen from pure Being, the ground of all being, into a refracted and estranged realm of existence. The importance ascribed to the knowing subject by Plotinus surpasses the position taken by Plato and paves the way for Augustine, one of the earliest of all existential thinkers. That later thinkers like Kierkegaard and Berdyaev should be influenced indirectly by Plotinus would be hard to deny. Time to them is *of* the subject from within his existence. In this respect we can say Plotinus is a pre-existential thinker, seeing time's vital relation to subjectivity.

On the other hand, Plotinus did not assert that time depends solely upon being known. The soul, he said, endures regardless of its immediate awareness of time, and this endurance in itself implies time. The reason for this, as given by Plotinus, is that the soul exists in relation to eternity.[20] Eternity is characterized as the *Totum Simul*. It is a unified being which engenders and embraces time and on which time actually depends. The self is the center of time yet dependent upon eternity for its existence. Here is another pre-existential insight, particularly of a religious character. Time's meaning and consequence is dependent upon eternity. Yet the restless soul is "fallen," and its time is a degradation from eternity.[21] This has much in common with what Augustine, Kierkegaard and Berdyaev have seen in their respective ways. To them man is one who exists "on the frontier of two worlds," time and eternity. Plotinus appears to have opened up the possibility of a new approach to time, directly paving the way for Augustine.

Before we take up another pre-existential insight on the part of Plotinus, it is noteworthy that one feature of the neo-Platonic view of time stands in marked contrast to that of Plato. Time is ever being created, yet ever vanishing in the eternal process of cosmic emanation from, and return to, the eternal Being of the "One." Oneness, by a process of emanation, yields plurality, which is ever being returned into unity. Time, then, is more effervescent, as it were, than in Plato's scheme, for it is ever being threatened by non-Being. Consequently, time is more of an intrinsic evil for Plotinus than for Plato; its plurality is forever being renounced from within the whole cosmic process, which is identified as Soul and moving *toward* unity even as it is a perpetual fall *from* unity. Yet, speaking of evil in general, Plotinus' scheme is too optimistic, as Dean Inge points out.[22] Since time is the product of the universal Soul's desire to manifest its powers and translate what it knows in eternity into another form, there is also the guarantee, so to speak, that nothing is lost, since, real as evil is, even in the form of time, it is not alone; it is always mixed with good. As for the existing man, he is surrounded by the spiritual world and is never far from it.[23]

Plotinus, we take note, held another pre-existential insight into time. It pertains to time's vital relation to eternity. While maintaining a gnostic and mystical union of the soul of man with the All-Soul, Plotinus, nevertheless, saw time and eternity as two distinct realms of Being. Both, he claimed, are intuited by the knower.[24] While the latter point is not our concern here, suffice it to say that this anticipates emphases on intuition by such varied thinkers as Kant, Pascal and Bergson.

Of more immediate concern to us here is the fact that Plotinus saw time as belonging to a kind of Platonic realm of becoming and as an image of eternity, its "standing Exemplar." Time is a kind of intrinsic copy of its eternal paradigm. For Plotinus it is a more mystical concept than it is for Plato. Even more important to us as we anticipate subsequent discussions, Plotinus in his third *Enneade* saw eternity as a "life," possessing everything in the present moment. This is a profoundly creative and pre-existential insight of far-reaching proportions. It includes the paradox of how eternity is a *Totum Simul* of a kind which implies both "movement" and "repose." Specifically, if eternity were strictly a state of "repose," the element of change and movement associated with time would disallow the relationship of eternity to time.[25]

Thus we must take note that, to Plotinus, eternity meant a far more dynamic reality than it did to Plato and Aristotle, since it consisted of both unity and diversity, identity and difference, rest and activity, permanence and change, subject and object. This is a paradoxical insight which appears to have been seized upon by Berdyaev, one which he has adapted to his doctrine of eternity and its importance to what he calls "existential time." It implies neither an Aristotelian dualism nor a Platonic dualism, but a less rational and more dynamic one of unity-in-duality. Embracing all tenses, it is closer, it appears, to that of the Heraclitean paradox of *Logos* amidst flux. In Plotinus, however, it is more akin to a mystical monism than to a rational ontology. Important is how Plotinus shifts away from any static interpretation of the eternal. This will be enlarged when we deal with that problem in Chapter IV.

We must now consider what Augustine did with the pre-existential insights which Plotinus introduced to the ancient world, especially in relation to Plato.

Existential Elements in the Augustinian View of Time

Somewhat like Plato and Plotinus, though more specifically and profoundly, Augustine, the distinguished Christian theologian of the fifth century, interpreted time to be centered in the knowing subject. This is basic to what makes Augustine an existential thinker, especially because he relates time not simply to man in general but to the concrete self. This is most evident in his autobiographical writing, known as his *Confessions*. What is thought of as duration he attributed to two functions of the mind: memory and expectation. The knowledge of history and prophecy are respective applications of these functions. Time, for Augustine, did not mean objective movement or measurement, as it did for Aristotle, but a mental product of concrete, personal experience.[26] Neither the past nor the future can be measured objectively, Augustine said. The origin or locus of time, then, is the person-subject of everyday life. Not a subjective idealism or psychology, this means outward things and experiences leave traces on the mind, and these are the real objects of knowledge. Time is not eternal motion or mere cyclic rhythm, but a matter of subjective awareness. Here Augustine is profoundly existential. Matched by his autobiographical approach Augustine sees how the knower engenders time. Whatever the relation to outward things, time's significance and reality are not known apart from their inner relevance to the concrete subject. At this point Augustine is akin to Plato and Plotinus in view of our previous observations, even as he anticipates Kierkegaard and Berdyaev in his concern for temporal existence and for the knower steeped within it.

Just as the past is known by the memory, Augustine asserted, so too the future is known by imagination or "expectation," the basis for anticipating coming events in the present.[27] Augustine states,

> For where did they, who foretold things to come, see them, if as yet they be not? For that which is not, cannot be seen. And they who relate things past, could not relate them, if in mind they did not discern them, and if they were not, they could no way be discerned. *Things then past and to come are.*[28]

Yet Augustine goes on to say, ". . . wherever they be, they are not there as future, or past, but present. . . . Wheresoever then is whatsoever is, it is only as present." [29] Past, present and future alike belong to the knower, who actually perceives and engenders time in the present. But Augustine, we must take note, also shrewdly enunciates the *present* of things past, present and future as the core of their reality.[30] Thus, together these tenses belong to the existential perspective of the present. Kierkegaard, as we shall see, rediscovered this principle a century ago. Central to the existential perspective is the precious present of our lives, the seat of relevant reality.

While Augustine sees the significance of past and future only in the present and regards time as always passing, he is close to the neo-Platonic idea adapted by Berdyaev in that all the tenses of time, despite time's pseudo measurements, are held to be real. We take note that both before and after enunciating the reality of the past and future in the present, Augustine shows that he is not satisfied with the denial of linear, or historic, time's reality. This anticipates what we shall say in behalf of Berdyaev and in criticism of Kierkegaard and the type of existential theologians of our day who minimize the role and reality of historic time, even while looking to a Platonic dualism often linked with Augustine. Actually, Augustine sees that the present could not *be* save for the reality of the past and the future.

If it appears that Augustine supports only the idea of time's unreality apart from the existential present, in the manner of Kierkegaard, due to his subordination of the past and the future to the present, let it be said that such an interpretation does not do full justice to Augustine. For instance, even after speaking of the "present tenses" of time, he says, ". . . I see three tenses, and I confess there are three." [31] And, ". . . no time is

41

all at once present." [32] Still plainer—with the writer's apologies for so early an anticipation of a Kierkegaardian abuse of linear time—he says, "But the present, should it always be present, and never pass into time past, verily is should not be time, but eternity." [33] Augustine concedes a real, but flowing, present. Thus it appears that even Berdyaev was not altogether correct in asserting that Augustine denied the reality of linear time; rather, Augustine lends some support to Berdyaev's own view of the *reality* of all the tenses while made *meaningful* only in the present, the existential present when eternity meets man in the moment. This important distinction anticipates much in the subsequent discussions.

Even more significant than this important observation, however, is the fact that Augustine glimpsed the basis for what all later religious existentialists have regarded as "the eternal now," while we shall see it employed by Hegel as well. One of the first thinkers to employ the idea, Augustine recognized the profound meaning of the "ever-present eternity." [34] Actually, it has much in common with the *Totum Simul* of Plotinus, though it is treated more dualistically. In addressing God, Augustine can say, " . . . all times are in Thee." F. H. Brabant is correct when he says, "This conjoins the Greek view of God as timeless and the Hebrew view of history as purposeful." [35] Yet even this leaves something to be desired, which we do not see solved until Berdyaev sets forth his more dynamic view of the time and eternity relationship. We must ask: How can the timeless and the timeful be related? Chapters IV and V will deal with this.

Augustine's "ever-present eternity," together with his profound insight into the present tense of the tenses,[36] seems to have inspired much of Kierkegaard's thought, especially his doctrines of "repetition" and "contemporaneity." These insights are basic also to Berdyaev's "eternal now," his more realistic view of "existential time" and its "eschatological dimension," the latter to be treated in Part II. But far more congenial to Berdyaev than to Kierkegaard is our above-mentioned critical observation, *viz.*, Augustine's retention of the paradoxical reality of linear time even apart from the primacy of the present and its relation to the eternal. In this respect, we maintain, Augustine prefigures Berdyaev more than he does Kierkegaard, while all three are existential thinkers who stress the paramount significance of the present and a meaningful time on essentially the same grounds. But this contention, like others introduced, must await subsequent treatment.

Actually, the very roots of "existential time" go back to the insights of Augustine. First, he saw time as belonging to the knowing subject, the self of existence; second, he saw the present moment related to eternity; third, he saw the present as primary, but not so exclusive as to negate the past and future of linear time. Modifying J. F. Callahan's view a bit, we must assert that Augustine's idea of time is more than "psychological." [37] While including the psychological it is more; it is "existential," involving the total self and its confrontation with eternity. Profounder than Aristotle's physical view of time and Plato's metaphorical view or even Plotinus' stronger metaphysical view, Augustine has a marked depth-dimension of the total self's involvement in time and its confrontation by eternity. It is this which makes it more mature and relevant to human existence and destiny. Neither the physical, the idealistic, ontological nor psychological categories can do this full justice. They cannot exhaust the meaning of the self or of the present moment, and that which gives them significance.

Rejecting the classical notion of cyclic time held by Plato and other Greeks, Augustine seemed to plead for the primacy of the *self* over against the necessitativeness or determinism of the impersonal cosmic forces. While Greek thinking places a premium on reason coming into harmony with the cosmos, Augustine could see the limitations of this. The self must answer to much more than a cold reason! Augustine also asserted that time cannot be measured objectively, though moving bodies can be.[38] Here we find that Berdyaev, though appreciative of Augustine's concern for the moral self, must take exception to Augustine's rejection of cyclic time. Admitting its reality within creation, Berdyaev, somewhat like Plotinus, recognizes its deficiency as a meaning-giving principle relevant to the creative, thinking and choosing self. Cyclic time, though real, is too external to yield any meaning to the concrete self.

In general, Augustine's main contribution to the existential view of time lay in his clarification of the mysterious present in relation to the knowing, existing self. Perhaps next in importance is his clarification of the relevance of the eternal present, together

43

with his refusal to negate the tenses of time in view of the primacy of the present. There can be little doubt that Augustine was existential, especially in his outlook on the problem of time, and that he anticipated much in thinkers like Kierkegaard and Berdyaev respecting the meaning of time.

Now we must ask: What has possibly contributed to the development of an existential perspective of time *since* Augustine? The answer to such a question demands a big leap ahead in the history of philosophy to the Age of the Enlightenment, where we find that the problem of time was reopened after considerable neglect.

Existential Elements in the Empirical View of Time

John Locke, whose seventeenth-century empiricism contributed much to the *Aufklärung* as a period of intellectual adjustment between the medieval and modern worlds, actually helped prepare the way, we believe, for the acceptance of an existential view of time. Locke did this principally by shifting the horizontal notion of time, still reflected in Descartes and Spinoza, from the objective physical plane, where Aristotle had left it, back to the subjective consciousness, which thinkers like Plato, Plotinus and Augustine had deemed to be its locus.

Descartes, the father of modern philosophy, had seen time as an incoherent series of instants in contrast to eternal truths comparable to geometrical propositions. One moment has no relation to another. Each is an independent unit in itself, with the miracle of divine will the sole factor in the appearance of the next, since God accounts for the creation of things. Time, then, is succession while, as for Spinoza, too, a subjective measurement of motion based on cosmic factors. Both thinkers saw duration as the objective attribute of created things, while not attributable to God, lest His essence be confused with his existence. For Spinoza, God is infinitely ever-present, so that in no sense is time to be attributed to God lest there be confusion with the popular idea of going on everlastingly. The eternal, then, amounts to a timelessness here. This for both thinkers is akin to an abstract changelessness. Spinoza is especially averse to time and change in his concern for a fixed monistic and eternal order.[39]

We have already indicated that Berkeley, despite his subjective idealism as well as because of it, reduced time to a mere measurement of motion. David Hume even went so far as to reduce time to a matter of sense perception. For him time meant a mere succession of instants like indivisible moments comparable to spatial atoms. But this disallows a continuous element of time, one implying duration. It is rather like a disjointed chain, since sense perception is a series of impressions.[40] In this respect Hume was not far from Descartes' incoherent time, while both had much in common with Spinoza in objectifying time, there being a defective interrelation between the subjective and objective aspects of time and its measurement. From a different angle, much the same can be said of Bishop Berkeley, since the subjective cognition of time is not really "projectionable" onto a measurable plane.

What did John Locke do to qualify this return to a measured, linear time? While for Locke the subjective was the front seat of empirical experience and understanding, he saw it from a more temperate standpoint than did Berkeley. It consisted of both external and internal factors, i.e., sense perceptions on the one hand, and deduced concepts on the other. Both, he thought, are essential to knowledge. On this basis, mental ideas to Locke were the height of reality. This includes time as the memory of cyclic recurrences.[41] While Locke's empirical view of time might be considered still too objective to be identified with the existential perspective and too exclusively mental in its subjectivity, it might be considered pre-existential for the reason that time centers for him in the subject. Unlike Descartes and Spinoza, for Locke time is largely subjective. While time here is held as a form of concept empirically arrived at, it is *of* the subject and relevant only *to* the subject, apart from whose mentality sense perception remains conglomerate. One might say that Locke opens up a bigger part of the existential view of time, though it, too, falls short of the self's wholeness.

But quite like Aristotle and the philosophers just touched upon, Locke interpreted time as a measured duration of experience. While this is not as atomistic as the positions taken by Hume and Descartes, it entails an objectified succession derived from sensation and reflection applied to remembered events and cyclic occurrences. Thus, time is actually left a mere train of ideas in continuity while subject to arbitrary division or measurement. For one thing, the future is regarded as a mere set of projected ideas; it remains unreal in any realistic sense and unrelated to the present. This empirical view, therefore, is to be contrasted with the existential views of Augustine and Berdyaev. Furthermore, Locke really sacrificed the permanence of duration in favor of the phenomenon of succession. The latter is the more real element for Locke, reflecting the primacy of sense perception in his scheme.

Included in Locke's view of time, however, is a temporal concept of infinity which is neither real in its own right nor identifiable with eternity, despite the fact that Locke would make it congruent to the eternal.[42] Again we take note of Locke's mental projection of infinite time. This idea remains sterile and inconsistent, we maintain, if for no other reason than that the future that it should logically entail is already regarded as unreal. Furthermore, Locke's theism does not harmonize with his notion of eternity as a "temporal infinity." He says that for God "all things exist every moment" and He "sees all things, past and to come." [43] This idea of simultaneity has something in common with Spinoza as well as with the *Totum Simul* of Plotinus and the "ever-present eternal" of Augustine; however, logically, it should be impossible for Locke to hold, since his "temporal infinity" is still a form of empirical time, an infinitely prolonged time, and it is ideationally projected at that.

Locke's idea here really calls for an existential perspective of time and eternity in terms of the present from an Augustinian standpoint, while even Augustine's version must await the more astute views of Kierkegaard and Berdyaev for improved meaning and broader implications. Locke's view of eternity is much too temporal, yet his idea of divine simultaneity as related to the knowing subject is a pre-existential insight. It is simply stifled in an overly temporal view of eternity, while not adequate when the tenses of time, especially the future, are not sufficiently realistic to require any simultaneity of God. The future, as seen above, is only a mental projection. By the same token, then, a temporal infinity must be a mere mental projection. This is inadequate as a truly revelatory and redemptive view of eternity, as we shall see in other contexts. It lacks a supra-temporal dimension or quality.

But by reintroducing the empirically subjective factor into

knowledge and the understanding of time, John Locke can be said to have prepared the way for another latent existential principle of time seen in the philosophy of Immanuel Kant. This must now be examined, followed by time's relation to the system erected by George F. W. Hegel, whose scheme was eventually challenged and offset by Soren Kierkegaard, the last century's "father of existentialism."

Existential Elements in the Kantian View of Time

As hinted above, there is a basic pre-existential factor in the philosophy of Immanuel Kant respecting our problem of time. Quite like the main thinkers previously considered, it is to be seen in Kant's profound concern for the knowing self. For Kant, time belongs strictly to the subject.[44] Unlike the objective claims of Aristotle, Descartes, Spinoza, Hume, and to some extent John Locke, time is not identified with motion, objects, sense perception or objective succession. It is literally of the mind, for Kant, and to that extent belongs only to the self.

In assuming his position Kant asserted that time is a given principle, a mental category or intuitive axiom. It is brought to experience rather than found by experience. It is imposed upon perception, not deduced or gleaned from it. Not in itself an empirical concept, time is an intuition conjoined with sense perception and becomes essential to any empirical concept. Time is an *a priori* form which is imposed on things by the subject.[45] It has three modes: succession, coexistence and duration.[46] Yet each of these shares in one basic dimension or quality, the successiveness of time.

Time, as such, becomes a subjective condition and is not a condition or quality inherent in things, either in themselves or as conceived. That is, while time is pure intuition and not inherent in objects, it has meaning only as *applied* to objects.[47] While it has an epistemological priority to all changes or movements of any kind, in the mind's consciousness of something time is not self-subsistent.[48] This is because time functions intuitively or is made relevant only in connection with perception.[49]

Time is conditional, then, to all appearances; it does not prove significant in a vacuum of hypothetical subjectivity but belongs to a person's actual knowing subjectivity, however refracted it may be. The mental appearances or phenomenal ideas are termed by Kant a body of "*a priori* synthetic knowledge," [50] a kind of judgment. Time is an essential form within the mind making these ideas possible.[51] As an intuitive, subjective condition of knowledge, time, then, is mental and has "objective validity only in respect of appearances, these being things which we take as objects of our senses." [52]

Having seen this conditional role of time, we can push the matter a step further. Time for Kant does not pertain to *das Ding an sich* or things-in-themselves but only to their empirical appearances to the observer. In contrast to Descartes and Spinoza, Kant sees how time lacks an "absolute reality," in this respect, while it has a "transcendental ideality." [53] It is positively nothing apart from the knowing subject. While having different modes and tenses, time has one dimension or quality, the successive, to which they all belong. Kant overtly states, "The present moment can be regarded only as conditioned by past time, never as conditioning it, because this moment comes into existence only through past time, or rather through the passing of the preceding time." [54] This in itself is not congenial to the more intense existential view of the present. Furthermore, time is always represented spatially, says Kant.[55] This is to be understood in view of the assertion that space is another mental category or intuition essential to knowledge and experience.

Time, then, is intrinsic to the epistemological dualism of Kant. It is an intuitional link between conglomerous percepts and intelligible concepts, while not guaranteeing any equation between the thing-in-itself, *das Ding an sich,* and the thing-as-conceived or experienced. As such, time as an intuitive principle belongs to the subject or "transcendental unity of apperception," [56] whose function it is to unify experience even as it synthesizes percepts on the one hand, and intuitive categories on the other. This is a "synthetic judgment" and amounts only to a refraction of *das Ding an sich,* thus reflecting the insufficiency of pure reason or *Vernunft.* In this respect time is a problem involved in the Kantian skepticism of reason.

While Kant may be said to divide the history of thought by his remarkable uncovery of the primacy of the subject, he seems to have submerged the fuller meaning of time. While pre-existential in his pointing to the basic importance of the knowing

48

self, Kant reflects a marked weakness respecting the *relation* of the knowing subject to time, especially from an existential point of view. It lies in the fact that the Kantian subject is too transcendent, abstract, or "objectified." It implies a concept of the self which overarches the concrete man who can say "me." It is more like the Platonic ideal man, who is also a mere "spectator," than like the *existing participant* in knowledge and experience. This points to two basic defects. (1) It bifurcates man as just described, and (2) it leaves time a mere mental category. This, in turn, reflects two other weaknesses: (a) It is an incomplete view of time and the experiential factors that contribute to it. (b) It keeps time as hypothetical as the transcendent subject to which it is attributed. Having suggested these two basic defects in the Kantian view of time we repeat that the knowing self is wedged apart from the existing self, and time as a mental category is not sufficiently related to the *existing* self for whom time is more than an axiomatic principle, since it is a vital personal problem. As a problem of intensity it is a combination of human anxiety, tension, insecurity, creativity and hope. For Kant, however, time is a mere ideational principle, not a realistic problem related to human eventfulness.

Where, then, lies the latent existential element in Kant's view of time? While having criticized it negatively, we can also appraise it positively. The positive factor centers in Kant's strong regard for the knowing subject as the center of time. This allows time to be related to the dialectic of knowledge and existence, to the extent that even Kant himself had to concede the problem to be another antinomy of reason.[57] Yet this in itself does little or nothing to make up for the bifurcation of the subject-self to whom time should appertain existentially. Kant's subject is too remote from the thinking, choosing, imagining, feeling self who should be seen at the center of the very problems being considered. The philosophical idea of time under scrutiny turns out to be next to irrelevant to time as experienced by men of the workaday world. It is neither satisfactorily related to human history on the one hand, nor to eternity on the other. Kant leaves eternity a matter strictly confined to a transcendental theology. It is free from time.[58]

In this respect, John Locke's empirical view of time came closer to the existence of the whole, concrete self than did Kant's view. Yet Locke was less shrewd at seeing how reason offers but a refracted picture of things. While Kant's skepticism of reason can be defended, it, too, proves next to irrelevant apart from the *concrete self* of existence. Kant fails to see time engendered by the total existing self, whereas to a greater extent Locke does. Thus, while a latent existential element is projected by Kant, anything comparable to "existential time" remains stillborn. In fact, even linear time which is allowed for in the form of the tenses is not shown relevant to the self in relation to experience. While the present is made dependent upon the past, Kant does not demonstrate how the intuited tenses are related to each other from the standpoint of an existing subject-self who exists in the present. One might ask: How does the present self intuit the *past?* The intuitions of succession, simultaneity and a dependent duration are deemed more basic than the events to which they should appertain. This is Kant's idealistic failure to regard man as a particular self rather than a universal self, also the failure to see the broader conditions which give rise to the consciousness and engendering of time. In this respect Kant falls far short of Augustine.[59]

Kant's concept of time remains abstract within his speculative view of the knowing subject. Does Kant fail to see the central problem here? Not entirely, we would judge, since he conceded the antinomy of time and could assert that even the intuition of time is invalid apart from its application to things in experience. This is a big point in Kant's favor, for it pushes the matter closer to the experimental, existing self than otherwise would be the case. But had Kant related himself as the *thinking man* to the subject about whom he centered the problem of time, he would have been closer to Kierkegaard and Berdyaev, but his dichotomy of the theoretical knowing subject from the existing self made both the self and the issue of time too transcendent and ideational.

Time is said by Kant to be infinite, yet he does not show how infinite time and finite time are related nor how eternity is related to either. The infinite time is but a prolongation of the finite. Kant asserts the thesis that the world begins in time, together with the antithesis that it does not belong to time, since time is also infinite.[60] Not only is this regarded by him as an unresolved antinomy,[61] but the dialectic of the problem anticipates that of

Hegel, although Kant does not resort to the rationalistic escape of synthesis employed by Hegel. Yet, lacking any real *end* of time, Kant offers no real solution in his appeal to the prolongation and regress of time *ad infinitum.* Here we broach the important teleological and eschatological implications of time. Kant is to be credited, we believe, for introducing these matters, at least indirectly, to modern philosophy. Hegel and the later process philosophers like Bergson, Whitehead and Alexander came to see the problem of the end as indigenous to their cosmic theories, while, as we shall subsequently see, each of them, together with the biological evolutionists, come to settle for inadequate views of the *telos.*

Actually, Kant sees time as something determined by the noumenal realm, which is above experience or is not symmetrical to the phenomenal realm. As a category, time is noumenal along with the transcendent self. It belongs to the same realm as freedom, immortality and God. As a mental principle this category brings about a tie between the noumenal and the phenomenal orders. Yet when related to succession and history, time is seen to be in opposition to the moral realm.[62] This causes a total contrast between history and the moral absolute. The latter is seen by Kant to be intuited as the Categorical Imperative, or the self's innate sense of "I ought." It would appear that the opposition and contrast here referred to would be more tenable had Kant linked the transcendent self with the concrete existential self, while, to a degree, it offers another pre-existential insight into the marked difference between the temporal and the absolute. It points to the relativity of human understanding, a subjective problem of the self.

Existential Elements in the Hegelian View of Time

Kant's failure to keep time related to the concrete self while belonging to the noumenal as much as invited the extreme rationalization of time by Hegel. For Hegel the real is the rational. This amounts to an inflation of the noumenal and its identification with the transcendent self as projected into a cosmic process of Reason. Thus the ideal or noumenal order is so integrated and identified with the phenomenal as to absorb it. In this way the Kantian dualism is resolved and the antinomies

51

synthesized. The Kantian categories are literally taken up into this system of Reason and identified with the vast dialectical process which, in turn, is identified with the cosmos. Time as an anthropological problem is now lost in this grandiose system. The infinite process really dissolves the reality of time as men know it in existence. Time is obscured in the eternal, monistic process of the cosmic Reason. As a cosmic, rational category it has nothing to do with the existing self or his subjective understanding of time. The only significant consciousness is that which is basic to the cosmic Reason-Spirit. One begins to wonder what happened to the conscious selfhood of the philosopher himself!

Specifically, Hegel's view of time must be understood in terms of what he speaks of as "Absolute Knowledge." This pertains to the Reason-Spirit or universal Ego as a cosmic consciousness in process of self-contemplation and self-fulfillment. It is the universal Subject turning in upon itself, or, better the Substance being turned inward to the Spirit, its complement. Hegel asserts of this Absolute Knowledge, "It is spirit knowing itself in the shape of spirit." It is the "pure-self-existence of self-consciousness." [63] In this context Hegel would have it understood that "Time is just the notion definitely existent, and presented to consciousness in the form of empty intuition." [64] This means time is "the pure self in external form" and grasped only by intuition. "Time therefore appears as spirit's destiny and necessity, where spirit is not yet complete within itself." [65] The self-reflecting nature of Spirit is actually identified by Hegel with the cyclic process of cosmic time as it transforms Substance, the object of its consciousness, into pure Subject. One might characterize this by saying that the perpetual knowing process of cosmic Reason "takes time" or, better, "makes for time," since it implies, in this epistemological sense, a beginning and end, though, paradoxically, it is an eternal process. Here the teleological problem of time is reintroduced and amplified.

Hegel overtly states, "The process of carrying forward this form of knowledge of itself is the task which the spirit accomplishes as actual History." [66] In this respect time and history are complementary while, critically speaking, we can hardly distinguish them as anthropological, since the process to which they appertain is so utterly cosmological. History is merely "the process of becoming in terms of knowledge, a conscious self-mediating process-Spirit externalized and emptied into Time." [67] As a matter of cosmic intuition, then, time is in and of the cosmic Spirit, not the human spirit. Such a concept is so objective that it is the very opposite of anything existential.

Actually, this rational cosmic process lacks a real end save as it is its own "final aim," says Hegel.[68] But, somewhat as in Bergson's later scheme, this end remains a mere potentiality and never a real consummation or fulfillment. While providing an ambiguous idealistic teleology, this kind of monism of Reason's dialectic-in-operation, as it were, discounts the eschatological element in the problem of time whereby eternity and time have a difference to be taken seriously along with whatever they have in common. The finite time-consciousness of men is simply swallowed up in the infinite time-process of the cosmos. Even cosmic time is dialectically negated and thereby minimized and obscured as a problem and reality. By Hegel's dialectic of thesis, antithesis and synthesis all events of time, all particulars, in fact, are absorbed in a cosmic dialectic which perpetually affirms unity *within* multiplicity, permanence *in* change.

Hegel accepts the idea of a cosmic, evolutionary development, but rejects the concrete reality of time as involving any realistic past and future.[69] An abstract "eternally present" process of Reason-Spirit, identified with God at work, becomes a rejection of what we have looked upon as common, linear or realistically historical time. Though Hegel subordinates history, even historical religion and revelation, to the cosmic process of Reason, he actually obscures the reality of the history to which he refers in his philosophy of history. Such a history can be real only for God, we take note, since its particularity involving events and men is dissolved in the total synthetic Process, which keeps primary what is universal and negates all particulars. There is no room for uniqueness here. The real is the ideal and the rational, not the concrete and existential. "Spirit," says Hegel, "is immortal; with it there is no past, no future, but an essential now." [70] Being and Becoming thus coalesce in this process. The eternal is within the process of change.

While Hegel dissolves time in his cosmic scheme, he is to be credited with seeing the idea of the "eternal now" in his own way, a principle we have seen opened up by Plotinus and Augustine and later taken seriously by existentialists like Kierkegaard and Berdyaev. While Hegel kept it immanental and rational, the latter thinkers see it as suprarational and basically transcendent. We might say, however, that to a degree Hegel's ideas of the "eternally present" and "essential now" are pre-existential. They have much in common with Kierkegaard especially and really anticipate Kierkegaard's own dialectic. The major weakness here is Hegel's strong tendency to keep them irrelevant to a temporal now or temporal stream of time or, better, to the concrete knowing subject who is the center of time and history.

History linked with time is completely subsumed under the sovereign everlasting process of Reason in Hegel's System.[71] The end is only projected as the necessary and immanental fulfillment of the rational design. The end is both immanent and imminent to the beginning. Thus history is merely a puppet show. As Hegel himself says of history, it is "providentially determined." [72] Shakespeare expressed it earlier: "All the world's a stage, And all the men and woman merely players;/They have their exits and their entrances." [73] Actually, for Hegel this applies even to the Christian revelation which he regarded as a historical or phenomenal unfolding of the eternal or noumenal process.

Kant's stress upon the noumenal as primary helped pave the way for the rational determinism of Hegel's System. For Hegel the rational, universal Absolute of Reason completely determines phenomena and the outcome of any temporal or unfulfilled existent. Thus time is detemporalized, as it were, by being constantly under a synthetic process which dissolves any particular events, moments and tenses by necessity. Such a harsh rational teleology leaves no room for either a realistic history of a sort or an eschatological dimension which refuses to see all things lost or obscured immanentally. Yet it points to an end ahead or beyond the present moment of the process, while very much related to it.[74] Both history and religious eschatology are reduced to mere aspects of cosmology. This is not congruent to a Christian revelation which involves a divine incursion into history. While Christianity is ranked with the absolute it lacks a realistic historical setting of any significance. Only the metaphysical yields truth, not the historical, eventful or concrete.

Influenced by romanticism's evolutionary idea, Hegel's scheme dissolves time and its role as a problem related to tragedy, anxiety, destruction and death. "The dialectic of the finite and the infinite is continually resolved but never consummated." [75] There is constant synthesis but no real fulfillment, no end in any temporal or supratemporal sense. This system fails to relate time to either an existence of tension or an end of actual fulfillment. The whole cosmic process is moving but going nowhere in particular. It really ignores man's enslavement to time. It "redeems" time only as it negates and obscures it. In contrast to this Berdyaev has said, "The incommensurability between history and individual destinies is a tragedy . . . which demands the end of history." [76] But any end which is relevant to history cannot imply the liquidation or absorption of time and history as does Hegel's end. It cannot ignore the particular selves and events to which time and history belong.

For Hegel all reality is in Becoming, the spark between the positive and negative poles of Being and non-Being. The eternal and temporal are immanent to each other. But it appears that Hegel was not true to this idea of polarity, for, unlike Plato, he makes into a synthesis what is neither a synthesis nor a total dichotomy but really a tension of interrelated opposites, indeed, a both/and paradox, as we shall assert in connection with Berdyaev. The opposites are functioning while relevant to each other without negating each other. This is what generates the live spark! F. H. Brabant provocatively asks the following:

Is temporal change merely the gradual unveiling of God's real nature? Or, is it in some sense a change in God's consciousness of Himself? If the first, then God's eternity seems to have no actual contact with human suffering and struggle . . . if the second is true, that God himself grows and learns and enriches His experience through the historical process, this seems to contradict all the traditional Christian definitions of His perfection. [77]

These pertinent questions have no solution in Hegel, and in moving in on them we see them as having no adequate answer until we examine closely the time-eternity relationship of Nicholas Berdyaev's type of existentialism.

But, as already hinted, Hegel made a pre-existential contribution in his unacceptable attempt to synthesize eternity and time dialectically. First, it clarified the issues together with enunciating the dialectical method which belongs to a polarity seen in most metaphysical problems. Second, it helped overcome the more Platonic and static ideas of eternity hitherto held by most thinkers save Plotinus. Eternity at least is not kept aloof from what belongs to Becoming. Whether or not satisfactorily handled, at least Hegel helped clarify what pertains to this, thus favoring a more dynamic view of eternity akin to Spirit. This much dialectically anticipates Kierkegaard and Berdyaev, again, while more so the latter.

But having said this I cannot quite agree with my esteemed senior colleague Richard Kroner when he asserts that by his dialectic of synthesis it was Hegel rather than Kierkegaard who inaugurated existentialism.[78] It is better to say that Hegel helped pave the way for it, as did Kant. Existential time is not a rational synthesis, as shall be clarified, while it is a paradoxical tension of relevant opposites. Hegel dissolves all tension. Here the neo-Platonic unity-in-plurality is closer to the issue at stake, for it preserves a paradoxical tension which Hegel's pure reason cannot tolerate, while unto the debilitation of a practical reason belonging to human existence and time. Kierkegaard saw the basic issues here and refused to dissolve the tension between time and eternity while allowing for both their relation and disrelation.

The existential view of time, it appears, has more in common with the pluralist position of Schiller [79] than with Hegel. Whereas Hegel sees eternity as making and dissolving time, Schiller holds that eternity transcends time while both time and eternity are real. This, in principle, agrees with Berdyaev's existential position and, to a degree, with S. K., insofar as S. K. preserved a duality. Schiller pointed to a matter significant to our thesis when he said, "Our dilemma, then, is this, that if the reality of time is denied the whole meaning and rationality of the world is destroyed at one blow." [80] Furthermore, eternity is such that it even participates in time, Schiller averred. This anticipates another existential principle and helps point to what we see clarified by Berdyaev both in his "existential time" and its "eschatological dimension."

The background for an existential perspective of time has come into view while its contour must be given clearer exposition and outline through a closer examination of the existential thinkers themselves. From Locke, Kant and Hegel, then, we will move directly to Kierkegaard who did so much to crystallize existential time for the contemporary world of thought.

Existential Elements in the Kierkegaardian View of Time

A century ago in Denmark, Soren Kierkegaard revolted against the popular Hegelian rationalism that had almost come to straitjacket theology and culture, especially under a state religion.[81] This he did upon taking a creative existential point of view as a thinker who would enunciate the priority of particulars to universals and the self and existence to any objective ontology. For S. K.* the self was concrete within existence, not abstract within reason. Such a self is neither a hypothetically transcendent knower like Kant's subject nor one to be lost in the cosmic Reason-Spirit of Hegel's monism.

A spiritual subject, the self of existence as held by Kierkegaard, is the center of relevant reality,[82] quite as for Augustine. As such, the self is a "synthesis" of the finite and the infinite, of time and eternity.[83] While this "synthesis" may appear to resemble that of Hegel's dialectic, actually it does not, for S. K. does not mean by this a rational synthesis dialectically satisfactory to reason. It is more like Berdyaev's paradoxical self with a both/and tension implied, though S. K. does not always think in these terms when stressing his either/or dialectic of moral and spiritual alternatives.

Being an ambivalent subject of both freedom and necessity, the self to Kierkegaard is "a synthesis in which the finite is the limiting factor." [84] Here time is the fundamental aspect of a person's mundane existence, an existence replete with anxiety, dread and despair. *Angst* is a sensitivity to one's finitude; *dread,* an awareness of possible absorption by non-Being; *despair,* a recognized meaninglessness of one's very existence.

While the so-called Real Self belongs to eternity, the basis of one's true *Existenz*, the existence-oriented self is steeped in the vicissitudes and fleeting phenomena of time. Fundamentally, time is regarded by S. K. as "succession," even infinite succession.

Following a somewhat Platonic pattern, S. K. attributes the realization of one's true self solely to divine revelation. Yet the

* Soren Kierkegaard.

57

existing self is neither a mere spectator of time's passing nor an automaton; he is a committed participant to whom time is a subtle problem. This makes the self the epitome of the paradoxical duality of Being and Becoming, even as it accounts for a man's nostalgic yearning for eternity from within time, a restless striving not always understood. Not a mere particle within an abstract process, Hegelian or otherwise, the existing subject lives intensely within the tension, which to Kierkegaard is "the frontier between time and eternity." [85] This is best offset by "the Moment," the existential present when the self, caught in despair of his meaning, is confronted by eternity and in that immeasurable moment finds his true *Existenz*.

In view of the foregoing, Kierkegaard says, "The existing subject is eternal but *qua* existing temporal." [86] Thus we see how the Kierkegaardian version of time *per se* has much in common with the Platonic realm of Becoming. S. K. gives us some important insights into this. Swinging on the wicket gate between time and eternity, man, he suggests, falls eventually into despair by expecting eternal happiness from things strictly temporal.[87] But when he sees his ironical situation and accepts his eternal *Existenz*, he experiences that true "Moment" of eternity-in-time.[88]

The Moment is the core of what we prefer to call "existential time" in its most positive sense. S. K. calls it "the finite reflection of eternity in time."[89] A Platonic element comes into view, we must note, though this "reflection" is not to be attributed to a common time as it is in Plato's Becoming, but only to the special moment of existential time. This moment is one of a sublime encounter.[90] It is an "atom of eternity," which imbues one's existence with an eternal quality in a way that lifts it above sheer temporal quantity. This deeper intensity of one's total existence is realized through what S. K. speaks of as "the moment perpetually affirmed." By this the abyss between time and eternity, the finite and infinite, is bridged.

For Kierkegaard, then, existential time is the most genuine; it is the intense "now" identified with eternity, the "only real present." Sin is that which is false and artificial; it is the losing of eternity-in-time, a confidence in sheer finitude, a settling for meaningless time and pseudo selfhood. Truth and righteousness, on the other hand, belong only to the great Moment of encounter, based on the "qualitative leap" of faith and ethical decision.[91] Seeing the intensity and depth of existential time in relation to its eternal quality of transcendence, S. K. regards chronological time as a matter of sheer human frustration. He can say, "Viewed pathetically, a single second has infinite value; viewed comically, ten thousand years are but a trifle, like yesterday when it is gone."[92]

Meaningful time, then, is not simply a quantity but a quality admitting the paradox of eternal Being in temporal Becoming, eternity-in-time. Experientially, this is the plenitude of true existence, the "fullness of time" of which the Bible speaks.[93] Included in this Moment is the thought that what has been in existence now becomes; the past is real only as brought by its significance and memory into the present. The latter was touched upon by Augustine but with less stringency. S. K. seems to close the accordian of linear time, keeping time real only in the vertical present. This is basic to his staccato-like idea that all of life is "repetition." There is a certain "contemporaneity" to all historical events, and ethical and spiritual choices belong solely to a present that is pregnant with the eternal.[94] It is this which allows the Christian to think of Christ as "our eternal contemporary." Eternity is seen by faith to be intersecting and "constantly permeating time."[95] By faith's present moment perpetually affirmed a person is not a mere spectator of time and history, then, but a maker thereof. History is no longer the meaningless series of events that was seen in an existence of anxiety, but now becomes meaningful and sacred. While S. K. does not enlarge upon this, Berdyaev does so and sees its profound eschatological implications for human existence, history and destiny.

As implied above, common time to Kierkegaard is a meaningless succession, and the present cannot be grasped from within its stream. Only "the eternal is the present," and the present is an "annulled succession."[96] This is S. K.'s Augustinian counterpart to Hegel's rationalized idea of the "eternally present." But there is still a deficiency in this idea, we maintain, lying in the Kierkegaardian view of the present. Unlike Augustine, as comparatively and critically examined earlier in this chapter, S. K. keeps the past and future of time *unreal* save as brought into the present. This is an important matter, for it means S. K. keeps linear or historic time ephemeral or utterly unreal.[97] It

59

is left illusory in the negative connotation of Plato's notion that time is a mere image.

Nor does Kierkegaard account for how an unreal past and future are *made* real in the present from a temporal standpoint, which can employ the ideas of remembrance and expectation such as recognized by Augustine and Berdyaev. Time is ephemeral in man's consciousness *per se*. Strange, then, that its problems should be so realistic to the existing man! Logically it should imply that existence itself is mere illusion and the evils that go with it as well. Here Kierkegaard has gone too far, he dissolves the actuality of time from the human standpoint almost as much as Hegel does in his way. Augustine anticipated this problem and asserted that if past and future are not real then the *present* is not time but eternity. S. K. stopped here. Augustine went on to qualify this by saying that if such is the case there can be no time at all, not even a temporally real present moment.[98] The present could only belong to God and eternity, then, and not to man and history.

Here is where Matthew Spinka's judgment that existential time is not a real time[99] is to be understood and yet corrected. It is applicable to S. K. but not really to Berdyaev, as we shall see. The issue is not one of depreciating the real as related to eternity but of determining to what extent the real is related to time. What does Kierkegaard really do on the strength of his argument? Logically, he keeps eternity related only to itself. But a person of existence is steeped in time, not removed from it altogether; therefore, the present which is his concern must not be negated altogether as a realistic temporal phenomenon, even when made significant and intensely qualitative by the eternal present. S. K. fails us here and provides for no eschatology related to history in any sense whatever. No involved future and no real end are seen here, only a negation and, in that sense, removal therefrom. The present alone is real, but the only real present acknowledged by S. K. is the eternal. This leaves common linear time and the anxiety and sinful tension associated with it now mere phantoms. Of what significance can eternity be to such an illusory existence?

Kierkegaard himself sees a problem here when he says, "It is a contradiction to forget the whole content of one's life and yet remain the same man."[100] In fact his negation of common time conflicts with another of his observations:

> A purely human courage is required to renounce the whole of the temporal to gain the eternal. . . . But a paradoxical and humble courage is required to grasp the whole of the temporal by virtue of the absurd, and this is the courage of faith.[101]

From the standpoint of the interpretation of time, these words should have flowed from the pen of Berdyaev, whose existentialism is consistently better balanced, allowing more consideration to be given to the time factor, even in the existential moment.

Anticipating improvements in Berdyaev, may we say that he does not succumb to Kierkegaard's abused Platonic idea of unreal time. S. K.'s eternity-in-time, as significant as it is, is too "timeless" to pertain to the concrete man of existence. The "fullness of time," as he sees it, is too remote from a man's perspective of time. It is all quality without a realistic quantity; a transcendence removed from the immanence of creation to which it is meant to be illuminating. It is eternal light without the temporal lamp; a luminous sun without eyes to see it. In this respect, Plato did not split the universe so harshly when he asserted time to be a moving image of eternity. While he saw a contrast he also saw a significant interrelationship, one which S. K. tends to destroy out of his distaste for a rational synthesis.

But this extreme reaction competes with S. K.'s own *paradoxical* "synthesis" of the finite and infinite centering in the man of existence. It also encumbers the legitimacy of another of his interests, "the fact that tragedy seeks support in the historical" and "needs historical reality more than comedy."[102] On the other hand, it corroborates the primacy of the transcendental as stressed by Kierkegaard and of which he says, "The religious seeks no support in the historic . . . the historic . . . is never finished . . . ."[103] and, "The religious is simply and solely qualitative dialectic and disdains quantity . . ."[104] Things temporal, historic and quantitative are completely "outward" to S. K. whereas, he says, "The religious lies on the inward sphere."[105]

61

All this seems to be crystallized in the basic question: "Is it possible to base an eternal happiness upon historical knowledge?"[106] S. K.'s question is important, but his answer, while provocative and helpful, appears deficient. May we anticipate the expanding argument here by a crossquestioning question: What human knowledge, even that of faith, is ever unhistorical knowledge? The issue may not be one of a *basis* in time but a vital *relation* to it.

* * * *

Pertinent to our basic contention that Berdyaev, more than other existentialists and pre-existentialists, keeps both time and eternity real while in relation, the preceding observations of the respective divisions of this chapter bring into range the fundamental problems involved. Having scanned the philosophical shoreline we have traced a chain of existential and pre-existential insights which charts us toward the Isle of Kairos, an existential time of far-reaching consequence. Drawing near and adjusting the lens of our equatorial we will train it upon that enchanting island whose ridge of time is pierced by a vertical peak snow-capped from the eternal source of time's rich meaning. It is upon this that we must now focus our attention.

NOTES

1 In another work, *The Pertinence of the Paradox*, I shall point this out with some detail in another context of thought.
2 Plato, *Timaeus*, A, B, C.
3 *Ibid.*, 37D, E. Cf. 38D and 38, b, 6.
4 *Ibid.*, 37E.
5 *Ibid.*, 38A, B, C, D, 39B, C, D, 47B.
6 *Ibid.*, 38A, B, C.
7 Aristotle, *Physics*, Bk. IV, Chap. 14, 223a, 16-23; 223b, 15, 23.
8 *Ibid.*, Bk. IV, Chap. 11, 219b. Cf. 219a, 8, 14.
9 *Ibid.*, Bk. IV, Chap. 12, 220b, 8. Cf. 221a, b. Cf. Epicurus who said, "It is impossible to conceive time in itself independent of the movement or rest of things," as cited by Clement Wood, *The Outline of Man's Knowledge*, p. 249.

[10] *Ibid.*, Bk. III, Chaps. 1, 2, 7. Bk. VIII, Chap. 10, 267b, 18-25 *De Caelo,* Bk. I, Chap. 9, 279a, 33; 279b, 18.
[11] *Physics,* Bk. VIII, Chap. 2, 252b, 9-12.
[12] *Ibid.,* Bk. IV, Chap. 14, 223a, 16-22, b. 15.
[13] *Ibid.,* 223a, 23.
[14] *Timaeus,* 39K, 42E.
[15] Cf. *The Phaedo* where one of the themes of Plato is the problem of the knower, and *The Republic,* Bk. VI, which deals with memory and the philosopher as a guardian of truth.
[16] Cf. John F. Callahan, *Four Views of Time in Ancient Philosophy,* p. 36.
[17] *Enneades,* III; 7:7, 8, p. 195ff; 7:9, p. 109f.
[18] *Ibid.,* 7:9, p. 110.
[19] *Ibid.,* 7:11, 12.
[20] *Ibid.,* 7:1, p. 96.
[21] F. H. Brabant, *Time and Eternity in Christian Thought,* p. 30.
[22] R. W. Inge, *Philosophy of Plotinus,* Vol. I, p. 232ff.
[23] *Ibid.,* pp. 22-24, 69ff.
[24] *Enneades,* III; 7:2, p. 98.
[25] This is something F. H. Brabant fails to see helping to remove "the frigid abstractness of the Platonic Forms" (*op. cit.,* p. 25) and making the eternal more dynamic and personal, while he does see it of Plotinus' fusion of subject and object in eternal life. Cf. pp. 26-28.
[26] *Confessions,* Book XI, par. 35, 36. Cf. 21, 32, where Augustine sees the existential problem of seeking to know time from within it. In *The City of God,* this is neglected.
[27] *Ibid.,* par. 37, 38.
[28] *Ibid.,* par. 22: italics mine.
[29] *Ibid.,* par. 23.
[30] *Ibid.,* 26.
[31] *Ibid.* Cf. 22, 21, 36, 37, 27.
[32] *Ibid.,* 13.
[33] *Ibid.,* 17.
[34] *Ibid.,* 16. Cf. 13.
[35] Brabant, *op. cit.,* p. 57f.
[36] Cf. *Confessions,* Bk. XI, 25, 26, p. 266f.
[37] Callahan, *op. cit.,* p. 204.
[38] *Confessions,* Bk. XI, par. 29-33, 36.
[39] Brabant, *op. cit.,* pp. 94-102.
[40] *Ibid.,* pp. 99-103.
[41] *Essay Concerning Human Understanding,* Bk. II, Ch. XIV, 1-6, 16. Cf. Leslie Paul, *The English Philosophers,* p. 118.
[42] *Ibid.,* 32.
[43] *Ibid.,* Chap. XV, 12, p. 91.
[44] *Critique of Pure Reason,* p. 75.
[45] *Ibid.,* pp. 75-91.
[46] *Ibid.,* pp. 236, 74.
[47] *Ibid.,* pp. 75, 79, 193.
[48] *Ibid.,* p. 76ff.
[49] *Ibid.,* p. 415n.
[50] *Ibid.,* p. 75.
[51] *Ibid.,* pp. 400, 440-449; 466-468, 475-478. Cf. 123, 131, 194, 197ff, 232.
[52] *Ibid.,* p. 77.
[53] *Ibid.,* p. 78f. This pertains to the knower's transcending capacity.
[54] *Ibid.,* p. 388.
[55] *Ibid.,* pp. 77, 167f.

56 *Ibid.*, p. 136.
57 *Ibid.*, p. 396ff.
58 *Ibid.*, p. 531.
59 Bertrand Russell in *A History of Western Philosophy*, p. 354, recognizes this deficiency in Kant. He states that Augustine's subjective time is far superior to that of Kant and adds that Augustine came closest to a solution of all early philosophies of time. Henri Bergson in *Time and Free Will*, pp. 232, 205f, 221f, also said Kant left the "free self" removed from the existing self but designated the subject who relates himself to himself.
60 *Critique*, A 396ff.
61 Cf. Berdyaev's criticism and quotation of Kant in *The Divine and the Human*, p. 195. Cf. S. K.'s statement, "Time is the category upon which pure thought must suffer shipwreck" (as quoted by Carl Michalson in a letter to the author).
62 Brabant, *op. cit.*, p. 114f.
63 *The Phenomenology of Mind*, p. 798.
64 *Ibid.*, p. 800.
65 *Ibid.*, Religion pertains to this but as that which falls short of absolute certainty.
66 *Ibid.*, p. 801.
67 *Ibid.*, p. 807.
68 "Introduction to the Philosophy of History," *Selections*, p. 349.
69 *Ibid.*, pp. 442, 357.
70 *Ibid.*
71 *Ibid.*, p. 440, 349f.
72 *Ibid.*, p. 353f.
73 *As You Like It*, Act II, Scene VII.
74 "Philosophy of History," *op. cit.*, pp. 354, 359.
75 Berdyaev, *The Divine and the Human*, p. 196.
76 Berdyaev, *The Fate of Man in the Modern World*, p. 89. Cf. Karl Löwith, *Meaning In History*, pp. 52-59, for elucidations pertaining to Hegel's secularization of the Christian view of history.
77 Brabant, *op. cit.*, p. 110.
78 Kroner's "Introduction" to *Hegel's Early Theological Writings*, p. 46.
79 Cf. W. W. Calkins, *The Persistent Problems of Philosophy*, p. 445f.
80 Schiller, *Riddles of the Sphinx*, Chap. IX, Sect. 11, p. 259.
81 Soren Kierkegaard, *Attack Upon Christendom*, pp. 78ff, 166ff, 191ff, 213ff.
82 *Concluding Unscientific Postscript*, p. 306.
83 *The Concept of Dread*, p. 76.
84 *Sickness Unto Death*, p. 45. Here "synthesis" is not a Hegelian idea, but meant to imply a paradoxical polarity, both aspects of which are real and related. It connotes a kind of mixture, as it were.
85 As expressed by Melville Chaning-Pearce in *Modern Christian Revolutionaries*, p. 29. Berdyaev uses the expression "on the frontier of two worlds."
86 *Concluding Unscientific Postscript*, p. 76.
87 *Ibid.*, pp. 505-508. Cf. *For Self Examination*, pp. 35-74, also *Philosophical Fragments* and *Sickness Unto Death*.
88 *Ibid.*, p. 75. Cf. *Stages on Life's Way.*, "religiousness B." Cf. *Concept of Dread*, p. 78.
89 *Concept of Dread*, p. 79.
90 *Ibid.*
91 *Ibid.*, p. 81f.
92 *Concluding Unscientific Postscript*, p. 84f.
93 *Concept of Dread*, p. 81. Cf. Galatians 4:4.
95 *Concept of Dread*, p. 80.

94 *Repetition*, pp. 3ff, 12, 33ff. Cf. *Either-Or*, Vol. II, p. 184.
96 *Ibid.*, p. 77.
97 Cf. H. V. Martin, *Kierkegaard, The Melancholy Dane*, p. 56ff.
98 *Confessions*, Bk. XI, p. 17. Cf. 13. "No time is all at once present"—though past and future are related to it. Cf. 21, p. 260.
99 Spinka's lecture on Nicholas Berdyaev delivered at Drew University and appearing in *Christianity and the Existentialists*, edited by Carl Michalson, p. 73. Spinka seems to forget that to Berdyaev the *chronos* is real, to which eternity *relates itself* in the existential moment. Cf. Spinka, *Nicolas Berdyaev: Captive of Freedom*, 178f.
100 *Fear and Trembling*, p. 54.
101 *Ibid.*, p. 59.
102 *Stages on Life's Way*, p. 396f.
103 *Ibid.*, p. 403.
104 Ibid., p. 401.
105 *Ibid.*, p. 399.
106 *Philosophical Fragments*, p. 323.

CHAPTER III

EXISTENTIAL TIME AND ITS DISTINCTIVE MEANING

Having introduced existential time as a concrete problem of existence and traced its chain of background in the history of philosophy, we are now in a position to magnify its meaning and distinctive features. Only after elucidating the meaning of existential time will we be able to vivify what we call its eschatological dimension. Tacking closer, then, to the main object of our pursuit we venture into an insular inlet of meaning, one which opens up vistas of fresh significance for time and human existence. First, we must sound out the specific types of time involved in this discovery. Here, Berdyaev is given the helm.

The Classification of Existential Time

Berdyaev is one thinker who does not try to escape the reality of time, even though he sees it cannot of itself vindicate its significance. To him there are three basic types of time, each of which is very real because they are relevant to existing men. They are (1) historic or horizontal time, (2) cosmic or cyclic time, and (3) existential time.[1] Though they are distinguishable, every man lives, or can live, in all three modes of time, neither of which can be dismissed as unimportant. They now must be examined separately and given a practical interpretation.

Horizontal Time

Horizontal or historic time is both a durational and successive stream. Its three tenses of past, present and future, all of which are regarded as important by Berdyaev, are "spectral," not objective.[2] This is to say they are real to the knowing subject and cannot be demonstrated to be relevant on any objective or neutral basis. Having a forward movement, horizontal time also implies a goal or end. This end is meaningless and unattainable in time itself, however, for it involves something beyond itself, somewhat like a river emptying into the sea. Furthermore, the future implied by the end of time conceptually includes a temporal infinity which cannot be grasped by a person's consciousness in a given moment. Yet to respect the idea of the *end*, Berdyaev shows that it must appertain to a time which includes a realistic future. But such a time cannot be equated with its measurement; therefore, horizontal time, though real and identifiable as *chronos*, is never to be equated with man's arbitrary clock time.

Time, to Berdyaev, is fundamentally a paradox, and to diagnose the meaning of the present is to begin to appreciate this. "The present is as inconvenient to sit on as the blade of a razor," said Homer.[3] Yet the present moment is very real to the knower. Its relation to the past is to be denied no more than the beam of light that strikes the eye can be said to have no relation to the "light years" of the sun's rays.

While not denying the reality of linear time as did Kierkegaard, with the possible support of an abused version of Plato's dualism and a one-sided interpretation of Augustine, Berdyaev really echoes Augustine when he describes the paradoxical nature of horizontal time. He states, "Its break-up into a past, which no longer exists, a future which does not yet exist, and a present which is in part already past, and in part still belongs to the future, makes it difficult to capture its reality."[4] But right here we confront a contradiction in Berdyaev. While he stresses the reality of horizontal time this quotation could also be pressed to defend Kierkegaard's position in that, as it stands, it expresses the unreality of past and future. This is not quite congenial to Berdyaev's total picture of things. As the center of time the present is "an infinitely brief instant," says Berdyaev. It is "a certain abstract point."[5] While Berdyaev sees the present as a mathematical point in linear time, and in that sense it is "abstract," he also sees its more innovative reality to the knowing subject of existence, i.e., its "spectral" or subjective relativity and existential relevance to the knower. The latter is the more tenable aspect of the present, since the idea of a mathematical point tends to be spatial. Though an elusive and subtle moment, the present, we reiterate, is very real to the subject. This alone does not refer to the *meaning* of the present but points to where lies its existence.

While both succession and duration are real to Berdyaev and together they constitute what he describes as *chronos* or horizontal time, he rejects the arbitrary measurements of time. They make for pseudo time and distort much of human existence. The popular notion of an ongoing, chopped-up timeline is a falsely objectified concept based on movement and successive events. It does not account for the durational continuity which is divided up into periods. This notion goes back to Aristotle's physical view of time and is applied to artificial standards of measurement typified by the calendar and clock. Indicating the problem, Nicholas of Cusa said, "The clock never strikes the hour, save when the concept biddeth."[6] It is the knower who accounts for time, not the pseudo standards imposed upon it. The comparison of time to a cinema of quickly succeeding "stills"[7] applies metaphorically to linear time, while if accepted as a description it becomes another objectification of time. Still there is a durational character to time which, as perceived by the subject, is also successive, because of its eventfulness. This is witnessed by the subject who participates in, remembers and anticipates events. Does the concrete man of existence dare to live on any other basis?

Cosmic Time

Cosmic time is radically different from the horizontal time of human history. Berdyaev really goes back to Aristotle in comparing it to a circle,[8] since it is not forward-moving like horizontal time but cyclical, rhythmical and repetitious. This also suggests the deficiency of employing the circle as the symbol of eternity, as has been the case in religious tradition. What to the poet is "the music of the spheres" is really cyclic time. It is to be seen in the cosmic seasons and the conduct of the planets, which provide the pattern or schedule of man's mundane existence.

The Greeks envied the rhythm of the cosmos. Philosophically, salvation to them meant a rational harmony with its order. Thus cyclic time with its determinism, especially as seen by the

Stoics, was a key to reality. But cyclic time tends to inundate historic time, even though it sometimes contributes to history's eventfulness through the rhythm as well as the cataclysmic events of nature. The biological necessities put upon men in their eating, sleeping and patterns of sex life would bespeak the rhythm of cyclic time. Seasonal rains, blizzards, famines and hurricanes as well as the relation of Pompeii to Mount Vesuvius would illustrate the cataclysmic factor.

Whereas historic time is rationally objectified by number and measure, cyclic time is even closer to being objective. This is reflected in the rhythmic cosmic processes of nature, which men do not control. Since necessitatively repetitious there is no real end to cyclic time, Berdyaev thinks, hence no forward movement, only a projected *telos*.[9] At this point Berdyaev is open to some question, for modern astronomy sees a temporal end to at least some of the cyclic process, if for no other reason than that the earth, if man does not blow it up himself, is expected to be destroyed by contact with either the sun or moon in an off-beat moment. Astronomers at Hayden Planetarium in New York speak of this as "the end of the world." Berdyaev, however, seems to qualify his view when he recognizes the *telos* to be both temporal and supratemporal, a matter reserved for Chapter VI.

Whereas historic time is largely man-centered, cosmic time is nature-centered, but not without serious significance for men who are related to nature even *as* men. Whereas horizontal time implies events and a beginning and an end, cyclic time is a necessitative perpetual process seemingly oblivious to either beginning or end, let alone events of a decisive moral and existential character. Threatening to overwhelm man by its impersonal process, cyclic time is, nevertheless, made basic to his measurement of time in the calendar and clock. But it is this objectivization of time which leads to man's enslavement to time, especially due to its pseudo measurements. This enslavement, related to anxieties over the past and future, constitutes "evil time," for Berdyaev. Time itself is not evil; how men regard it can be. Thus the evil of time is a subjective problem of human existence.

Berdyaev maintains that while the cosmic process is related to a man's physical existence and thereby contributes to his

69

interlude of historic time on earth, it does not account for the knower who perceives both cosmic and historic times. The mystery of the existing knower and his consciousness cannot be bypassed. It is fundamental to our problem. Cyclic time is related necessitatively to all men alike; it is something that *must* be thought, so to speak. But horizontal time is more "particular and private," meaning different things to different persons in their specific situations. Cosmic time is restrictive; historic time is more free, though commonly made restrictive by man's arbitrary and objectified measurements of time under the pressures of cosmic time. We might say that events in cyclic time are general, deterministic and rhythmical, whereas events in historic time are particular, moral, less predictable and more innovative. Cyclic recurrences are insistent, whereas horizontal events can be creative, decisive and selective. Historic time at least occasions a moral relevance, while cosmic time is utterly amoral in itself.

Cyclic time is akin to natural necessity. In this respect it accompanies the organic scheme of birth, growth, maturity, senescence and death. Since it is a perpetual rhythm, it is important to take note that cosmic time cannot imply progress. It belongs to the cosmic laws of necessity but not human freedom. Speaking about human life in this context, columnist Hal Boyle once remarked, "It's such an odd and unpredictable rhythm of pain and pleasure, despair and wonder—this being a prisoner in the pattern of time." When the medieval monk washed the face of a sundial the words that greeted him were, "Brother, it's later than you think!" Cosmic time yields little more than a "timetable of worries." This must be recognized as an enslavement. Sensing this the Psalmist wrote, "We spend our years as a tale that is told." (Ps. 90:9.) And unless life is linked with a higher dimension of time it is apt to become "a tale told by an idiot, full of sound and fury, signifying nothing."[10] Sophocles, too, referred to such bondage:

> Fair Aegeus' son, only to gods in heaven
> Come no old age, nor death of anything.
> All else is turmoiled by our Master Time.

What to human existence appears to be "death's dateless night" is closer to being dated by cyclic time. In this respect cosmic time is harsh and fatalistic. Does it still have full say about man's destiny? Not if he is *a* man, a particular moral and existing self not to be obscured by either a materialistic process or an idealistic universal. Man can be involved in the cosmic process without being completely inundated by it.

Cyclic time involves change, but it is an evolutionary necessity rather than a personally creative or apprehensive innovation. While it is pertinent to the person in existence who cannot altogether escape its strictures, in itself cyclic time so much as reduces him to a mathematical digit as it throbs out the rhythm of the cosmic process. Thus time is both cyclic and more than cyclic to Berdyaev. The phenomena of the cosmic panorama affect all men, yet can neither account fully for the temporal drama of human existence nor give it meaning. The grandeur and rhythm of the cosmos are meaningful primarily because they can neither explain nor account for the unique creature of time who perceives and appreciates them. Said an observer to a young astronomer expounding the cosmic splendor of astral systems and their light years with almost derogatory inferences about man's infinitesimal place in the cosmos, "But remember, sir, you are the astronomer." Indeed, the timetable of the cosmos is awesome, but only to a being who is subject to more than its stereotyped rhythm. Such a subject-being is not a mere spectator of time but an engenderer of time. Metaphorically, he is comparable to the projector and film designer to which the film strip and reels of time must be related and qualified to be consequential. Time belongs to his consciousness more than to the world.

Existential Time

With the concrete knower at the center of existence, historic time is frequently distorted by its pseudo measurements and objectified standards. Such expedients manage either to mislead or discomfit a person as he looks to the past or the future. The conservative may look to the past for what is classically beautiful, happy or perfect often to neglect the creative opportunities of the present, while the progressive often looks with utopian anticipation to the future, only to remain frustrated over the

71

present. But both demonstrate how historic, horizontal time is so incomplete and shattered in itself. Thus, not only cyclic time but even linear time is linked with a person's anxiety and tragic existence.

Berdyaev says that the inclination to objectify time and restrict human life to its artificial measurements began with and illustrates the Fall, when pretemporal man fell out of harmonious relation to eternity, and time became a "decomposed eternity." Here Berdyaev is more neo-Platonic than biblical, while contributing to an existential version of the biblical myth of the Fall. There are two ways out of this enslavement: one, by surrender to the necessities of nature and the blind rhythm of cosmic time, only for a man to become less than a man: the other, by living intensely and qualitatively in the present by seeing events submerged in existential time, an intense meaningful time, especially as related to eternity. The choice is an existential one: either one's utter capitulation to a meaningless existence or one's faith in an eternity that yields a meaningful existence and destiny. To see this is to see the preeminence of a choice as the individual contemplates his existence.

While very real, neither horizontal nor cyclic times have meaning in themselves, Berdyaev shrewdly affirms. The significance of these times is to be seen in their relevance to the knowing subject-in-existence. Accompanying this is a "historical dynamism" which bespeaks a purposeful end to existence.[11] This cannot be accounted for by an objective cyclic time or an evolutionary process with a *telos,* as we shall see, but demands a supratemporal as well as temporal *eschaton* which sees time's *end* in vital relation to eternity.

It is in view of the foregoing that *time and things temporal gain real meaning only through the "break-through of the transcendent,"* as Berdyaev puts it.[12] This is the *ekstasis,* the interruption of time when eternity invades it. It is the dynamic moment of *true or meaningful time, existential time. In this existential moment eternity is seen to endow common time with a supratemporal quality not limited to the linear and cyclic patterns of the cosmos and existence.* The present moment is now no mere "fragment of time" but an intense instant of meaningful time. This kind of time when seen in relation to history with all its "tragi-comedy," [13] as Berdyaev expresses it, makes history more than just so many past events but a meaningful series of events.

Interpreting this, we might say that as *Historie* (common, less personal history) can become *Geschichte* (the more biographical and crucially moral nature of events) so now *Geschichte*, while not alienated from *Historie*, becomes *Heilsgeschichte*. Secular history becomes sacred history; common time becomes uncommon. The events pertaining to this are both temporal and supratemporal. As samples of existential time they are not limited to horizontal and cyclic times but are like the single "point" where the vertical intersects the horizontal, where the *vertical quality of eternity imbues the horizontal quantity of time with a higher dimension.* This point is the "present instant" of *true* time,[14] i.e., existential or meaningful time. Here is a dynamic eternal *now* made relevant to moments or events in common time, thus giving them a depth, quality and intensity from beyond themselves, while not precluding their relation to common linear time. This is fundamental to the thesis propounded at the outset of this work and is germane to what makes Berdyaev's existential point of view superior to others.

Existential time, then, cannot be expressed simply in terms of horizontal or cyclic time, while neither can it ignore them. It is time belonging to the subject's present moment when touched by and imbued with eternity. Just as the self transcends things so, too, it is transcended. This applies to such a moment of depth. Thus an otherwise finite moment can be experienced with the intensity of an infinity. Berdyaev saw this pertaining to one's moments of worship, artistic creativity, emotional rapture and, in a negative sense, even in suffering.[15] A moment, then, can be either what Soren Kierkegaard called an "atom of eternity" or an obnoxious, evil endlessness. But there can be victory over the latter with its negative and repellent infinity through the positive, spiritual communion with the Eternal.

Both kinds of intensity are existentially relevant, but the one is an enslaving kind of intensity, the other liberating. The latter is seen reflected in the Passion of Christ and the ministry of the Apostle Paul, for instance. Paul knew and even welcomed "the fellowship of His sufferings," as expressed in Philippians 3:10. There is a depth and quality in such moments that cannot be measured or defined. It is the special dimension that existential time has that ordinary linear and cyclic times lack. Berdyaev says,

> Existential time is not calculated mathematically, for it depends upon the intensity with which one lives, upon our sufferings and our joy. In it creativity is brought about and leads into ecstasy; one can symbolize it by a point, which expresses a movement in depth.[16]

The failure on the part of rational and process philosophers to see this accounts in part for the remoteness of their theories from the concrete existence of men and their inability to give meaning to human tragedy and human destiny as well as to ethical decision, aesthetic creativity and religious inspiration.

Existential time is distinctively paradoxical. It bespeaks the opposition and yet the interrelation of time and eternity. This very factor is what makes common time uncommon. While we shall subsequently enlarge what this involves, suffice it to say here that this is the locus of Berdyaev's resolution of the fundamental philosophical problem of the one and the many or the principle of permanence as enunciated by Parmenides versus the principle of flux as enunciated by Heraclitus. Eternity as something dynamic rather than static accounts for this interrelation of opposites. "Eternity itself," says Berdyaev somewhat in keeping with Plotinus, "must be understood dynamically, not statically; in it absolute rest coincides with absolute movement."[17] This calls to mind the doctrine of *actus purus* held by Thomas Aquinas but proves itself much less of an abstraction; something more personal and dynamic. The Eternal Now is seen meeting the temporal now and affecting it existentially. It is because of this, as Augustine somewhat similarly saw it, that each moment of time is made relevant to eternity and potentially serviceable to it. But this rests upon an eternity which, so to speak, takes the initiative and makes itself relevant to time, for time in itself is meaningless, though real. Time is either empty or filled. To be meaningful the eternal must fill it. This relationship has been seen more shrewdly by Berdyaev than by either Augustine or Kierkegaard.

With this as our description of Berdyaev's classification of time we must ask: How is time known? Having but touched upon this in the background given in the previous chapter, let us turn our attention to another basic aspect of time and its existential interpretation.

The Knowledge of Existential Time

Like most of the basic problems of philosophy, time cannot be understood apart from the epistemological problem. We already have indicated that the existential perspective sees the problem of the knower himself at the heart of the problem of time. Plato, Plotinus, Augustine and Kierkegaard saw this each in his own way and, to lesser degrees, Locke and Kant also did. We have seen how Berdyaev has certain roots in common with all these thinkers, whereas it is his way of moving beyond them which is crucial to the over-all picture of time and eternity as the basis for a meaningful existence and destiny.

There are two fundamental aspects of the knowledge of time which must be clarified. Berdyaev, somewhat like Augustine, sees them to be memory and what he calls the "prophetic spirit." These demand examination and interpretation.

Memory and Existential Time

It was the problem of memory which led Augustine to introduce the idea of the "eternal now" by which he saw that the past lives on in the present.[18] Yet Plato had seen the significance of memory also, and his theory of "recollection" implied intuited "memories" of a pre-existent life. "Memory," says Berdyaev, "is undoubtedly man's most profound ontological principle, the one which cements and preserves the unity of personality."[19]

Time implies changes in a person, but the remembrance of the changes helps keep the knowing self a unified being in the midst of change and temporal succession. It contributes to duration in this respect. But the existential perspective enhances the meaning of this relationship. The past, for Berdyaev, is real even in the horizontal sense, though memory brings it into the present, making it relevant to a person's "now." Thus, a past event is "contemporized," as it were. It is made significant in the present, but, unlike Soren Kierkegaard, Berdyaev does not contend that it is unreal apart from the present. "The present past is distinct from the past regarded from the standpoint of the present," says Berdyaev.[20] Kierkegaard overlooked this, but Augustine did not.

We must concede that while Augustine made a parallel observation, his version of the distinction between "the past" and "present of things past,"[21] when taken out of context, lends almost as much support to S. K.'s view of linear time's unreality as to Berdyaev's view of its reality. Augustine sees a present of each tense related to the knower's "memory," "sight" and "expectation," respectively. This means that the tenses have consequence only in relation to the subject's present. Yet Augustine, as earlier denoted, was reluctant to deny the reality of the tenses of linear time. In general, then, he gives more support to Berdyaev than to Kierkegaard, even more than Berdyaev seemed to realize.

In the existential moment, Berdyaev asserted, the subject "transfigures" time inasmuch as he "integrates the past in the present and in eternity."[22] This is the epistemological aspect of man's eschatological role. But questions arise such as the following: How can the evil of the past be done away? How can the good be preserved? A function of memory is to help remedy the mortal disease of time which these questions express. Berdyaev distinguishes "disintegrated time" from "integrated time," the latter making the past relevant to the present. Thus memory helps overcome time's disintegration. It is partly because of this that it can serve as a "temporal agent of eternity." [23] This is a profoundly important thought, to which we must return below. It somewhat parallels S. K.'s idea of "contemporaneity" save that it gives a greater role to the human faculty than does S. K.'s idea of the Moment of Encounter. Existentially, memory helps retain what is good in the past. The past, then, is not all evil, nor unreal. To know the past in the present is to know a past event that is relevant to the present; hence it is real, not fictitious. The objective is not lost in the subjective but comes alive with significance in the subject's present. Thus time is known inwardly while fed by the memory of the existing self who is the locus and innovator of time.

Berdyaev could say, "My knowledge of truth is my own relation to truth." [24] More than tautologous, this points again to the primacy of the existential subject and pertains as much to the knowledge of time as to anything else. Basic to his critique

76

of all objectification of thought, Berdyaev observes, "The subject is ultimately real, 'existential,' and only the subject is capable of knowing reality." [25] This has much in common with S. K.'s basic contention. Only the subject can know time, Berdyaev maintains, for *time is in the subject,* not the subject in time. This is also in keeping with Berdyaev's description of a "philosopher's tragic situation," his being wrapped up existentially in the very things he seeks to understand.[26]

Contrary to Plato, who said a man was a "spectator of all time and all existence," [27] Berdyaev sees a thinking man as an ardent participant in existence and much involved in the very time he knows. Plato kept the problem related more to the universal or ideal man than to the man of existence. But quite in agreement with Plato, Berdyaev sees how the philosopher as a lover of truth and a guardian of society must have a good memory. This matters, however, only as the philosopher thinks as a participant in human existence. Autobiographically Berdyaev consistently says,

I have . . . never been able to acquiesce in the ephemeral, perishable achievements of time, in all that lives but for an instant. The happy moments of my life have continually escaped my grasp. I could never be reconciled to the fact that time is in a perpetual flux and that each moment is devoured by and vanished into, the succeeding one. This terrible aspect of time has caused me intense and unspeakable pain.[28]

This is a profoundly existential reflection showing us how Berdyaev was as dissatisfied with the notion of time's unreality as was Augustine, if not more so. Nothing is to be gained by denying time's reality, lest life's anxieties as well as its joys be deemed logically fictitious.

Somehow the knowing self must find his relationship to eternity, but not by settling for an illusory or effervescent time. Only an existential perspective can allow for it. While for Berdyaev time as *chronos* is a "decomposed eternity," it is still a realistic matter that shares in being through the self. Of what relevance to a man is an existence, the time of which is unreal? Unless the temporality of human existence is real, however defective it is, it is difficult to concede that it can be redeemed eschatologically or be given meaning and destiny. Likewise, of what significance is a philosophy not born of the pangs of a real temporal existence seeking to fulfill itself? Memory must play a significant role for any philosopher, especially the one who would be true to his existence. "Knowledge is largely remembrance," says Berdyaev,[29] and memory a kind of "*a priori* awareness" in the Platonic sense of recollection,[30] as it creatively illuminates the present moment from past experiences. Thus memory helps keep one's existence and selfhood intact, even as it contributes to the knowledge and relevance of time.

Berdyaev even allows for the very memory of one's "prehistorical spiritual existence" contributing to one's present selfhood. But this is a Platonic theory which seems to account for human intuition. Included here is an intuitional "remembrance" of divine wisdom attained through "communion with the *Logos*"[31] from "before" the appearance of one's consciousness in time. While akin to the Platonic doctrines of recollection and pre-existence, Berdyaev sees them existentially, thus linking memory not only with time but with eternity; however, we wonder if this much is but an attempt to strengthen his mystical gnosticism even as it remains more neo-Platonic than Christian. Here Berdyaev unnecessarily goes overboard and almost adopts Plotinus' theory that the soul intuits eternity as well as time. This should hardly be necessary for one who looks to Christ and God-manhood so intently as he does.

"The doctrine of pre-existence is profound," states Berdyaev, "for it rests upon a remembrance of existential time."[32] While we question whether Berdyaev really clarifies the relation of pre-existence to the existential time experienced from within a mundane existence or, better, in relation thereto, one strength of his suggestion is that even past events could have been existential, and, remembered as such, they too contribute to the present in a doubly existential manner. This helps to account for a *Heilsgeschichte* which includes *Historie*. Kierkegaard fails to reckon with this or its equivalent in the time-eternity relationship. It is possible that a Christian's contemporaneity with Christ is affected by previous moments of a similar kind, and they, in turn, are influenced by such moments as experienced by others.

This means that existential time must not be divorced from historic time, though it is not identical with it.

This also lends counter argument to any denial of the reality of the past. Kierkegaard neglects the possible existentiality of past moments, since to him all of the past is unreal apart from the present, whereas Paul Tillich, an existentialist theologian with more in common with Berdyaev, recognizes the problem. Tillich really stands with Berdyaev in refusing to annul the past as well as the future, for these tenses are conjoined in the present. A tension to reason, the existential perspective of the tenses is, nevertheless, inevitable.[33] Thus, a past moment is not necessarily lost, especially as a past existential moment qualified by the eternal. This is to say that an existential moment that has slipped into the past, unlike an ordinary past moment, is of special enduring value.

Defending Berdyaev's claim that the past is real and that only a real past could be existentially remembered in the present—not to overlook the thought that *only a realistic historic time can be redeemed eschatologically to any glory of the Eternal—may we suggest the basic relevance of these observations to Christian theology today.* For instance, the Apostles of the early Church not only witnessed to the existential event of Christ's Incarnation and Resurrection in relation to the eternality of the Word but also in relation to their remembrance of the past of his historic appearance in time (Cf. I John 1:1-4; Luke 1:1-4; John 1:14, 2:22.) Furthermore, however imperfectly perceived, they remembered the past existential moments when he confronted them with his eternal Word and Person. This helps to account for the eschatological consciousness of the Apostolic Church. When Paul was confronted by the risen, living Lord, he recognized him even to the extent that later he remembered he was addressed by one who said, "I am Jesus of Nazareth whom thou persecutest." And earlier Paul had witnessed the stoning of Stephen who even at the point of death prayed to Jesus.

The Christian of today must rely upon the New Testament *kerygma*, the preached proclamation of a crucified and risen Son of God, while recognizing within it a *remembered* "faith portrait" of the one who was the Word made flesh. While biblically our faith rests not upon a scientific or rational "photograph" of the historical Jesus but upon an interpreted witness, we contend that it presupposes an actual Jesus of history who posed for the portrait and apart from whom we would have no record or "portrait" of the Word revealed in an event. Here we see how man's memory is what Berdyaev referred to as "an instrument of eternity," not just time. The *kerygma* gives witness, then, both to the divinely eternal and to the anthropologically temporal aspects of the Incarnation.

When "the Word was made flesh" it embraced an eventful *chronos* remembered by some to have been just as real as that flesh. This implies that *the reality* of historic time must be retained in the New Testament witness and *kerygma*, lest theology settle for a *temporal* version of a Docetic Christology. While one temptation is to rationally overstress an appeal to the historical Jesus that he might be idealized, a matter quite insecure today, the other temptation is to minimize the historical Jesus on the grounds of the claims based on *Formgeschichte* that his historicity is objectively insecure and perhaps untenable. But it must be denoted that while the scientific discipline of biblical criticism does not define the faith discipline of dogmatics, the believer still adheres to the *kerygma* which witnesses to the Eternal Word, who was *remembered* by the Apostles *to have entered time even as they had faith in him from within that time.*

Edwin Lewis has asserted in view of contemporary biblical interpretation that the "Christ of faith" and the "historical Jesus" are *one* and need not be dichotomized in our thinking so as to be of no mutual relevance to the revelation.[34] While we deem it to be in error to identify the two rationally, they can be said to refer to the same person only as we give primacy to the "Christ of faith" in terms of "existential time" as we have described it. Not a matter of rational synthesis from the standpoint of either biblical criticism or Christian dogmatics, Jesus and Christ are interrelated or associated, faithwise. We do not know exactly where one begins and the other leaves off, but the two are two-in-one by the faith perspective of the Apostles, not by an objective, scientific reason. Only "eyes of faith" could see the redemptive Word in the Word-bearer and his message, but it is also true that the same "eyes of faith" were confronted by the risen eternal Word through a person who was remembered

80

and who had met them in *their* time and history. Yet it became a *Historie* qualified and elevated to a profounder *Geschichte* of crucial significance to them when they met him faithwise in his unique "man-God" presence as the crucified but victorious risen Lord of Life.

The powerful relevance of the latter centered in a "divine-human encounter," but one which was mediated and expressed by the former. If not, how was the Living Word even recognized as Jesus? We may glimpse Jesus and fail to see the Christ, but we cannot be confronted by the Christ of the Word without seeing him as Jesus. Were this not the case there would be little, if any, occasion for the Apostles to give witness to the saving Christ in terms of Jesus of Nazareth even to the extent of embellishing their witness with mythological thought forms, as *Formgeschichte* critics like Rudolf Bultmann contend. Without the Word-bearer with a role to play in relation to history we lack the distinctiveness of the Word. Unless we see Christ in terms of Jesus we can see no grounds even for a faith-embellished portrait of him. While a satisfactory equation cannot be written out rationally, we can still have a Christology which keeps a link between Jesus and Christ. It lies, we maintain, in a balanced existential perspective, one which interprets the faith encounter with the living Christ in terms of an existential moment of time qualified by eternity and sees the memory of the witnessing apostles as an "agent of eternity." The role of the historic time factor is not to be obscured here but elevated and enhanced by a *balanced* existential view which refuses to negate or neglect the time factor in the "now." While not relying on it objectively as the redemptive source, this still respects time as a redemptive agency or medium. Berdyaev is right in saying that a person's present encounter with the living Christ is affected by his being remembered, since "the historic Christ for the Church's past which goes back to the first disciples, now becomes my past, my memory and my history." [35]

We have seen this in the faith encounter known to St. Paul when on the Damascus Road he sensed One say, "I am Jesus of Nazareth whom thou persecutest." But having said that the apostolic faith and memory witnesses to the Incarnate Word and that a Christian's faith relies upon this witness and remembrance of an actual Jesus in history, we are *not* saying that either the historicity of Christ or the historicity of the Incarnation can be scientifically established. Not belonging to the scientific discipline, both matters, nevertheless, *belong to the faith encounter and doctrinal witness.* Both the temporal and supratemporal elements are involved in this basic New Testament paradox.

Memory, then, can contribute to the meaning of history even as it gives assurance of history's reality and eventfulness. Berdyaev says that even antiquity is retained in the present, so that the disintegration of time is overcome by its correlation of the tenses. This principle we have adapted in terms of the *remembered event* and remembered personality essential to the revelation of the Christian *kerygma.* History, *while very real,* now becomes *more* than so many events; it is also mythical or meaningful in ways not understandable to either rational or empirical thought. "Myth," says Berdyaev, "is the story preserved in popular memory of a past event and transcends the limits of the . . . objective world . . . ." [36] Existentially, the great historical epochs of revelation coexist in view of this, and a myth can resuscitate a truth submerged in the human spirit and symbolize either a people's heritage or destiny, indicates Berdyaev.

In this respect *symbols can interrelate the temporal events with the metahistorical.* They express what is inexpressible, while truly existential. Note here, they can be interrelated existentially, not identified rationally. This applies, we maintain, to the Incarnation as an existential event related, but by no means limited, to history while also a revelation and symbol of transcendent Truth. It is the eternal act of God dramatically portrayed on the stage of history, but significant only because it is more than drama and more than history while involved in it. Similarly, the Fall is a symbol of an existential problem of men in time while it is a supratemporal matter, too. Berdyaev thinks of it as a pre-existent, prehistoric matter. Also, the Apocalypse is an eschatological symbol of the end as a supratemporal matter while related to this world of time.

Memory, then, intensifies the moments of time even as it helps cement them together in duration. Memory in the above-discussed sense also helps make "the eternal present" more vivid as it relates a past moment qualified by eternity to our present. This is seen in the apostolic *kerygma,* a message which centers in the significance of the Incarnate Event. Berdyaev even states,

> The historical memory is the greatest manifestation of the eternal spirit in our temporal reality. . . . Without it history would not exist. . . . All historical knowledge is remembrance, one or another form of the triumph of memory over the spirit of corruption. . . . Memory is therefore the eternal ontological basis of all history.[37]

In this respect, memory is important in preserving great existential moments or keeping them relevant to our lives in the present. It is not altogether passive, but creative. In some respects it is even selective as it "forgets" lesser associations with some past events. This we see reflected even by the writers of the Scriptures (Cf. John 21:25). Berdyaev realized the psychological implications of this problem when he came to write his autobiography. For him it was a "process of selection which goes through an experience of victory over time," [38] This is an existential choice and victory without being a repudiation of chronological time's reality.

Prophetic Spirit and Existential Time

There is another facet of the knowledge of time which is as essential to man's existence as memory, while perhaps an even more creative faculty of the knowing subject. It is what Berdyaev calls the "prophetic spirit." Parallel to Augustine's interpretation, this suggests the knower's relation to future time.[39] The prophetic spirit, what Augustine called "expectation," links a person's present with his future. It apprehends the future just as the memory embraces the past. Yet prophecy, to which this faculty of the knower is basic, is no mere prediction of events to come; it is seeing the future's significance in terms of the eternal and interpreting this to the present, a present of both eternal significance and temporal realism. Thus, like memory, the prophetic spirit is also an instrument of the eternal Now which embraces all tenses.

This becomes important to understanding the contemporaneity of the tenses in existential time, for by it the *future is made relevant to the present. While only the* faith-perceived *eternal present can provide this relevance,* all anxiety and anticipation, even moral promises and purposes, prophetic insights and Apocalyptic symbols which look to the future and thereby contribute to the reality of time, would be utterly nonsensical were there no realistic future that could be relevant to the present moment. While this pertains especially to the more spiritual and creative moments of life, it is not unrelated to other moments of intensity. When in 1927 Colonel Charles Lindbergh performed his great aeronautical feat he did much thinking above the watery billows. One thought that came to him as referred to in *The Spirit of St. Louis* (p.90) was this: "I'm flying in a plane over the Atlantic Ocean; but I'm also living in years far away."

In light of all this W. E. Hocking errs, we believe, in viewing the future solely as an illusory division of linear time. Leaving it unrelated to the existential subject in the present he treats the future as "wholly nonexistent." [40] But a fictitious future justifies the reality of neither a person's tragic apprehensiveness on the one hand, nor his prophetic consciousness on the other. Furthermore, *even the existential present cannot give meaning to an unreal future.* Bergson, somewhat like Hegel, also projected a pseudo future. While seeking to deliver men from duration's spatial illusion he denied the reality of both the future and the past.[41] Nor did Bergson see an eternal present to make the tenses relevant to each other; he simply dissolved them in cosmic duration's *élan vital.* But could the existing man live on such principles? Hardly. He could trust no one and nothing that involved the future. Every human bond, hope, vow, pledge or promise would be ridiculous.

Berdyaev recognizes the prophetic spirit as an epistemological instrument of the eternal present in the temporal present. By it the sheer timeline is transcended as the future is made integral to the existential present. A man's living on the frontier of both time and eternity is now prophetically instrumented. *He can look to the future without being solely futuristic* because the eternal present is a "process of incessant creation." [42] This qualifies the view of the future implied by horizontal time. It allows no "scientific prevision" which regards the future as something objective, determined or static. It sees no cut-and-dried temporality, but *a dynamic "eternal now" which embraces the future*

84

in the present without obviating its reality in the time stream.
This, too, is pertinent to our basic contention.

Thus the past and the future are more than transitory. They are seen to have a supratemporal relationship to the present. Without this existential cohesion, time and history would not only be meaningless but illusory and unreal. Berdyaev says, "The creative process of the present can only be faithful to the best of the past. The ineradicable power of the past must be transmuted into a future creativity and become its agent." [43] This enhances man's eschatological role in a temporal existence. His existential moments of creative insight, whereby he helps bring new things into being, can serve the fulfillment of his destiny and make him a co-creator with God, especially as he looks to the end in the future while above any measurable temporality.[44] This is of marked significance in relating spiritual insight and revelation to a historical culture and in guiding society toward a meaningful end of time.[45] Only such an end can mean fulfillment.

What is the knowledge of time, then, but the spiritual activity of the knower? "Time is in man, not man in time," Berdyaev stressed. Richard Niebuhr also enunciates this principle of Berdyaev, saying:

Time in our history is not another dimension of the eternal space world in which we live, but a dimension of our life and of our community's being. We are not in this time but it is in us. It is not associated with space in a unity of space-time but it is inseparable from life in continuity of life-time.[46]

Niebuhr's case would be even stronger, however, if he would distinguish the temporal present from the eternal present and then show their relationship. This would clarify the existential moment, prevent the absolute dichotomy of past and present, and give support to memory's function. Niebuhr's "internal history," "subjective events" and "esoteric" thought here have kinship with Berdyaev but seem to require elucidation of the existential present's relation to both time and eternity. Thus, true or meaningful time is an existential matter epistemologically, and must be interpreted from within the spirit-subject, for it belongs to the knower's very existence.[47]

Karl Heim is another contemporary of Berdyaev who has come to see that time belongs to the self, and is not an objective reality as is commonly assumed by the scientist. No one can escape "my time now," Heim reminds us, whereas the scientist usually disregards this *now* on the assumption that all physical relationships are the same irrespective of the *now*. In harmony with the foregoing arguments from Berdyaev's perspective, Heim states, *"The now is filled with history which still vibrates within it. . . .* We cannot conceive *a real passage of time* without presupposing the ego which plays a decisive part in bringing this passage of time about." [48] Thus the Platonic illusoriness of time, the Hegelian liquidation and Kierkegaardian negation of it as well as the cosmic rationalizations of it are all erroneous. Time, then, is an innovation of the concrete knower in existence, to whom memory and prophetic expectation are essential activities which contribute to time's stark reality.

Having glimpsed what is essential to the knowledge of time and how the "eternal now" is related thereto, we must further consider how eternity makes existential time so distinctive.

The Distinctiveness of Existential Time

Whenever a man patterns his life by cosmic time's necessitative rhythm, or allows himself to be bogged down by the measurements of a pseudo-objectivized linear time, he encumbers his existence and enslaves himself. Berdyaev contends that a person cannot be liberated from such an artificial existence until he thinks and lives in terms of what we have described to be true or meaningful time, existential time.

The Occasion for Meaning and Destiny

Existential time becomes for Berdyaev the very basis of a most vigorous interpretation of existence, history and destiny. This interpretation is inspired mainly by the revealed Christian principle of God-manhood and sheds a unique light on the problems of eschatology. The distinctiveness of existential time for the understanding of existence and its end lies in what we have touched upon as its qualitative intensity, that which makes it superior to cosmic and horizontal times. It is this transcendent

86

quality which allows existential time to give deeper meaning to human existence and its temporal problems of history and destiny. "The infinity of existential time," says Berdyaev, "is a qualitative infinity, not a quantitative." [49] While this quality is of eternity, it is irrelevant to men save as it relates itself to time's quantity. This is a matter Kierkegaard would not concede. But such is the unique revelatory Event of Christ.

Cosmic time with its impersonal, necessitative and cyclic constraints renders no significance to man as a moral, spiritual subject with a destiny. It keeps him a mere daguerreotype of nature. Whereas cosmic time binds a person by its stereotyped strictures, existential time liberates him. Berdyaev says, "The secret of life is to live in the existential present, for this is to live in eternity." Not meaning to overstate the phrase "live in eternity," Berdyaev at once adds, "Time [the *kairos*] is to be experienced as an eternal present to which past and future refer." Even more specifically Berdyaev says, "*Existential time must not be thought of in complete isolation from cosmic and historic time; it is a break-through of one time into the other.*" [50] It is a confrontation and invasion of the eternal into the temporal, what Paul Tillich also refers to in the biblical term *kairos* as distinguished from *chronos* or common linear time. *Kairos* is time qualified by eternal relevance, time that is of significance to the Eternal because it is disturbed by and invested with the eternal.

Tillich sees how *kairos* is the key to overcoming temporal estrangement from eternal Being, "the ground of all being" in existence. Christ yields the New Being through his once-for-all revelation of the "fullness of time" from which time, history and culture receive a new depth. Christ is the paradoxical centre of history in perfect *kairos*. This is akin to Berdyaev's position save for the primacy of Tillich's ontological frame of reference. *Kairos* is that by which God judges and redeems time, that by which the Unconditioned reconditions the Conditioned. But more shrewdly than Berdyaev, Tillich sees how *kairos* is related to the Christian doctrine of justification of the sinner, for Christ implies an involvement in a sinful existence that it might be conquered from above itself. [51]

Kierkegaard's equivalent of *kairos* is the "Moment." It is known in the intensity of the present when the man who comes to despair finds himself confronted by eternity in that moment; it is then that he sees the meaning of his redemption. Berdyaev sees the great potentialities of this existential moment. For him it is basic both to the redeeming of man's spirit personally and to the ultimate transforming of history and the entire cosmos.[52] This becomes an eschatological matter based on an "inward time" which is not subject to mathematical formulation or rational expression. In this respect, existential time is authentic spiritual time, so to speak, consisting of moments that are qualitatively intensified by a positive relation to eternity. They are taken up into eternity to the extent that eternity has been "taken up with" them.

A meticulous distinction is now in order, however. Berdyaev says, "A moment of existential time is an emergence into eternity. *It would be untrue to say that existential time is identical to eternity, but it may be said that it is a participant in several moments of eternity.*" [53] Not depreciating the element of *chronos* as in S. K.'s version of the Moment, Berdyaev sees existential time more in terms of the experiential intensity of a person's sublime moment as best seen in creative or religious ecstasy. Positively, it is a communion with the Eternal-in-time. In this respect, existential time is at the fringe of eternity, while not to be identified with it completely. It is a both/and paradox of interrelation, leaving us conceptually with a meaningful tension not amenable to pure reason. Negatively, in Berdyaev's own words, "Suffering is a phenomenon of the existential order, but it is objectivized in mathematical time and appears to be infinite in the quantitative sense of the word." [54] The latter is a horror of infinite time, the pseudo infinite, rather than a communion with eternity.[55] It is on this basis that Berdyaev attacks the old orthodox doctrine of hell, which is commonly expressed in terms of a deficient temporalistic concept of eternity as infinite time.[56] The odiousness of any suffering lies in its being de-existentialized into an objectified, evil time with an implied pseudo-infinity. Thus hell cannot be eternal, for eternity is qualitative and belongs to God! At this point Berdyaev could have been more consistent in relating hell's temporal reality to his own doctrine of "celestial history," since hell does not exist without being of pertinence to God. Celestial history implies the time-embracing aspect of a dynamic eternity not immune or oblivious to time.

Yet Berdyaev retained the idea of hell as a paradox of the problem of time and eternity. While Berdyaev is not too clear here, we might deduce from this that "heaven" is "eternal" (qualitative) while "hell" is "everlasting" (quantitative).

The Basis for the God-Man Relationship

To a degree, we are ahead of our story for we have had to hold off a close examination of the character or nature of eternity. Be that as it may, existential time as the occasion for a meaningful time, and destiny is given its major clue in the Christian revelation of *God-manhood*. That clue is not merely a principle and symbol, but *an event,* the Great Event of the Incarnation *when the Eternal invaded history.* Berdyaev shows keen insight in saying,

> The full significance of an event in the life of Christ moved in existential time; in historical time it only shines through the burdensome environment of objectification. The metahistorical is never contained within the historical, history always distorts metahistory in adjusting it to itself.[57]

While this corresponds to Karl Barth's assertion that revelation is history while history is not revelation, yet to be examined, it does not deny the mutual relationship between historic time and eternity in the great existential Event and its significance. Applying this, again, to the problem of the Jesus of history, we must assert that the revelatory significance of the event demands the God-manhood of the Christ who in his unique Sonship portrays eternity-in-time. Here is the perfect existential Event, which sheds light upon the enigma of time. In the light of its Messianic and eschatological implications, this Event, as we shall see more clearly, becomes the Key to the Kingdom, for it gives a vital "metahistory" to the world of time. Christ, the Eternal Word, entered time and, by faith in Him in the present, a deficient time is made efficient to His purpose, sublime in the eternal Now and relevant to His eternal End.

Kierkegaard also saw the importance of God-manhood to the understanding of existential time. A person can participate in the eternal when in "the Moment" he sees what Julius Bixler, interpreting S. K., describes as ". . . the ingression into history of the absurdity of the Incarnation." [58] Only as a man in the darkness of an otherwise meaningless existence and time chooses himself in this light and accepts eternity's disclosure of his Real Self in his eternal *Existenz*, S. K. maintained, can a man know himself.[59] This is the Christian existential answer to the Socratic dictum: "Know thyself." When man is confronted by God in the existential moment, and when he commits himself to the paradox of Being in Becoming as reflected in the Incarnation, only then is the abyss between time and eternity overcome for him. The meaning of life and the solution to time is found only in relation to the Eternal as realized in the paradoxical moment of existential time in which the eternal meets the temporal. It is this paradox, together with its qualitative meaning and spiritual nature, which is distinctive of existential time.

*   *   *   *

Having seen the momentous and far-reaching meaning of existential time, we are constrained to look to the chief sources of its distinctiveness within eternity. This demands a more meticulous examination of the nature of eternity, that the full revelatory significance and eschatological dimension of existential time may be accounted for. Having sounded out the time factors which constitute the Isle of Kairos while keeping our attention on her central point of interest, we must ask: What is there about eternity that caps the majestic peak [60] of Kairos with such redemptive splendor? It is this that next demands our scrutiny even as it anticipates the second part of our study, the eschatological dimension of existential time.

NOTES

1 *Slavery and Freedom,* pp. 257, 259.
2 *The Meaning of History,* p. 69. Time for Berdyaev is engendered not only by anxiety and aspiration but by creative acts. Heidegger stressed only the evil aspect of time, its relation to "anxiety" and "dread," the orientation of a meaningless *Dasein* in death, which implies a future and end. Cf.

Heidegger, "What is Metaphysics," pp. 355ff and "An Account of 'Being and Time'" in Heidegger's *Existence and Being*, p. 25ff. Much like Sartre, Heidegger despairs of finding meaning to his time-imbued despair such as the nothingness identified with imminent death. Cf. Jean-Paul Sartre, *Existentialism and Humanism* and F. H. Heinemann, *Existentialism and the Modern Predicament*, Chaps. VI and VII; Guido de Ruggiero, *Existentialism*, 1946; N. Bobbio, *The Philosophy of Decadentism*, 1948; R. M. Querido, "A Philosophy of Despair," "*The National Review*, Vol. 129, Sept. 1947, pp. 237-241; X. V. Douglas, "Sartre's Existentialism," *Virginia Quarterly Review*, Spring, 1947, pp. 244-260; David Victoroff, "The Christian Sources of Modern Existentialism," *Sobornost*, Series 3, Summer, 1948; also the following works by F. C. Copleston: "Existentialism and Modern Man." *Aquinas Papers*, no. 9, 1949, Oxford; "Concerning Existentialism," *The Month*, Vol. I, London, pp. 46-54; and a review in *Philosophy*, Vol. xxiv, Oct. 1949, p. 356f.

3 As stated by Rosenstock-Huessy in *The Christian Future*, p. 167.

4 *The Divine and the Human*, p. 178. Cf. Augustine, *Confessions*, Bk. XI, 14.

5 *The Meaning of History*, p. 69.

6 As quoted by Aldous Huxley in *The Perennial Philosophy*, p. 186.

7 Bergson alluded to this in *Creative Evolution* long before Dean Inge referred to it in a meeting of the Aristotelian Society reported in *The London Times* back in the 1920's. Upon seeing this article we have since taken note of Inge's own reference to the occasion in *God and the Astronomers*, p. 79, where he argues for the reversibility of time. Berdyaev would concur. Cf. *Slavery and Freedom*, p. 228.

8 *Slavery and Freedom*, p. 257. Cf. Aristotle, *Physics*, Bk. IV, 223b, 29, 24. While cyclic time is attributable to Greek thought it was not foreign to Hebrew thought. Cf. first part of Ecclesiastes 3:1-8. Nor is it unrecognized in the N.T. Cf. e.g., James 4:14, Acts 1:7.

9 The relation of cosmic time to the end will be considered below in Chapter VI with a special critique of modern process philosophies of the end made pertinent to and judged in the light of Berdyaev's eschatology.

10 Shakespeare, *Macbeth*, V, 5.

11 *Solitude and Society*, pp. 99, 108f.

12 *The Divine and the Human*, p. 178. This is known through faith, *gnosis* and creative experience, especially in relation to Christ. (Cf. p. 87 below.) It is "crucial" time broken into or disturbed by eternity. Cf. Heb. 6:5.

13 *Ibid.*, p .177. Cf. *Dream and Reality*, p. 243. Cf. *Solitude and Society*, p. 112. "The evil engendering instant remains the slave of time, and fails to attain to eternity."

14 *Slavery and Freedom*, p. 260f. Cf. Jean Guitton, *Le Temps et l'éternité chez Plotin et Saint Augustin*, p. 359 as quoted by Rosenstock-Huessy, *The Christian Future*, p. 72, "In Christianity the time of every human existence receives a superior quality in its smallest fragments."

15 *Ibid.*, p. 261.

16 *Essai de Métaphysique Eschatologique*, p. 232f (*The Beginning and End*, p. 206) .

17 *The Divine and the Human*, p. 112; *Destiny of Man*, p. 295.

18 *Confessions*, Bk. XI, par. 35, 37, 16; Bk. X, par. 35.

19 *Solitude and Society*, p. 102. Cf. p. 106.

20 *Ibid.*, p. 100.

21 Cf. Augustine, *Confessions*, Bk. XI, par. 26.

22 *Solitude and Society*, p. 100.

23 *Ibid.* This is not meant to be Platonic.

91

24 *Dream and Reality*, p. 13.
25 *Ibid.*, p. 286.
26 *Solitude and Society*, Meditation I. Cf. above, Chap. I.
27 *Republic*, Bk. VI.
28 *Dream and Reality*, p. 29. Cf. p. 42.
29 *Solitude and Society*, p. 107.
30 Cf. Plato, *Phaedo*, 73-76.
31 George Seaver, *Nicholas Berdyaev*, P. 117. Cf. Berdyaev's *Dream and Reality*, pp. 1, 35 for his personal sense of pre-existence.
32 *Essai de Métaphysique Eschatologique*, p. 234.
33 Tillich, *The Protestant Era*, p. 8, *The Interpretation of History*, pp. 129, 135, 146, 18.
34 *Biblical Faith and Christian Freedom*, pp. 103f, 147. Cf. D. M. Baillie, *God Was in Christ*, pp. 37, 49. This is also the thesis of James Moffatt, *Jesus Christ the Same*, p. 11.
35 *The Meaning of History*, p. 161 (1936 ed.).
36 *Ibid.*, p. 21. Cf. *Dream and Reality*, pp. 284, 91, 82. In relation to the *kerygma*, see D. M. Baillie, *God Was in Christ*, p. 21.
37 *Ibid.*, p. 73. When Berdyaev speaks of "the ontological" he means Being as spiritual existence, not as projected Being. Theologically, it seems to have kinship with the biblical "I am" and Eckhart's idea of God as Being-Spirit, for all being is Spirit to Berdyaev, while not in any pantheistic sense. Cf. Berdyaev's "Deux Études sur Jacob Boehme" in his French translation of Boehme's *Mysterium Magnum*, Tome I, p. 5ff.
38 *Dream and Reality*, p. 284. Cf. pp. iv, v, vii.
39 *Confessions*, par. 10. Cf. Berdyaev's *Dream and Reality*, p. xii, *Solitude and Society*, p. 197. In *The Destiny of Man*, p. 295, Berdyaev seems to use the term "imagination" quite in apposition to "prophetic spirit."
40 Hocking, *The Meaning of God in Human Experience*, p. 429.
41 *Time and Free Will*, pp. 81, 190 and *Creative Evolution*, pp. 15, 34. Cf. Pringle-Pattison, *The Idea of God*, p. 374f.
42 This is brought out here in contrast to Bergson who attributed incessant creation to his *élan vital* in an evolutionary sense, while Berdyaev sees a creative eternality in the dynamic and existential sense. Bergson's *élan vital* remains an unfulfilled potentiality; Berdyaev's eternal now dynamically redeems the times which have yet to be fulfilled in the end. Cf. Chapter VI, below.
43 *Towards a New Epoch*, p. 74f.
44 *The Beginning and End*, pp. 158-163, 174, 179.
45 *Ibid.*, pp. 165, 169f, 172f.
46 *The Meaning of Revelation*, p. 69. Cf. 68-73. Spinoza in his *Ethics*, p. 254, saw this problem of "dichotomy" also.
47 Cf. Lamont, *Christ and the World of Thought*, p. 69. Lamont has some highly existential insights, I maintain. More like S. K., he denies the reality of past and future (p. 74f), but he can say, "Time ranges itself around the Present precisely as my world ranges itself around me," and, "The present stands out from the rest of Time in dimensional pre-eminence," (p. 76f). But Lamont has minimized the influence of past events and experiences with other persons and their wills upon the present (p. 95). Can there be a real present without a real past and a real future? Are they completely objectified?
48 Heim, *Christian Faith and Natural Science*, pp. 58-60. This view is influenced considerably by Martin Buber's "I-Thou" principle of knowledge and personality, as is Berdyaev's position. (Cf. pp. 102-104.) Italics mine. Cf. Buber, *I and Thou*, pp. 11, 101f. "All real living is meeting."
49 *Slavery and Freedom*, p. 260.

50 *The Meaning of History*, p. 197 and *Slavery and Freedom*, p. 260.

51 Cf. *The Interpretation of History*, p. 250ff. In the light of the Incarnation and *Logos* Tillich makes much of this. Cf. his work, *The Protestant Era*, p. 27f, 46f, p. 33ff, and *Systematic Theology*, Vol. II, p. 90, 150. Cf. Berdyaev, *Spirit and Reality*, p. 163. May we take special note that *kairos* is *chronos* "disturbed" by eternity, as both Tillich and Berdyaev bring out. Cf. the N.T. use of both "times" attributed to Christ, e.g., *chronous ha kairous* in Acts 1:7. Note the eschatological implications of *kairos* in Luke 21:24, and Acts 17:24-26 and its spiritual quality and relation to the future in Acts 3:19. Also how the believer is called to "redeem" in Eph. 5:15f.

52 Berdyaev, *Slavery and Freedom*, p. 111. Cf. S. K., *From Sickness Unto Death; Stages on Life's Way*. The cosmic relevance of Berdyaev's view has roots in St. Paul's more mature eschatology. Cf. Andrews, *The Meaning of Christ for Paul*, pp. 242ff, 17f, 55, 115, 143f, 173ff.

53 *Slavery and Freedom*, p. 261. Italics mine. Not to be pressed rationally! Note the both/and paradox, a relevant tension!

54 *Ibid.*

55 The "anguish" of death and "terror" of eternity are matters which both Berdyaev and S. K. deal with, the latter most profoundly in *Fear and Trembling*, Chap. I.

56 Berdyaev decries the sadistic idea of an "eternal" hell, for the eternal belongs only to God; yet he does not dismiss the reality of hell. It is a chosen alienation from God. Cf. *Destiny of Man*, p. 277ff. and *Slavery and Freedom*, p. 261.

57 *Slavery and Freedom*, p. 262. Cf. *Freedom and the Spirit*, p. 35ff.

58 Bixler, "The Contributions of Existenz-Philosophies," *Harvard Theological Review*, Vol. 33, Jan., 1940, pp. 35-63.

59 Cf. *Concluding Unscientific Postscript*, p. 505ff; *Concept of Dread*, p. 78ff.

60 Augustine in *Confessions*, Bk. XIII, par. 13, footnote 2, reminds us that in the Scriptures Christ is likened to a "mountain."

CHAPTER IV

EXISTENTIAL TIME AND THE NATURE OF ETERNITY: I

Upon considering the problem, background and meaning of existential time, we have seen how it has a special relation to eternity. That this depth dimension, transcendent quality and intensity of existential time may be magnified it is important that we focus our attention upon the intrinsic nature or, better, character and attributes of the eternal so that the full meaning of existential time may be appreciated.

This endeavor entails the basic question: What is the relation of existential time to the fundamental properties of the eternal? Approaching the answer from a philosophical standpoint in this chapter, we shall enlarge upon it from a more theological standpoint in the next chapter, which opens up the discussion on the eschatological dimension of time in Part II of our comparative study. To answer the question before us, we must first find our bearings in the problem and then proceed to examine the existential and pre-existential views of eternity.

The Existential Problem of Eternity

The "eternal now" or "ever-present eternal" has been seen to be essential to existential time. But for this to be fully appreciated we must treat the time-eternity relationship not only from the standpoint of time but also from that of eternity *per se*. This demands the examination of the fundamental religio-philosophical attributes or properties of eternity, the source of existential time's distinctive quality and eschatological dimension. Perhaps no issue moves us closer to the awesomeness of the ultimate and divine than does that of eternity. But before turning to existential interpretations given to it in the history of thought we might well be reminded of the basic problem involved.

Thinkers in general have conceived of eternity in essentially

94

three different ways: [1] (1) eternity as unending or infinite time, (2) eternity as something timeless, (3) eternity as including time. But it appears from a Berdyaev-like perspective that none of these concepts is quite adequate, though perhaps the latter comes closest to having existential pertinence. All three either tend to make eternity temporal, keep it unrelated to time or let it completely absorb time. A more dynamic view of the nature of eternity and its relation to time must be found if man is to have a destiny which makes him more than a slave to time and his temporal existence. While Kierkegaard saw the basic issue involved here, Berdyaev and, to a lesser extent, Karl Barth, as we shall indicate in the next chapter, point to such a solution. With this in mind we can consider immediately the existential and pre-existential insights into eternity which have been entertained in the history of philosophy. We must turn first to classical Greek philosophy and neo-Platonic thought followed by the more characteristic existential insights of Augustine and Kierkegaard.

The Pre-existential Views of Eternity

Eternity in Classical Philosophy

Presupposed by Plato was an eternal Model of creation. It is related to the cosmic World-Soul which has no beginning in time. At first the Model was described as a "living being." [2] But Plato, it appears, really departed from the implications of this. Basically, the great Greek thinker refused to attribute any kind of succession to Eternal Being because all time or change, he said, belongs to the realm of becoming. As number, time is movement and diversity, said Plato, but as the image of the eternal, it is uniformity. [3] This view keeps the eternal static, unified and immutable. There appears to be nothing "living" about it. Thus it becomes questionable whether time as the seat of change can emulate a static eternity or the realm of Becoming have a vital relation to Being. Plato fuses eternity with the "unchanging," "everlasting" and "perfect" in his eternal forms of beauty and goodness. Mathematics likewise points to eternal ideas.

In *The Republic* Plato presents a dialogue between Socrates and Adeimantus in which the question is asked concerning God:

"But may he not change and transform himself?" The answer settled for is this: "If he can change at all he can only change for the worse, for we cannot suppose him to be deficient either in virtue or beauty." [4] This reflects the static logic and idealism of Plato, a tendency which has frequently reappeared wherever a theistic doctrine of divine sovereignty has been stressed with causal logic.

Yet the discussions about God in *The Republic* frequently impress us by the personal connotations in the references to God in ways that seem to compete with a static idealism. An unbending Absolute completely averse to change would seem to disallow this even as it would yield no vital relationship to anything else. In fact, God is elsewhere said to take no heed of human affairs,[5] and emotional or anthropomorphic attributes like grief or joy are not to be ascribed to God.[6] Yet, Plato on occasion seems to argue for more than an unbending or static Ideal. In *The Cratylus* he has Socrates saying, "There must not only be stable objects but also a stable subject to know them." [7] This has possibilities more congenial to a dynamic eternity and biblical theism, but whether it is consistent with most of what Plato says must be questioned, as our preceding observations demand.

Despite Plato's doctrine of the Demiurge,[8] an intermediate or lesser god and state between Being and Becoming to help account for creation, the Platonic eternal is too immutable to be related to the changes of time. The classical view is defective because of this static timelessness which keeps it removed from time. Eternity here is a remote, transcendent, unredemptive and unexistential concept. Thus Plato's dualism affords us no real philosophy of history, nor does it prove amenable to a vital eschatology. It seems too abstract to be pertinent to human existence. Save for its timeless values or patterns, its unity cannot affect temporal plurality, anxiety, tragedy and transience. In view of this Berdyaev is right in rejecting the Platonic Ideal of eternity.[9] The objective *nous* of the eternal idea lacks a vital *pneuma* whereby it can relate itself to time efficaciously.

Had Plato been truer to his original pre-existential insight into a "living" Being identified with eternity,[10] it is possible that he could have done much to prevent its Parmenidean infrangibility and thus contribute more to the pre-existential view of

96

the problem of time. Timelessness is hardly attributable to a spiritual state of being, at least not one which makes itself relevant to men of time. Yet Plato may have become aware of a problem here, for in his *Sophist* (245, 249) he does not view Being with such sheer timelessness. There is room for both rest and movement. The Eleatic Stranger says,

> And, O heavens, can we ever be made to believe that motion and life and soul and mind are not present with perfect being? Can we imagine that being is devoid of life and mind, and exists in awful unmeaningness in everlasting fixture?

Theataetus replies, "That would be a dreadful thing to admit, Stranger." As for rest and motion in eternal Being the argument leads to a claim upon "both." This seems to anticipate the mystical view of Plotinus.

Roger Hazelton, in stressing this dynamic element in favor of making Plato appear more congenial to the biblical revelation, looks upon Plato's eternity as both including and transcending time.[11] This "inclusive transcendence" may be a possible interpretaion, but it seems to neglect Plato's more consistent stress upon the immutability of the eternal. Even so, while it may be more of a paradox, it does not do much to allow for an incursion of the eternal into the temporal. And if it did, we would have to assert that Plato, to a degree, anticipated Christ. This poses a problem for the Christian idealist but not for the Christian existentialist.

While time is said to emulate eternity in the Platonic dualism, the two are quite disparate by nature. In fact, Plato sees no end even to the phenomenal world.[12] Similarly, the very soul of man is deemed immortal and without beginning or end.[13] There are really two realms of immortality, or two kinds, on this basis: the timeless, and the potentially timeless linked with the man of time. The parallel would be Being and Becoming. But for the basic dualism to be resolved, we contend, there should be something of Becoming in Being to allow it to have a vital relationship with the temporal. This would call for a dynamic, not static, eternity of Being, something dynamic or "living" whereby eternity can embrace time, while neither dissolving its reality nor negating itself. Such a solution is not found in the typical Plato, while we see it anticipated by Plotinus, then glimpsed from afar by Augustine, approached boldly by Kierkegaard, one-sidedly adapted by Karl Barth, and completed and consistently applied only by Nicholas Berdyaev.

Aristotle's view of eternity is even less dynamic than that of Plato. To him eternity is an infinity of time in a purely futuristic, horizontal sense. Quite inconsistently, however, he holds that the eternal Forms of the absolute, quite like Plato's Ideas, are changeless. Actually, Aristotle does not reconcile the "changeless" with his infinity of time, though the changeless Forms are seen immanentally stamped into the things of this changing world.

As seen earlier, Aristotle identifies time with motion. Yet he seems to contradict his idea of eternity as an infinity of time when he says, "No motion can go on to infinity." The complement of this is that "No process of change is eternal." [14] An untenable contradiction in Aristotle's position seems apparent. Furthermore, his failure to see eternity as intrinsically different from time and his aversion to ascribing any kind of change to it makes his position quite sterile of any consequence to the realm of time and history. This, together with his horizontally terminated "now," yields no dynamic or living character to the eternal. Eternity in this immanental dualism remains abstract *nous* or Absolute Being and totally removed from a vital relationship with the particulars of time, save as its Forms immanentally blueprint the things of Becoming.

The eternal activity of God, for Aristotle, is the contemplation of his own Being. While this points to a kind of absolute subject, it is comparable to a thinking-thought in which mind or subject and object are one. Interested in protecting its perfection, Aristotle does not grant this divine mind any vital relationship with the world of Becoming or time. As the Unmoved Mover the eternal is an unchanging *Totum Simul* while causing movement by attracting the universe to itself.[15] The forms are really aspects of this attraction, like the oak of the acorn. They bespeak the design and ultimate potential of all things.

Adapted to the idea of God as *actus purus*,[16] this cold concept of the eternal was adapted by St. Thomas Aquinas in the framework of his medieval theology. Retaining the Aristotelian idea of an immutable eternity, Aquinas pressed it further and defined it as "simultaneously whole," "interminable" and having "no succession." [17] He seems to contradict himself, however, when he goes on to assert with a degree of pre-existential insight that "God communicates His eternity" and immutability.[18] We must ask: Does not the "communication" of eternity to time involve more than an immutability in the perfect act of the Eternal? And what of the nature of the Act itself? Thomas states, ". . . as some receive immutability from Him, they share in His eternity." [19] While the immutable is the source of motion for Aquinas just as the Unmoved Mover is for Aristotle, we must ask: How can the immutable absolute be shared without being more than abstract, pure Being, even if described as *pure act?* While the "act" of the Unmoved Mover causes its effects, it does not share of itself but is only, as Aquinas says, as "an agent is present to that upon which it acts." [20] Such a rational approach to the eternal leaves it too stiff and unbending to communicate itself and help solve the problem of time and redeem it eschatologically.

As E. P. Dickie has stated of the Thomistic concept of God, "There is no room left in the divine nature for God's personal communication of Himself in love to mankind. . . . Creation, indeed, . . . can make no difference to God, can add nothing to His perfection. And redemption loses most of its meaning." [21] Berdyaev is right when he says of the Thomists, "By the precepts of Aristotelian philosophy they have changed the God of the Bible into pure act, and excluded from Him all inward motion and every tragic principle. The absolute cannot issue from itself and create the world. Movement and change cannot be attributed to it." [22]

Indeed, such an eternity cannot be linked with a personal God. Though Aquinas attributes "act" to the nature of God, and this much is an improvement on Aristotle's Unmoved Mover, it is still an impersonal essence of "unmoving" movement, a rational abstraction lacking sufficient dynamic character to be able to deal with the changes of another order. As Aquinas himself says of God, "He cannot acquire anything new, nor extend himself to anything whereto He was not extended previously." [23] How can this concept of God allow Him to "move" or "act" in any way beyond Himself unto a redemption of creation? As seen above, there is no capacity for change and succession or their relevance in such an abstract concept: it is too rational to be dynamic in character so as to have a positive relationship with time.

Even when baptized Christian, the Aristotelian-Thomistic concept of the eternal essence remains absolute and timeless, therefore, too remote from historic time and its problems. Such an eternity can hardly belong to the Living Being of revealed theism. Disallowing a sufficiently dynamic "eternal now," this abstract absolute "Act" lacks the character or quality whereby it can relate itself to time. Conceptually, as a projected infinity of time, it has no real relationship with the concrete finite stuff from which it was projected as infinite.

In the main, then, neither the Platonic nor the Aristotelian views yield an eternity existentially adequate to the meaning or redemption of time. What, then, has the neo-Platonic position to offer us concerning the interpretation of eternity?

Eternity in Neo-Platonic Philosophy

Plotinus greatly improves upon Plato and Aristotle, we believe, at the point of boldly expressing an eternity which combines "Eternal Movement" and "Repose." [24] We have seen but foreshadowings of this in Plato's *Sophist* and as attempted rationally in the Aristotelian-Thomistic idea of God, while, as already suggested, it falls far short of the full dynamic character which such an eternity demands, especially to be relevant to human existence.

Congruent to his assertion, cited in Chapter II, that the soul or knower is linked with eternity even as it engenders time, Plotinus here provides another pre-existential insight, one which points to the paradoxical tension of unity-within-plurality and Being in Becoming. While eternity remains for him a Model of time as in Platonism, Plotinus shows with pre-existential insight that if eternity were strictly repose or changelessness all that is outside the divine could not be related to it. This supports our above-stated contention that there must be something of Becoming in eternal Being. In principle, this also anticipates and supports Berdyaev's acceptance of a pneumatic rather than an idealistic static view of eternity. This is fundamental to our thesis, for it is only on such a basis that time and eternity can be seen

100

to be related, while their respective realities are neither denied nor obscured.

In his scheme of cosmic emanation from "the One" and the return thereto of "the many," Plotinus is not averse to an eternity of movement and activity. Plotinus sees time as the activity of the eternal Soul. Not turned in on itself in self-contemplation as in Aristotle's view, but active in an outgoing creation and generation, this eternal Soul produces life and time out of willful act. That is, the Soul translates what is of its eternal world into another form, the temporal. The eternal Spirit or *nous* is not in time, but time is in it.[25] Actually, time is also of the soul of man, as seen earlier. This is contrary to various modern cosmic views of time which, as we shall see, obscure or depreciate the knowing subject's role. It is a paradoxical two-in-one pantheism, for it seeks to relate eternity and time without negating the reality of either.

Yet Plotinus seems to leave himself open to a contradiction. He claims that eternity is an unchanging essence oblivious of past and future. This is really opposed to his idea of "eternal movement" and activity in God and his remarkable pre-existential and even quasi-biblical description of eternity as "God made manifest, declaring what He is." [26] Eternity is a cosmic ascent and time a descent. Though the temporal "descent" is a form of evil since less than eternity, the men involved have a "share in eternity," says Plotinus.[27] Here we see his attempt to blend his pre-existential insight into man "sharing" in eternity with his idea of a cosmic mysticism. This is supported by the idea that both time and eternity are intuited by the knower, the one being of the cosmic process, the other being an everlasting state.[28]

Plotinus' mysticism provides a more consequential view of eternity than do the theories of Plato and Aristotle, an eternity which can relate itself consistently to time from the standpoint of its own nature and intrinsic activity. This, together with his pre-existential epistemology of time, dealt with in Chapter II, challenges the more stringent dichotomy of eternity and time held by Plato and Aristotle. In his third *Ennead* Plotinus sees the *Totum Simul* of the eternal Soul as a "life" that possesses everything as present, i.e., "all things at once." This entails a fusion of subject and object of a kind much more dynamic than that of his Greek forerunners. Yet the eternal is still a kind of paradigm of the temporal, quite as for Plato.[29] While the cosmic process is pantheistic, the time-eternity relationship has greater pneumatic quality and redemptive possibilities than in Plato's view. F. H. Brabant has even dared to say that it "goes far to change the frigid abstractions of the Platonic Forms into the Christian conception of Heaven."[30]

Plotinus, then, did not yield entirely to an objective concept of Being. He saw eternal Being to be quite free and dynamic, more like *pneuma* than *nous*. Eternity is a kind of Becoming-Being, so to speak. This anticipates Berdyaev's view with its application to the undoing of the knotty problem of permanence and change from the standpoint of eternity and time.[31] It provides the Becoming in Being which we have seen to be a needed factor in eternity, particularly to be existentially meaningful.

While this neo-Platonic view of the eternal is much more congenial to Berdyaev's existential solution of the problem of time than the classical view, the mysticism of Plotinus has some weaknesses which must be avoided. Berdyaev, even with his strong mystical tendencies, appears to be quite aware of them. He sees that Plotinus is preoccupied with a mysticism of "the One" to the extent that man is ultimately absorbed or "lost in God." Thus, all plurality and individuality are eventually negated.[32] This does not lend itself to a Christian immortality and end. Theoretically, time must be absorbed in the end, not exactly fulfilled and consummated. In addition *the One* is only "attainable through an abnegation and abstraction of the plural world."[33] It must include an abnegation of time, not its fulfillment. This is reflected also in what we called a contradiction in Plotinus' view of eternity; nevertheless, his attempt to retain a pneumatic quality in eternity is a profoundly existential insight which helps illuminate the *Totum Simul* or eternal Now by interrelating permanence and change rather than dichotomizing them, on the one hand, or identifying them, on the other.

Among ancient philosophers Plotinus was exceptional in that he saw the problem of time related to the nature of eternity as well as to the knower and the meaning of destiny. His basic idea of the emanation of the temporal from the eternal, plurality from unity, prefigures Berdyaev's idea of time as "a decomposed eternity," while his idea of the *return* of the *many* to the *one* prefigures Berdyaev's eschatological doctrine of the transfiguration of time and the cosmos. Yet the bipolar monism of Plotinus includes the idea of time being swallowed up by eternity in the return of the many to the One. Ontologically, this monism is no more congenial to the bipolar existentialism of Berdyaev than to the classical dualisms of Plato and Aristotle; nevertheless, the neo-Platonic mysticism and pattern are somewhat paralleled by Berdyaev in his eschatology of cosmic transfiguration. While Plotinus has an ontological theory in which time is dependent upon eternity, his concept of the eternal, it appears, really disallows their eschatological relationship in a real end. It implies the repudiation of time in time's end, while that end can hardly be more than hypothetical, since it is eternity's activity which makes for time. How can this dynamic eternity be so inactive, as implied by time's end?

Time is ultimately liquidated rather than embraced redemptively in Plotinus' scheme. Berdyaev, on the other hand, looks to an "eternal end" which, as we shall see, illuminates and transfigures time and the temporal order while preserving the reality of both the temporal and supratemporal aspects of the end. This allows a legitimate biblio-eschatological "return" to the eternal, since both the temporal and eternal elements are retained in the existential end. Thus Berdyaev has much in common with Plotinus' pattern while retaining the reality of time more realistically in terms of concrete existence. This helps account for existential time's eschatological dimension in Berdyaev's philosophy. It points toward another aspect of our basic contention. It will be enlarged upon in Part II.

The Existential View of Eternity

Eternity in Augustinian Theology

Strange to say, Augustine did not follow through on the implications of his profoundly existential view of time. When it came to its relationship to the nature of eternity, Augustine reverted to the abstract Platonic idea of Being. It can be said that Augustine's view of "the eternal present" has some similarity to Plotinus' *Totum Simul,* but it is not as dynamic. Yet while stressing eternity's changelessness he could say that all time belongs to God.[34] This attempts to combine a Greek view of a timeless God with a Hebrew view of historical purpose. The paradox of the Incarnation is what bridges the gap here, but the question remains whether the eternity to which Augustine refers can provide for an actual incarnation in time.

Had he sought to blend his existential insights into time, the present and the "eternal now" with the more dynamic view of eternity held by Plotinus, we venture to say that Augustine would have developed a more consistently existential eschatology through the application of the supratemporal implications of the *now* to the end. One serious consequence of his idealistic concept of eternity is that, as it stands, *The City of God*, Augustine's classic on eschatology, is largely futuristic, pointing Roman society (Becoming) to the Ideal Church (Being).[35] The equivalent is an institutional church reflecting the Kingdom of God, a Platonic adaptation.

Time is the essence of change, Augustine indicated in the above-mentioned work, whereas he said that in eternity there is no change.[36] Here we see eternity conceived Platonically again as an immutable timelessness.[37] In his essay on "The Trinity" Augustine also insists upon the "timelessness of the Godhead."[38] But, we ask, can a timeless eternity and Godhead be related to time? We think not. Furthermore, such a view of the nature of eternity is inconsistent with, and does not account for, Augustine's own doctrine of "the eternal present,"[39] which did much to make Augustine a precursor if not an exponent of the existential version of time. No chunk of idealistic ice can be related to the temporal "now and then," even if labeled "the eternal." To refer to but one specific problem, it makes impossible the idea of providence, which Augustine respected.

Not seeing both sides of the existential clue to the time-eternity relationship, Augustine failed to enlarge upon its implications. Concentrating only on the time side of the matter, he was prone to keep the nature of the "eternal present" too static through a sterile Platonic concept of eternity, even as he thereby jeopardized the revealed meaning of God as a living Spirit. An abstract idealistic eternity is congenial to neither the creating, revealing and redeeming roles of the divine person nor to the eschatological meaning of time and creation.

It also appears that Augustine's concept of the immutable Godhead based on Platonic ontology disallows his own two-sided doctrine of *caritas*, a reciprocal relationship of love between God and man. Yet it is congenial to his progressive eschatology of "the city of man" becoming "the City of God," the latter being treated as a projected ideal and future end of the Church. But it would better blend with the one-sided view of *agape* as interpreted today by Anders Nygren,[40] save for the fact that the N.T. *agape* is a self-giving love to which no ideal, Platonic or otherwise, can do justice. An immutable eternity not only disallows Augustine's doctrine of *caritas,* an attempted synergism of *agape* and *eros,* but is hardly reconcilable to the self-giving quality of *agape* itself, let alone the doctrine of revelation. Furthermore, it remains too immune to time to give occasion to the existential moment. Thus the Platonic idea of eternity is out of harmony with Augustine's particular observation that "God moves the spiritual creature through time." [41]

A century later, Boethius held an idea of eternity akin to that of Augustine but more congenial to the Scholastics. "Eternity," he said, "is the simultaneous and complete possession of infinite life." [42] The *Totum Simul* to Boethius implies immutability in an abiding present. Eternity is said to lack nothing of the future or past and, therefore, includes divine foreknowledge but not an Augustinian predestination. While Augustine held to a moral freedom in man it had little place respecting divine election and providence. Thus Boethius anticipated issues significant in Thomism as well as the later debate between Calvinistic and Arminian theologies. Aquinas tried to relate immutability with the *actus purus,* as we have seen, while accepting the *Totum Simul* of Boethius, in contrast to the followers of Duns Scotus, who rejected a divine simultaneity as well as an eternity with a beginning and end.[43] Yet Aquinas, in his *actus purus,* tried to protect the transcendence of eternity over time as a matter of kind rather than degree.

A dynamic eternity such as that held by Plotinus but missed by Plato and Augustine points more toward the existential solution which, we maintain, Berdyaev eventually uncovers. But what of eternity as held by Kierkegaard? How does the discrete Dane of a century ago pose and sharpen the issues involved in understanding existentially the nature of eternity?

Eternity in Kierkegaardian Philosophy

Drawing closer to what we anticipate in Berdyaev, we must also consider Soren Kierkegaard's insights into the nature of eternity. Kierkegaard did not quite side with Augustine's Platonic idea of eternity. He saw the eternal to be the redemptive factor that lends meaning to time through the existential Moment which liberates man from his temporal existence of sinful finitude. For this to be true, however, the "eternal now" could not be static in nature. Here S. K. helps vivify an important existential insight.

To S. K. eternity is not the static ideal Being that it was largely for Plato and Augustine. Rather, it is described as Being-in-Becoming. Of this paradox Kierkegaard says, "The infinite and eternal is the only certainty, but as being in the subject *it is in existence* and . . . the *eternal becomes* . . . it comes into being." [44] The qualitatively transcendent element of the existential moment thus springs from an eternity, which relates itself to the present. Eternity, then, intersects time in "the Moment." This insight is based on the revelation in Christ. It might best be appreciated in the light of Kant's frequently overlooked admission that only "a transcendental theology" can yield an understanding of eternity. [45] This is something Hegel failed to reckon with when he monistically identified eternity with a temporal process of cosmic immanence and interpreted God as the Spirit of spirits. [46] But what to Nicholas Berdyaev and Paul Tillich is the *ekstasis* or divine incursion of time by the eternal in *kairos,* Kierkegaard only approaches as he speaks of the "touching" of time by the eternal. We are prone to think that this Kierkegaardian expression is a deliberate choice meant to suggest the uniqueness of the existential Moment while toning down eternity's intense interrelationship here with moments in a linear or successive time real in its own right. [47] The same will be seen in the interpretation of the distinguished dialectical theologian of today, Karl Barth.

Kierkegaard holds to a heterogeneous paradoxical dualism of "either/or" rather than a dynamic paradox of "both/and," which we would deem neither a heterogeneous dichotomy nor a homogeneous synthesis, but rather a mutually relevant tension of opposites. "Either/or is the token which insures entrance into the unconditional . . . the key to heaven!" says Kierkegaard in his *Attack*. Yet he often speaks rather carelessly of a "synthesis," as we have seen, one which he means to keep irrational, mysterious and closer to what we regard as a "both/and" tension. Even so, this idea remains deficient from the standpoint of his time-eternity relationship. Eternity intersects an unreal time in the subject's existential Moment. The eternal and transcendent God confronts a man involved in an illusory time. But the latter tends to minimize the actual seriousness of the problem and its reality. While a man's true *Existenz* belongs to the one, qualitatively, his mundane existence and selfhood belong to the other, quantitatively. The abyss here is healed for the concrete self only when in the Moment of encounter with the Eternal, and by "the moment perpetually affirmed" through a faith of "radical obedience" to the revealed will and Grace of God, he realizes where lies his Real Self.[48]

Whereas S. K. leaves his paradox in a transcendent dualistic pattern of eternity and time, Berdyaev's bipolar position rejects both an ontological dualism and monism wherein either transcendence or immanence engulfs or negates the other. While S. K. does not look as deeply into the nature of eternity *per se*, he sees how it is essential to the meaning of time and things temporal. He stoutly asserts that only the eternal can be present.[49] This being the case, there is no realistic temporal present, we reiterate, only a seeming one. This together with a denial of the tenses of time makes time a delusion in every sense. The idea is utterly Platonic.

Denying the unity of thought and being as held by Hegel, S. K. severely attacks the rational monism of Hegel,[50] but this does not disqualify Kierkegaard's own regard for time and eternity as a paradoxical "synthesis," though we believe the term unfortunate. Not a rational but irrational "synthesis," it represents a meeting of opposites in a kind of mixture rather than compound, one in which Being is related to Becoming, however "thin" the relationship guaranteed by S. K. At this point Kierkegaard helps correct Augustine's more unbending Platonic concept of the eternal, while also putting in question Hegel's rational blending of the time-eternity dialectic. Kierkegaard at least sees that only a dynamic eternity not constricted by an idealistic concept can relate itself to time in any sense.

Kierkegaard then makes the "eternal now" the basic clue to meaning, one which is quite relevant to men in the "instant" or existential Moment. Eternity is not seen here as the infinite extension of a time line but a point infinitely extended in all directions simultaneously. This transcends any and all limits of a temporal moment. Chaning-Pearce speaks of this great Moment as follows:

> In that instant the inward and the eternal meet in a timeless here and now reached through and within, yet ever beyond, our space-time continuum. There is the point of intersection where the longitudinal line of human life, love [eros], thought and time meet the vertical line of of eternity and the down-pouring love [agape] of God. For the Christian, for Kierkegaard, that instant of interesection is the cross of the incarnate Christ. There is the paradox of faith.[51]

This great Moment is also basic to what S. K. refers to as "repetition" and "contemporaneity." [52] Repetition implies that what *has been* now *becomes* for a person. Contrary to the Platonic doctrine of "recollection" which asserts that what *is* has been, this means a bringing of the past, deemed unreal in itself, into the present moment. A past truth or event may be realized or lived in the present. This provocative insight allows for a "contemporaneity" of the present moment of faith with the past event of Christ.[53] It allows that a Christian is contemporaneous with Christ, insofar as he enters the existential moment and is confronted by eternity.

One basic way in which a Christian is contemporary with Christ lies in his witness, which implies that he must suffer for the truth if he loves it. "Only one thing is it possible to remember eternally: having suffered for the truth," says Kierkegaard in his *Attack*.[54]. Even providing a chain of existential moments, as it were, such commitment confers an eternal contemporraneity on whatever looks to Christ for its significance. Employing this principle, W. M. Horton has said, "Jesus is fulfiller of Old Testament prophecy and the decisive act of God in history, for by him the eternal and the universal in Judaism is disentangled from transient and local elements and made available to all mankind." [55]

Spiritually, this enhances the meaning of the believer's communion with God through a relevant revelation in the Moment of faith. Ethically, it implies that the "original choice is constantly present in every subsequent choice." [56] Even so, S. K. fails to correct the Platonic notion of an unreal, illusory or merely reflective time. Rather, he seeks to give time status and meaning only in the existential moment linked with eternity, the only true or real present. We can appreciate this endeavor, but not without a sensitivity to its Christological and eschatological repercussions. The Christological factor was touched upon above in relation to Berdyaev's view of existential time as having a role for memory to play as an agent of eternity even in this sort of repetition and contemporaneity. Kierkegaard is prone to accentuate the "Christ of faith" at the expense of an adequate interrelationship with the "Jesus of history." We can say this despite the fact that we could concur that a rationally defined Christology is impossible. The eschatological implications of this await our discussion of Barth's theological view of eternity.

It must be stressed that for S. K. only "the eternal is the present," and this cannot be grasped from within the common stream of time. Unless a person is "contemporary" with this absolute, it is unreal or irrelevant to him. Faith in a unique revelation is the sole possibility of this. While the eternal present is not the same as the temporal present, time and eternity "touch each other" in the present, the existential moment, as a tangent touches a circle. This "atom of eternity," as it has been called, is regarded by S. K. as "the finite reflection of eternity in time." [57] Here we see another Platonic coloring of S.K.'s position.

More important to our immediate concern is this: while the eternal is seen to intersect time in the present moment and is seen "constantly permeating time" [58] on the basis of the shifting present, Kierkegaard still does not quite side with Plato and Augustine in leaving the nature of eternity a static immutability. While he seems to do so at times, as in his discourse entitled "The Unchangeableness of God," where he speaks of the God Who exists while unchangeable in the eternal present,[59a] thus raising questions in the reader's mind as to how God can then reckon with time and finitude, let alone provide the conditions for their appearance or even "give men time," this we must interpret to be S. K. at less than his philosophical best. Kierkegaard's basic position allows us to say that eternity *as* the present, eternally, copes with the present, temporally, and the two "presents" meet as one in the existential moment. In fact the Instant is the "breaking through of the eternal," in contrast to a common instant of time "filled with emptiness," as S. K. puts it.[59b] Thus we see that eternity is a dynamic, suprarational reality of qualitative and redeeming significance. In this respect S. K. goes much further than Augustine to account for an eternity which can both meet and give meaning to time. S. K. does this by his paradoxical "synthesis," an irrational mixture of Being and Becoming in the form of eternity-in-time.

Yet S. K.'s irrational "synthesis" or paradox here gives too little consequence to the time side of the Moment. Only the eternal is truly the present and the real. But if time, including linear time, is unreal, we must contend that the temporal present under discussion is altogether unreal or a delusion. Augustine saw the problem here and said that if such is the case only eternity is real, intimating that we might as well cease our discussion of time. Too frequently this is overlooked by the interpreters of Augustine. If time is unreal, we must ask: To what does eternity relate and reveal itself in the existential moment? Logically, the answer must be "Nothing!"

While S. K. seeks to give meaning and status to the present through the eternal present, actually his version of existential time amounts to eternity relating itself to an illusory temporal existence, thus trying to redeem what is basically unreal. Such a stringent dualism endangers the reality and common sense of accepting any time at all. Kierkegaard then dissolves in his way what Hegel does in his. Time and temporal ills are relegated to a form of non-Being. This almost justifies Matthew Spinka's claim that existential time is really "no time at all," as previously mentioned.

But this is attributable only to S. K., we maintain, not to Berdyaev. For Berdyaev an inauthentic existence is not deemed unreal along with its evil time, while for S. K. it is. Thus, S. K.'s "eternal present" really embraces itself, its own present [60] on the one hand, and "touches" only an illusory present on the other. In contrast to what we shall see more clearly in Berdyaev, this jeopardizes the redemptive property of eternity and the uniqueness of its existential Moment, just as it also detracts from the reality of the evil that is being redeemed. Kierkegaard's otherwise sound "leap of faith" now appears to be an escape of a kind which we would judge he did not intend. This is due to the constraint of a quasi-Platonic ontology in or out of disguise.

Our observation here is given indirect support, we find, by John Marsh when he states that Reformed theology, which greatly influenced S. K. through Luther, and much of which goes back through Kierkegaard in its contemporary form, is "Platonist in method." [61] But whether this must be the last word in the existential perspective of theology and the problem of the time-eternity relation is still debatable. Berdyaev would have us see the inadequacy of all ontological systems. While Kierkegaard has not duplicated Plato's ontology in its entirety, he has subscribed to a pattern closely allied with Plato's ontology while in a way which does less to allow a serious element of Being to belong to the Becoming of human existence even though deemed far less than pure Being. That is, he so depreciates the *chronos* of existence that it becomes unreal rather than refracted or deficient. Berdyaev does not do this, for even time as a fallen state or "decomposed eternity" *is* something; it belongs to a real human existence however disoriented it may be.

While S. K. held that only eternity is *present,* he disallowed its relevance to anything but a pseudotemporal present. He denied the past and the future in his concern for the existential moment. But, as shown above, both Augustine and Berdyaev assert that there can be no present without a linear past and future. Thus, S. K.'s existential moment is related to no real temporal present, no realistic time, in fact, and his eternity is related only to itself, the only real present. While his idea of eternity has more dynamic quality or "life" than those of the classical and rational concepts of eternity, including that of Augustine, S. K.'s view has less dynamic quality than the eternity held by Berdyaev, for it relates itself directly only to one tense of time and a very obscure one at that. Furthermore, by keeping linear time unreal, S. K. fails to unfold the eschatological dimension of existential time in relation to the future. This gives no meaning to history on the one hand, and no hope relevant to life in this world on the other.

Though there is a potential here which gives man a new out-

111

look, it is one that is an uplook but hardly conducive to a look around and ahead, as it were. While this much is *basic* it is *not sufficient* for a mature or complete Christian perspective of existence and destiny. The only history S. K. can acknowledge is one which is "sacred" by means of the existential moment and the "contemporaneity" it affords the man of faith. Kierkegaard goes so far as to say the following: "If the contemporary generation had left behind them nothing but the words, 'We have believed that in such and such a year God appeared among us in the humble figure of a servant, that He lived and taught in our community, and finally died,' it would be more than enough." [62] This is good, but hardly stronger than S. K.'s time-eternity relationship. It puts a premium on belief, while minimizing the divine person-event of the past and his temporal medium, as related to the witnesses whose reports revolve around certain events, not just their meaning or significance alone.

The statement would be more plausible had Kierkegaard given a stronger role to the time factor, even apart from the inability to date or measure it. Our faith must be seen related not only to our own staccato-like existential moments but to those of others before us. This kinship could hardly have come about without the media of durational time. For S. K., Christ is of eternity and central to a sacred history which is not allied with a beginning and end, as in common or secular history which is past and gone. Again, this is good but not good enough. It is a complement to S. K.'s idea that an eternal happiness cannot be related to a temporal, historical knowledge. [63] Granted, this protects the *basis*, but it does not protect the *relation* involved. It means that while Christ was *in* history he was not *of* it. This, too, is noteworthy, but it does not account for the occasion for Christ even being *in* history while not of it. His being *in* history is no accident or inconsequential matter, since it pertains to the divine act of revelation and redemption. This S. K. does not protect. In other words, for him "sacred history" or *Heilsgeschichte* stands altogether outside of common history. [64]

This is what contemporary theologians of the neo-Reformation school like Barth, Brunner and Bultmann have exploited to various degrees under the direct or indirect influence of Kierkegaard. But does it tell the whole story of the relation of the Christ of eternity to the Jesus of history or the Incarnation?

Kierkegaard would reply, "The Christian fact has no history, for it is the paradox that God once came into existence in time." [65] We can and must appreciate this, but we cannot concede that Kierkegaard has reckoned with all its implications. Even the "fact," the "history" and the "time" packed into this quotation from S. K. are extremely significant ingredients, which must not be ignored. Without them, would we recognize even faithwise Him who confronts us in the great Moment as God in Christ? Hardly. While we see through a glass darkly, we must at least see through the smudged glass of temporality and finitude to which God has chosen in Christ to relate himself.

S. K. tends to link time and history with sheer chronology or the pseudo measurement of time. This is one seat of his error; hence his extreme aversion for anything of time. While S. K. is accordingly impatient with an orthodoxy which speaks to the critic of Christianity primarily in terms of what God has done in the past centuries—a legitimate impatience—he is prone to **overlook that we know little of a Christ of the existential pres-**ent save for his disclosure in terms that the apostles remembered and understood in terms of a realistic past. Even the Christ who appeared to Paul identified himself as Jesus of Nazareth, thus becoming all the more relevant to Paul in terms of his very limited relation to Jesus. The existential encounter was primary, but its temporal relationships were an important aspect of its necessary relevance. Thus, a sacred history must not only be identified with the *source* of its meaningfulness, *viz.,* eternity and the existential moment of encounter, but must also be related to the terms by which the encounter comes about or is made relevant and more intelligible to men. There must be an empirical *Historie,* then, if there is to be a meaningful *Geschichte* in terms of a *Heilsgeschichte.* No need to speak of a "sacred history," then, if there is no time or history that can be made meaningful or sacred. This is not a rational synthesis, however, but it is an existential association. The parallel is a divine Grace that saves a *real* man, however sinful or fallen he may be.

Another aspect of our criticism of Kierkegaard is this: What knowledge does man have, even a faith-conditioned knowledge inspired by God, which does not have some temporal connotation or form, even when it is a knowledge of or about eternity?

113

One's faith is still involved in the human refraction of human finitude and temporality, or else it remains irrelevant to the man of time and existence. If not, the faith is not man's in *any* sense, and such a faith is no glory to God. A faith inspired by divine Grace is one thing; a faith imposed on a man is another. It is utterly imposed if man's time is as insignificant an instrument as S. K. makes it out to be.

While S. K. is right in not claiming that faith rests on any objective proof or theoretical gloss of all antinomies related to a divine truth revealed to human existence, an almost disastrous connotation in his view is that a *perfect* act of faith is called for. One can only have an absolute relation to the Absolute! The great abyss hardly allows this—unless the Incarnation is a sufficient answer, one which conjoins both sides of the abyss between time and eternity that the man of faith may be existentially "contemporary" with the Absolute. S. K. seeks to assure us of the latter but only as the "sacred history" involved is outside history.[66] But can the eternal Absolute be incarnate unless in some sense reconciled to history? We think not, for "God was in *Christ* reconciling the world unto himself," as St. Paul says.

Though mundane history is not the source of saving knowledge, neither is it totally alien thereto, for it is an instrument, medium or vessel. While a faith datum, the Incarnation bespeaks this instrumentation as do some consequences within history apparent to both believers and unbelievers, the latter at least in a dependent sense. The Church is the conspicuous sign of this. To regard the time of Christ's manhood and ministry as in no way a matter of common history is to obscure the divine *ekstasis* and the redeeming influence of the Incarnate Person-Event upon history and world destiny. Christ's advent entails a missionary commission which implies movement within history and throughout the world. Leslie Paul is quite right: "Without men moving through both sacred and secular history it is inconceivable how Kierkegaard should be presented with a conception of Christ that can become contemporary with him." [67]

A more balanced view is required. While S. K. is right in warning us not to look primarily to history, he endangers the agency or medium of history used by God. The apostles were contemporaries of Christ in their way that we might be in ours.

It is nonsensical to infer that the Incarnate One is contemporary for us in the very same way he was for them. For the apostles he had both inward and outward contemporaneity. Not all eyes that saw him, however, beheld the Christ, but those who did were common men of time who saw another who proved himself uncommon! Whom they saw was not disrelated from how they saw him. Thus the Incarnation was an event in a time qualified by eternity, a *chronos* made *kairos*.

The eschatological counterpart to this includes a realistic future and end. If not, eternity must be said to be dealing with illusions in dealing with men of time, history and existence. We must affirm that eternity does not deal with illusions! The God of creation and redemption is not schizophrenic! Eternity does not redeem a fictitious time any more than a fictitious sin and evil. Thus, S. K. must be said to neglect what Charles Williams has referred to as the "conversion of time by the Holy Ghost." [68] S. K. allows for no time to convert! He provides well for that which converts but not that which is to be converted. Granted, the latter is not the center of Christian faith, but it is the problem to which faith must appertain; hence, it is the setting of faith and its drama of redemption. S. K. actually stifles the eschatological potential of existential time, disallowing a realistic future as much as the past. Only the present can be interpreted *sub speci aeterni*.[69] This gives no significance to the future and the end. It means that a human existence related to the past as well as to the future is of no consequence to the meaning of human existence and destiny. Kierkegaard seems to forget that the past and the future could include "existential presents," feeding the present encounter with God. If this were not so, the apostles would have had no ambition to write the scriptures or give witness to a *kerygma* meaningful *now* in terms of a past lived in relation to Jesus Christ and a future lived even in the world in terms of a hope inspired by Jesus Christ.

While S. K. says eternity in this existential context is a type of Being-in-Becoming, a principle of revelation based upon the Incarnation, he does not show how a moment of revelation can be a "fraction of eternity" from the standpoint of a realistic time or history. It is utterly timeless. Yet S. K. still seems to sense a problem here, one which he really does not solve but smooths over in other contexts of thought. He states, for example, "The eternal is infinite in content, and yet it must be made commensurable with the temporal, and the contact is in the instant." [70] But said instant is really a mere bubble of effervescence. In the context just quoted, S. K. concedes a plain contradiction. But is such a plain contradiction a relevant one, one truly paradoxical even? That can be debated, for opposites-in-meeting must be related with relevance to each other to meet and meet meaningfully.

Though S. K. is protecting what is deemed an "absurdity" to reason, he is in danger of making it an absurd absurdity; that is, one which is not even relevant to the *existing* man of faith who is still a man of time. Kierkegaard is willing to sacrifice the reality of time, even the present thereof, to gain status with eternity through the eternal Now. This is a betrayal of the subjective aspects of a realistic manhood, which in itself is not praiseworthy of the new manhood gained in the true *Existenz* to which he looks. Kierkegaard writes, "I am able to make from the springboard the great leap whereby I pass into infinity. . . ." This is a return to pure Being in a way which smacks too much of a Greek immortality, while meant to convey the idea of true *Existenz*. By this S. K. says, "I gain myself in my eternal consciousness." [71] But this is a kind of "risk" which renounces the reality of that from which it leaps by faith. Why leap then? Why leap from a fiction? Why leap from an illusion, a time not real in its own way?

For all his strength, what is Kierkegaard's main weakness? It is that he renounces as unreal what he might better repudiate as an erroneous limited perspective. The two are not the same. Inauthentic existence is not the same as a form of non-Being. Evil in the temporal sense is a misconstrued, fallen condition but not to be treated as illusory; it is at least mixed with a form of good belonging to the created order, particularly to the existential subject whose time it is, however warped. To recognize as real only the eternal divine Being is unfair to temporal creation and the eternal God and *Logos* Whose order it is and Who wills to redeem it. Kierkegaard actually makes time a form of non-Being while sometimes referring to it as a form of Becoming. This is the case despite his legitimate differentiation between the eternal's entrance into time and existence on the one hand, and the history of Christianity on the other.[72]

By nullifying the reality of successive time S. K. threatens the very relevance of eternity to time and debilitates the fuller meaning of existential time. It is as though the historical stage, setting, events and personnel of the divine drama of redemption were of negligible significance to the divine plot and the communication of its truth. This anticipates Barth's view of revelation. While S. K. resists the attempt of the old orthodoxy, or any other rational scheme of religion, to appear plausible,[73] he does so at the risk of making it either impossible or historically irrelevant. Shrewdly recognizing the advantage of the free-thinking rationalist to undermine such plausibility, S. K. would conserve the Gospel through its implausible paradox.[74] But we fear that S. K.'s version of the paradox is too heterodox in its opposing facets to provide for the time-eternity co-incidence. This is not even genuine paradox, since it weakens the contact between the opposites in tension.

For S. K. time is something which ends, whereas the eternal and existential do not. Thus he compresses the real end along with true or existential time into the Now in such a way as to dissolve and bypass any realistic end in future time. The only end is, paradoxically, no end at all, the qualitative, transcendent eternal present. Here is the precedent *par excellence* for Karl Barth's "otherworldy" theology. The folding door of historic succession is slammed together against the central doorpost; the accordian is closed tight! Time's duration and succession are collapsed. This amounts to a one-sided redemptive time, hence a debilitated and immature version of *kairos*. This calls to mind again our thesis that eternity meets and redeems a realistic *chronos* lest we have neither *kairos* nor *eschaton*. A redeeming eternity does this without threat to the reality of itself or the abnegation of that which it redeems.

*   *   *   *

We have traced the developments in the outstanding philosophical concepts of eternity in the history of thought from Plato to Kierkegaard. This has brought us to the borderline between philosophy and theology from the standpoint of a profoundly important problem, that of eschatology. But further refinements of the matter are important from the religio-philosophical standpoint. Having come to see the existential perspective of the issue through the mind of Kierkegaard, we must enlarge this area of thought with a comparative approach to Berdyaev and the distinguished contemporary theologian Karl Barth. Plunging us more directly into what we call the eschatological dimension of existential time, we are at the brink of Part II of our comparative study.

What does Berdyaev do to enhance this special quality of existential time in view of the doctrine of eternity? How does it compare with the insights of the dialectical, neo-orthodox theologian Karl Barth? These questions broaden the importance of what we have led up to, even as they show the importance of theological answers, critically evaluated, to the perennial and ultimate questions posed by philosophy. Thus we must further consider the meaning of eternity and its significance to time that we may better grasp the eschatological dimension of existential time and establish the distinctive meaning of the End of time.

Thus, having begun to understand what there is about eternity that adorns the peak of Kairos, we can examine it further from the standpoint of its self-revealing, luminescent beauty and strength. What is there about eternity that not only makes *chronos* become *kairos* but makes *kairos* point to *eschaton*? This demands further treatment of the nature of eternity from a distinctively theological perspective.

NOTES

1 Cf. Pringle-Pattison, *The Idea of God*, Chap. XVIII.
2 *Timaeus* 37, D-E, 38D.
3 *Ibid*, 38C, 39E. Cf. A-D, 39B, 47B.
4 *The Republic*, II: 381. Cf. II: 380.
5 *Ibid*., 365. Cf. *The Laws*, X, 889ff; XII, 948.
6 *Ibid*., III, 388. Contrast Genesis 6:6 and Luke 15:7.
7 As cited by Brabant, *op. cit.*, p. 7 (Jowett, I; p. 388).
8 Cf. Plato's *Timaeus*, *Sophist* and *Statesman*, contrast *The Republic* and *Laws*.
9 Berdyaev, *Spirit and Reality*, p. 105. Cf. pp. 17-19. Dean Inge in *God and the Astronomers*, p. 75, gives credit to Plato for allowing "timeless values"

to belong to "the world of events." Inge uses this as the argument against a rigid dualism, but actually, in terms here set forth, it is inadequate for "baptizing" Plato's ontology.

10 Plato, *Timaeus* 37E.

11 *God's Way With Man*, pp. 120-124. Hazelton attacks Emil Brunner who, too, sees Plato's timeless eternity. Cf. Brunner, *Eternal Hope*, pp. 47, 53. But Hazelton is striving for an analogical position, which mitigates the paradoxical factor. He strives to make appear semi-immanental what is still a paradoxical tension, while not necessarily a Platonic dualism. Thus he looks wrongly to Berdyaev for consistent support. Berdyaev sees eternity as making a victory over time by redeeming it with meaning and destiny. Plato hardly proffers us this. Cf. Berdyaev, *The Meaning of History*, p. 63f, 67f. While Berdyaev sees time as real and "rooted in eternity," it is a "decomposed eternity" due to a fallen man and cosmos rather than intrinsically "anchored in the being of eternal God," as Hazelton claims in terms of his "converted Platonism" (pp. 123, 124). Yet Hazelton's intentions show creative insight in searching for a view which claims "the eternal not only grounds the temporal but bends into it and responds to it" in terms of the Christian revelation. But in such an idealistic framework the evil of time belongs to God as much as time does, while its redemption is either inevitable or unnecessary.

12 R. W. Inge, *God and the Astronomers*, p. 75.

13 *The Republic*, X, 608ff, 614, 617. Cf. VI, 498, C.

14 *De Caelo*, 279B, 28-30. Cf. *Physics*, Bk. VIII, Ch. 2, 252b, 9-12.

15 Cf. F. H. Brabant, *op. cit.*, p. 22f.

16 *Summa Theologica*, I, 12, 1, p. 92.

17 *Ibid.*, I, 10, 1, p. 74f, Cf. 10, 4, p. 78.

18 *Ibid.*, I, 10, 3, p. 76.

19 *Ibid.*, I, 10, 3, p. 77. The neo-Thomist, Jacques Maritain dramatically expresses the Aristotelian-Thomist concept of time in his essay "The Mathematical Attenuation of Time" in *The Freedom of the Intellect*, pp. 63-101. He relates the matter to the theory of relativity but, essentially, no fresh light is given.

20 *Ibid.*, I, 8, 1, p. 63.

21 *God Is Light*, p. 153f. Cf. H. F. Rall, *Christianity*, p. 312, where *actus purus* is seen to make God morally deficient and incapable of compassion and incarnation.

22 *Slavery and Freedom*, p. 84. Cf. *Freedom and Spirit*, p. 216 and *Spirit and Reality*, pp. 16, 18, 19, 105. Cf. the consequences of this in *The Destiny of Man*, p. 38.

23 *Op. cit.*, I ,9, 2, p. 71.

24 *Enneades*, 7:1, p. 96.

25 *Ibid*, 3:7:11. Cf. R. W. Inge, *God and the Astronomers*, p. 76f.

26 *Ibid*, 7:5, p. 102.

27 *Ibid.*, 7:7, 11, pp. 105, 113.

28 *Ibid.*, 7:1, p. 96.

29 *Ibid.*, 5:6, 1.

30 Brabant, *op. cit.*, p. 25.

31 Cf. Berdyaev, *Solitude and Society*, pp. 46, 53; *Slavery and Freedom*, p. 49f; and *Spirit and Reality*, pp. 111, 75.

32 Cf. Matthew Spinka, *Berdyaev: Captive of Freedom*, p. 104.

33 Berdyaev, *Spirit and Reality*, p. 151.

34 *Confessions*, 11:13. The latter anticipates the Barthian view.

35 *The City of God*, Vol. I, Bk. 5, Ch. XVIII, p. 165ff.

36 *Ibid.*, Vol. I, Bk. XI, Chap. 6. Cf. Chap. 4, end, and Chap. 5. Cf. *Confessions*, XI, 13. Eternity is "ever-fixed" and "whole."

[37] *Ibid.*, Vol. I, Bk. 12, Ch. X, p. 345f.

[38] Bk. XV, 47, The Library of Christian Classics, Vol. VIII, *Augustine: Later Works,* p. 175f. Berdyaev in *Spirit and Reality* speaks of the Platonic idea of eternity, which we have seen adapted by Augustine as ". . . an escape from the whirlpool of cosmic fatality" *(Spirit and Reality,* p. 105. Cf. pp. 17-19.)

[39] Cf. *Confessions,* Bk. XI, 16, p. 261. Cf. 9, footnote p. 257. Eternity simply *is.*

[40] Cf. Nygren, *Agape and Eros,* Pts. I, II, III. While an outstanding three-volume study of the problem, it maintains a one-sided position on the God-man relation, one which is quite congenial to the view of the Word and Grace in Barthian theology. In general, I think Augustine's *caritas* or an "agapesized *eros,*" so to speak, is truer to the N.T. story of redemption as well as its eschatology as seen by Berdyaev. Its existential nature is also seen through the two aspects of the meaning of *ekstasis,* (a) the irruption of the eternal, (b) the term's relation to "ecstasy," an element of *eros* as subjective response, inspiration and communion.

[41] As attributed to Augustine by Thomas Aquinas, *Summa Theologica,* I: 10, 5, p. 80. We cannot agree with Hazelton's claim for Augustine as for Plato that "eternity may and does become temporal," (*God's Way With Man,* p.122), and that Augustine's answer to the problem of time and eternity is Plato's inclusive transcendence, a more neo-Platonic idea which Hazelton attributes to Plato in which time is enveloped by eternity.

[42] As cited by F. H. Brabant, *op. cit.,* p. 64.

[43] *Ibid.,* p. 65-67.

[44] *Concluding Unscientific Postscript,* p. 75. Italics mine.

[45] *Critique of Pure Reason,* p. 415.

[46] Cf. Chapter II for our reference to Hegel's view of eternity.

[47] Since making our evaluation of S.K.'s position we have found that J. V. Martin in *Kierkegaard, the Melancholy Dane* confirms what we say here (pp. 59f, 68). He also says S. K. denies linear time, p. 56, and confirms our statement about eternity "touching" time "as a tangent touches a circle" (p. 57). S. K. himself says on p. 67 of his *Training in Christianity,* "For in relation to the absolute there is only one tense: the present. For him who is not contemporary with the absolute for him it has no existence."

[48] Cf. *Sickness Unto Death* and *Stages on Life's Way.* Cf. "Religiousness B," a stage based on faith and the incarnation in contrast to reason and immanence. For the quotation see *Attack Upon Christendom,* p. 81.

[49] *The Concept of Dread,* p. 77.

[50] *Concluding Unscientific Postscript,* p. 112.

[51] *The Terrible Crystal,* p. 51.

[52] S. K., *Repetition,* pp. 3ff, 12, 33ff.

[53] Cf. Tillich, "Existential Philosophy," Part III, *Journal of the History of Ideas,* Vol. V, No. I, Jan. 1944, pp. 44-70.

[54] S. K., *On Authority and Revelation,* pp. 58, 63. *Attack Upon Christendom,* p. 249.

[55] *Our Eternal Contemporary,* p. 13.

[56] *Either/Or,* Vol. II, p. 184.

[57] *The Concept of Dread,* p. 79.

[58] *Ibid.,* p. 88. Unlike Berdyaev, S. K. does not seem to relate suffering to existential moments save as spiritual despair, the subjective condition or "prelude" to faith.

[59] (a) *Edifying Discourses,* p. 257. Cf. "Eternal Happiness," p. 110ff and (b) *Attack . . .,* p. 281.

[60] T. H. Croxall in his *Kierkegaard Studies,* p. 130, confirms this, I find, in

his assertion that to S. K. the eternal is "forever contemporaneous." He adds, "For eternity knows no past or future. It is the everlasting Now, always present . . ."

61 Marsh, *The Fullness of Time*, p. 16. Collins in *The Mind of Kierkegaard*, p. 250, says S. K. stressed the unchanging nature of God as transcendence. This confirms our immediate observation. But Marsh on a biblical basis retains, akin to Berdyaev, both *chronos* and *kairos* as "running time" and "filled time" (Chap. II), and says, "Sacred and secular history are distinguished but not separated" (p. 117). This is unlike S. K. and Barth, as we shall see. Marsh also sees revelation as "God's speaking" and "man's hearing" (Chap. I). *Kairos* is not only "filled" (O.T.) but is "fulfilled" (N.T.). Cf. Chaps. V, VII. The Kingdom is also both present and future. While Marsh does not seem to see the inadequacy of a Platonic framework to express this much eschatologically, his basic argument for biblical time is much in accord with our thesis that the dialectic of time and eternity is best understood in terms of "existential time" as we have seen it with the help of Berdyaev. A Platonic concept of eternity does not do this justice.

62 *Philosophical Fragments*, p. 87. Cf. p. 51ff.

63 *Training in Christianity*, pp. 66-70, and *Philosophical Fragments*, p. 323.

64 *Training in Christianity*, p. 67f.

65 *On Authority and Revelation*, p. 60.

66 *Training in Christianity*, p. 67. Cf. pp. 27ff, 66-70.

67 *The Meaning of Human Existence*, p. 187. This also hits Barth who, in his *Epistle to Romans*, 1957 ed., pp. 277, 314f, 57, says "The Truth of God is not liable to the 'flux of history'. . . ." His "thoroughgoing eschatology" makes sacred history disparate from secular events and strictly the *Krisis* of all history.

68 *The Descent of the Dove*, p. 15.

69 *Concluding Unscientific Postscript*, pp. 195, 272f.

70 *On Authority and Revelation*, p. 130.

71 *Fear and Trembling*, pp. 47, 57.

72 *On Authority and Revelation*, p. 58f.

73 *Ibid.*, p. 59f.

74 *Ibid.*, pp. 57-64, 103-105.

CHAPTER V

EXISTENTIAL TIME AND THE NATURE OF ETERNITY: II

Having come to see the strong relation between the meaning of eternity and existential time from an existential, philosophical standpoint, it is necessary to enlarge the implications bringing into sharper focus the provocative meaning of eternity from a more theological standpoint. The basic eschatology of Nicholas Berdyaev provides us with a substantial liaison between the philosophical and the theological perspectives from within a more balanced existentialism than we have managed to find in the creative work of Soren Kierkegaard. This is important. Not only does it enhance the central meaning of existential time but offers us the basic principles of what we have called its "eschatological dimension." Thus, in Part Two we shall be able to see more clearly how *kairos* not only gives depth to the present but to the future and end as well. Upon examining Berdyaev's clarifications of eternity we shall follow them with a comparative study of Karl Barth's insights into the matter before closely examining the meaning of the *eschaton* in subsequent chapters.

Eternity in Berdyaev's Religious Philosophy

One of Berdyaev's basic contributions to the existential conquest of the problem of time lies in what we have but touched upon as the dynamism of eternity. What does this really mean and imply? Divine nature, character and perfection, to Berdyaev, do not mean a static idea of divine Being or ideational substance ascribed to the Absolute. Rather, they imply a dynamic life of spirit and freedom. Such a view of eternity, based upon the free and spiritual theism of the biblical revelation, is not extrinsic to personal will, creativity, suffering, emotion, purpose and love. Its nature is one of Spirit (*Pneuma*) and must not be reduced to a rational concept. To ascribe Pure Being to the aseity of the eternal is possible only in terms of the biblical "I Am" and should not be regarded as a rational deducement. Basic to this dynamic eternity is *the coexistence of unity and duality*.[1] It calls to mind the paradoxical *Logos* of Heraclitus in his *Cosmic Fragments*. We have also seen it prefigured in the mystical metaphysics of Plotinus and sharpened as an issue of existential thought by Kierkegaard. Berdyaev has seen where this demands a fuller treatment and interrelationship consisting, we might say, of a blend of what we have seen to be basic to these diverse thinkers.

Berdyaev profoundly sees how only an eternity of a dynamic and mystical quality can enter into a vital relationship with time to redeem it. This has kinship to the New Testament *kairos,* a kind of time which is far from irrelevant to God, corresponding to the "seasons of the Lord" and divine acts involving history. This is seen to be possible and actual in an existential time characterized as the "irruption of eternity into time, an irruption in cosmic and historical time, an addition to and fulfillment of time." [2] As this epitomizes the dynamic character of an eternity that is relevant to time, so, too, it allows Berdyaev to defend the reality of both linear time, or history, and an eternity related not only to the present and past but also to the future and the end. A paradoxical mystery, such an eternity can be expressed only in terms of "a symbolic or mythological consciousness." [3] It is not subject to any rationalization, definition or manipulation satisfactory to a reason which presumes to be sufficient unto itself.

In view of this, Berdyaev does not hesitate to state under the inspiration of the biblical revelation, "Eternity is eternal newness, eternal creative ecstasy, the dissolving of being in divine freedom." [4] This means that God and eternity are to be understood as dynamic Spirit rather than abstract, rational, ideal Being. Only faith grasps something of the former, whereas reason postulates the latter. In contrast to the position we see taken by Paul Tillich in this regard, Berdyaev asserts, "God is not essence but existence." [5] God is the eternal Subject, not an object of rational projection and contemplation. Tillich still insists that God is Essence or the Being which is "the ground of all being" and fallen existence, the latter a strictly finite category.[6] But Tillich shows how he himself is theologically victimized by his rationalization of the divine. He has constructed an ontologized existentialism under the influence of Heidegger so as to become first, a philosopher and second, a theologian. His "bridge-building" is one which still over-accommodates the secular philosophic mind of the age. This is done, basically by ontologizing the divinely eternal in terms which are still secular.

But we cannot identify the revealed Spirit-Subject with an objectified Being-Essence, at least not without tying the hands of God by making His revelation conform to the human molds of reason. Tillich simply does this in a new way. His is a scheme which differentiates Being from existence but refuses to attribute existence to God. But this being the case, logically, Tillich should not subscribe to *kairos* as he does, since absolute Being or Essence is too unbending a category to be a subject, let alone a free and redemptive subject which can cope with, redirect and save the fallen time of which, in principle, it is the "ground." Unless the infinite and eternal has a strong element of existence, it is still immune to the temporal and finite existence it would save.

Berdyaev assures us of something that Tillich cannot. While Berdyaev sees that only a symbolic representation of eternal freedom can be made, he does not settle for mere symbolism in the manner of Tillich, who reduces all outside of Essence to fallen being and mere symbol. To Berdyaev, God, as revealed, is the great "I-Am" or Person-Spirit-Subject who discloses Himself even as He addresses Himself to man who, though a creature of time and existence, is His "other." For Tillich this is reduced to sheer anthropomorphism. The stress on freedom which Berdyaev makes is designed to protect this spiritual relationship between God and man as well as the dynamic relationship between eternity and time. It is much closer to the biblical picture of the divine and eternal than the static category of Being still retained by Tillich, which makes God an "It."

We would not defend Berdyaev's stress on freedom at every point including his cosmic theory of "meonic freedom"; nevertheless, it is an attempt to preserve the dynamic character of the eternal in a way that most historical theology has failed to do and will continue to do so long as the Greek categories are retained ontologically rather than as working patterns. Theologians and philosophers have either shied away from this problem or failed to see its implications.

Not only asserting with Kierkegaard that existence is Becoming and that eternity is Being-in-Becoming as it meets time in the Instant, Berdyaev boldy contends, to use ontological language, that Being *is* Becoming, i.e., embraces Becoming to itself even as it is also Being-in-Becoming. While S. K. sees Being-in-Becoming he is not as bold as Berdyaev in acknowledging an element of Becoming-in-Being. Berdyaev's spiritual "metahistory," which is quite neo-Platonic in pattern, helps to account for eternity's dynamic nature which can make itself relevant to a realistic, common time and not be immune to human history. This is to say that the nature of *the eternal can embrace time and reconcile itself to historic change,* thus redeeming time by giving it meaning, even though it belongs to a fallen, refracted order. The infinite is reconcilable to the finite, eternity reconcilable to time. The personal Spirit-Being of God can alone account for the element of permanence being reconcilable to change.

Time, then, is not altogether alien to the intrinsic life and nature of eternity, for Berdyaev. Time belongs to creation since it centers in man's consciousness and existence. Moving beyond S. K.'s disdain for a realistic linear time, *Berdyaev not only faces the problem and implications of man confronted by eternity in the Moment but also of God confronted by time in that Moment.* In other words, for Berdyaev the existential moment is a meeting of the Spirit-Subject of God who engenders eternity and the spirit-subject of man who engenders time. While the respective spirits are akin, their respective "times" are qualitatively different, though neither is oblivious to the other and their meeting still depends upon the redemptive initiative of the eternal. This is central to our stated thesis, its clarification and defense. Eternity and time are seen to be interrelated without loss of reality to either, something Berdyaev's existential view provides more vividly than any other existential position.

Berdyaev in essence says that there is no warrant for restricting the reality of all time to the human side of the time-eternity relationship or to terrestrial concepts of time. When this is done, time is strictly seen to be a complete denial of eternity; hence, it is not even a means of any kind to an eternal purpose or eschatological activity. Like the created order as a whole,

126

time is of no consequence without some roots in eternity.[7] While time is a kind of "decomposed eternity" to Berdyaev, it is not sheer non-Being or unreality. Even inauthentic existence is real though it is a sort of counterfeit. Here we see where Berdyaev joins the phenomenal philosophies, including Kant's dualistic criticism and English empiricism, in seeing no direct relationship between time and ultimate essence, but he approaches the matter from a different standpoint. Retaining a duality of time and eternity, he still refuses to claim that eternity remains unaffected by time and history. Rather, time is of concern to the eternal, which is *Pneuma* rather than *nous* or *ontos*. But here we must recognize not only an evil or false time of anxiety and pseudo measurement, or even a real but empty time of duration and succession, but a good or true time, which can be represented only as "some interior stage or epoch of eternity itself." [8] Thus, not all time is alien to eternity. While there is a false time associated with its artificial measurements and a realistic but meaningless history, eternity does not negate all *chronos*. Therefore, Berdyaev, can say, "For time, our world, the whole of our world process, from the moment of its inception to that of its end, represents a period, an aeon in the life of eternity, a period or an epoch rooted in it." [9] On the surface this appears to be an ontological assimilation of time by eternity, but only if we refuse to move further into Berdyaev's thought of eternity as dynamic.

This is not a monistic immanental theory. It is a dualistic interrelation of transcendence and immanence which chooses to settle for neither extreme. "History," says Berdyaev, "is the result of a deep interaction between eternity and time; it is the incessant eruption of eternity into time." [10] Referring to a meaningful *Geschichte,* this combines the existential and the metahistorical approaches to the problem. It is a way of giving metaphysical, though not a rationally ontological, basis for what he and Kierkegaard have seen to be of existential significance. While secular history is not negated here, Berdyaev is really pushing the argument in the interest of a Christian view of history, one based upon the consciousness of "eternity manifesting and incarnating itself in time."

Here we see how a sacred history is not kept alien to secular history but uses and elevates it. While there is a constant struggle between time and eternity, a revealing eternity breaks the chain of an otherwise distorted and meaningless time. Though eternity seeks a victory over time, it does so without denying time.[11] The victory is won very much from within or, better, in relation to the time process itself, which amounts to a mixture of good and evil time in man's consciousness. It is not a victory which causes us to leap out of time entirely. That would be an escape from existence, an existence which, admittedly, is both fallen and steeped in time's finitude. Thus we see how time has rootage in eternity, while not, we must assert, in a manner of Greek ontology, so much as in a manner of pneumatological relations, first, by creation as time depends upon the created man and, second, by redemption as time depends upon the eternal for its significance. Man can have no real destiny save as his *time* belongs to God's purpose.

But this pattern of the time-eternity relationship cannot be fully appreciated until we see the significance of Berdyaev's creative idea of "celestial history." [12] This is a kind of eternal time, so to speak, time particularly as God apprehends it and deals with it. It is time viewed more from the standpoint of the eternal, while only in terms of the revealed truth which faith takes seriously. It is time in terms of what was set forth above as an "interior epoch in eternity itself." [13] In other words, a God of redemption finds the time that belongs to His created order to be of some consequence to His eternality, and this, subjectively, is His "celestial time." As God has invested himself in men and the time of men, so, too, He has allowed the time of men to be of some concern to His eternal purpose. The entire biblical story of redemption implies an intersection of terrestrial and celestial histories very much related to both the origin, existence and destiny of men.

In general, we have come to see how eternity is not altogether a timeless category even though its transcendent quality is paramount. Unlike Plato and Augustine, as well as Kierkegaard to some extent, Berdyaev points us to a faculty of "timefulness" within eternity, if we may speak of it thus. Not enamoured of a rational immutability and unafraid of being accused of finitizing the divine sovereignty or of polluting the infinity of the eternal, Berdyaev moves further into the paradoxical understanding of God than perhaps any other thinker has dared to do. If he is thus accused, let it be understood that this consistently dynamic concept is more "complimentary" than "insulting" to the nature, character and power of God. Berdyaev does not try to rationalize this the way Edgar S. Brightman does in his monistic concept of a finite God who must contend inwardly with evil and finitude. Rather, the idea of "celestial time" is one which concedes to the eternal a capacity to grant the appearance of time and a capacity to cope with it.

Celestial time is a suprarational, faith-perceived mystery belonging to the paradox of a pneumatic Being-in-Becoming. As this is the pattern seen from the perspective of human existence, it is made so and provided for in terms of a faith-perceived divine existence. A static divine essence could know nothing of this. Only a dynamic divine essence, the aseity of which is in keeping with its creative and redemptive acts can account for it. While there is a distant kinship here with the *Actus Purus* of Thomas Aquinas, we can but repeat our earlier claim that Thomas falls short of retaining the dynamic spirituality of God in his ontology. Such is the case, it appears, with any ontological theory. Let it be remembered that Berdyaev's is a pneumatology which makes no apologies for the meeting of opposites without total synthesis. This is acceptable, however, only to a faith perspective, and it is fundamental to Berdyaev's religious existentialism. It places his total philosophy on the borderline between general philosophy and dogmatic theology. It shows, too, how philosophy is driven to theology for the ultimate answers to its persistent questions, while at the same time theology must employ the splendid tools of thought which philosophy proffers it without succumbing to the unwieldy rational claims of the tools *per se*.

What is the big clue to Berdyaev's position as here set forth? Without question it is the Incarnation of Christ, the great New Testament event to which Christian existentialists consistently look. It is the Unique Event which discloses time's meaning by eternity's incursion into time. But in this regard Berdyaev goes beyond S. K. in unveiling how the dynamic nature of eternity can and does disturb, invade and even use sheer historic, linear time. We have seen how S. K. with his antitemporalism only allows eternity to deal with the present image of its own Now. Thus we can better understand why and how Berdyaev pushes the meaning of existential time further into the light of what a redemptive eternity entails. Yet Berdyaev makes an important distinction when he asserts that "eternity does not coexist with the temporal order." [14] Thus, it would be unfair to say that the two elements are either disparate or coalescent; neither two nor one, they are two-in-one by existential relation. This is true both from the standpoint of "celestial history" and of "existential time." Eternity and time are paradoxically interrelated, then, but not identified. Neither a rational synthesis, again, nor an either/or dichotomy, here is a relevant both/and tension, a legitimate paradox.

In this respect, the existential moment becomes the purest time of all, i.e., the most genuine and meaningful to human existence and destiny, since closest to eternity without obscuring the time-element involved. While linked with common time, with its tenses and durational as well as successive and even cyclic features relevant to man, the existential moment has the *plus* of eternal quality given to it. Qualified by the eternal through the *ekstasis* of eternity-into-time, it is comparable to the New Testament *kairos*. Not sheer *chronos* or common time, it does not ignore or defy *chronos* but raises it qualitatively to a new and higher level. Kierkegaard, in effect, denies *chronos* and thereby mitigates the redemptive meaning and consequence of *kairos* as well as the resultant *eschaton* related to both. Berdyaev does not to this. He does not appeal to eternity almost to remove men from time but to redeem them from its sinful, enslaving finitude while they live existentially within it.

Actually, Berdyaev is the truer existentialist at this point, for he accepts historic time as an experiential part of man's concrete existence. How is this the case in terms of the Incarnation? The answer would be something as follows: In Christ eternity entered times as "the Word made flesh." While the eternal Word and the human form of that Word are not an absolute unity, they are an interrelated unity of opposites. This involves an interrelationship of eternal purpose and unveiling with the temporal means of divine appearing and acting. Not a rational synthesis, here is a relevant paradox of a kind which is neither Docetic on the one hand, nor Nestorian on the other. Just as both Jesus and the Word are real, so, too, both historic time and eternity are real. The common history of the man Jesus is real and is used by the eternal, but in and of itself is not of the eternal, nor does it yield the eternal. The parallel may be seen in Jesus' own words, "He that seeth me seeth the Father." Yet not all who saw Jesus saw in him the Father. Here is the issue. It is a both/and tension, we maintain, amenable only to "eyes of faith." But of profound consequence to contemporary theology is the fact that even the eyes of faith are given a human and temporal form by which to see the divinely eternal. Celestial time thus implies that eternity implements terrestrial time and makes it serviceable to the existential moment of faith, which feeds on both the eternal Word and its temporal form.

Berdyaev boldy faces up to the problem of God and change. Doing so far more than most ontological thinkers, he also does so more consistently than the other existential thinkers we have considered. Going to neither the Parmenidean nor the Heraclitean extreme, he maintains a dynamic eternity which vitally interrelates the two factors of the one and the many, permanence and change, transcendence and immanence, eternity and time. The *dynamic* nature of *eternity*, again, *is to be expressed in terms of neither ontological dualism nor monism,* the distinction which most historical theology has regarded as the criterion of intelligible form. Basing his metaphysics on neither the transcendent nor the immanent alone, and interpreting it neither from God's standpoint nor man's alone, Berdyaev's initial insight centers neither in God nor in man but in *God-manhood.* This is the fundamental clue and the paradox of his balanced existential eschatology. It stems from the New Testament revelation: "God was in Christ." It overcomes the static concepts and harsh logic of rational and idealistic schemes seeking a unified view dependent on either a monistic or dualistic ontology. God-manhood is a revealed principle,[15] while belonging to the superlative existential Event which bespeaks the dynamic nature of the Eternal who has invaded time. It is the time of a unique man in concrete existence who is identified with the redeeming Eternal Word which he brings to other men in such a down-to-earth time and existence. Thus eternity invests itself in time to redeem it. And what does it mean to redeem time but to salvage it from meaninglessness and a directionless oblivion and give it both renewed status and purpose.

We stated above that Berdyaev existentially expresses the

dynamic view of eternity introduced by Plotinus but neglected by Augustine, while adapted to a certain extent by Kierkegaard. Berdyaev does this by seeing the Eternal Spirit as both Being and Becoming—if we may use ontological categories to express a paradoxical mystery and existential tension. Quite like Plotinus, Berdyaev states, "In God absolute rest is inseparably connected with absolute motion. It is only in our rational consciousness and in our natural world that rest excludes motion, and that motion is incompatible with rest." [16] This principle also blends with Berdyaev's idea of personality being the same or a permanent self within a changing self. While it applies to men, it also applies to the biblical idea of God and the dynamic nature of eternity which, for Berdyaev, includes "celestial history," the divine perspective and relation to time.

Thus Berdyaev boldly challenges the rational notion that any movement, succession, change or development on the part of, or in relation to, the eternal is in opposition to the perfection of the divine nature.[17] This is most significant. The Spirit-Person of the eternal both *is* and exists. This is to say that God in His eternality is not immune to change and can relate Himself to time even as He transcends it. The idea challenges the orthodox view of God as well as the interpretation of theologians like Ulrich Simon, whose less dialectical "theology of crisis" identifies the doctrine of sovereignty in traditional manner with the immutability of God.[18] Immutability is a Greek notion that sterilizes the dynamic nature and freedom of eternity and logically leaves it immune to the temporal crises of men, even as it makes a biblical revelation unintelligible, if not impossible or irrelevant from that standpoint.[19] *Only a dynamic eternity not remote from the past and future of time can redeem the times,* Berdyaev would say, and thus provide a meaning to history and give occasion to the eschatological dimension of existential time. This is apropos to our main argument that, seen in relation, time and eternity neither coalesce nor negate each other.

In view of eternity's self-relation to *kairos* by means of its *ekstasis* into time as seen most clearly in the Incarnate Event and those moments of faith and encounter which look to it, it is noteworthy that Berdyaev, while recognizing that only symbols can express this relationship, does not reduce the event to mere symbolism in the manner of Paul Tillich. Berdyaev sees that while the historicity of Jesus is not the basis of his significance, nor the heart of the revelatory Event, one cannot minimize, distort or deny the historical factor belonging to the Incarnation. The latter is far more than symbol, myth or analogy. The historicity of Jesus belongs to the Christ Event even though it is not a matter of rational proof or speculation. It is a problem belonging to this relationship between history and "celestial history." It is one which a historical science cannot touch since it belongs to the existential "break-through of the noumenal world into the phenomenal world." [20]

Respectful of modern and contemporary contributions to New Testament scholarship by means of higher criticism, Berdyaev overtly says, "A historical biography of Jesus cannot in actual fact be written . . ." He then goes on to say, "But that only proves that the reality of Jesus Christ is borne witness to by the faith of the Christian community . . ." [21] This, as we interpret it, implies that the "Christ of faith," while uppermost in significance and essential to the faith of the Christian *koinonia,* is not out of relation to, nor removed from a dependence upon, the "Jesus of history." The latter is no less than the temporal form of the former. Here is a shrewd and important insight often overlooked today by such neo-Reformed or "crisis theologians" as Karl Barth and especially Rudolf Bultmann under the influence, direct or indirect, of Soren Kierkegaard.

The "reality of Jesus" to which Berdyaev refers includes an actuality in historic time even as it keeps Jesus as the Christ related to eternity and the Word of divine truth and activity; however, as an event it is not to be objectified in calendar time or dates but appreciated only through a "free faith" necessitated by neither rational argument, orthodox logicizing, nor scientific objectivity. Faith builds on neither objective knowledge nor objectivized theories. Yet Berdyaev challenges any view which depreciates the reality and role of historic time as related to the revelation of the Word in the Incarnate Christ. The eternal Word (*Logos*) manifested himself in terms of concrete temporal manhood. This is subordinately given witness in the *kerygma* which includes, as we interpreted it earlier, a faith portrait which presupposes a man of time who posed, as it were, for the portrait. As Berdyaev suggests, divine revelation is a spiritual event which "shows itself in symbols in the facts of history." Here is a unity-in-duality once more.

While Jesus is historical, he demands more than a historical biography. This something "more" is given witness by the writers of the New Testament, for his is a "spiritual biography," an evangelistic witness. As the Eternal Son Christ is not to be objectified in history, however related to it. With Kierkegaard here, Berdyaev has come to see that neither a harsh orthodox logic of dogmatic identification nor a soft liberal logic of historical idealism is adequate. But what S. K. was prone to dichotomize in terms of time and eternity Berdyaev has chosen not to, and rightly so, for we still have an association of opposites without rational identification. In the light of this relation sacred history, then, is not common history but existentially qualified history, "sacred metahistory." [22] It is a faith-perceived truth given in terms of terrestrial history by virtue of its connection with events and personalities; however, it is seen to reflect "celestial history" as the plan and purpose of God only as it becomes relevant subjectively through a faith encounter, which recognizes the Word as the eternal language of God transposed into the temporal language of men. God speaks, but man also hears even if imperfectly. Faith in Christ as the Son comes via the *kerygma*. But this proclamation is a witness given through a memory which, as "an agent of eternity," gives us an important, though subordinate, witness to an actual Jesus of history through whose works, death and resurrection the *kerygma* inspires the great moments of faith.

Thus, the Incarnation implies that a historical, temporal form implements the eternal Word. The Word is dramatically revealed on the stage of time amidst the scenes of history. The leading role was given to the Word-bearing and Word-personifying Son of the Eternal Playwright, who would convey to men of historical existence the meaning of their existence and its destiny. The same Son was not only the Word-bearer but the personified Word, both in terms of eternal Love and the divine *Logos*. The Logos which to the Greeks was an abstract principle of order is now seen as the dynamic Spirit of truth and love.

This is possible through an eternity that copes with time. Philosophically, Berdyaev's view of the *Logos* reminds one of Heraclitus' view which, often misinterpreted since Aristotle, is a paradoxical interrelation of permanence within change, unity within multiplicity, or, in this case, eternity within time. Religiously, Berdyaev's view of the *Logos* involves an eternity whose redemptive dynamic gives to time a special eschatological depth. This it does neither by absorbing it nor by negating it as a reality, for time is of man's consciousness and realistic existence. How does this interpretation compare with that of Karl Barth's theology today?

Eternity in Barth's Theology

Karl Barth, perhaps the most provocative exponent and fountainhead of neo-Reformed or dialectical theology, also has come to address the meaning of eternity. In his great series *Die Kirchliche Dogmatik* he, too, enunciates his regard for a time element indigenous to the very nature of eternity. This has kinship with Berdyaev's position, save for the fact that the "other-worldliness" of Barth demands that he restrict time's reality to eternity *per se*, something Berdyaev would not do.

Actually, Barth is even more stringent as a transcendental dualist than is Kierkegaard, who influenced his thinking around the turn of the century. In the preface of the second edition of *Der Römerbrief* Barth wrote: "If I have a system, it is limited to what Kierkegaard called the 'infinite qualitative difference' between time and eternity . . ." This early assertion is retained but later modified, first, by Barth's deeper look into eternity and second, by his shrewder treatment of Christology. Respecting the first adjustment, "While time is not eternity," says Barth, "neither is eternity timeless," he adds, "for it is togetherness and interrelation of past, present and future. . . . Eternity is God himself. . . . But time is willed and created by God as one of his different realities." [23] Time is of God and belongs to man only as he belongs to God by faith or is in relation to eternity, i.e., only as "our time remains in His hands" from beginning to end. Thus Barth asserts the reality of time only as a *given*, since it depends entirely upon being willed and created by God. [24] Thus Barth refuses to entertain the idea of a time of any consequence when innovated by man's consciousness.

While this view neglects what we have recognized to be existential time, even as it overlooks man as an engenderer of time, it must be credited with helping to enunciate what we have described as a dynamic eternity. In fact Barth is quite specific about the time that is *of* eternity. He states in *Die Kirchliche Dogmatik*, Band II,

> The eternity of God is in itself *beginning, succession and end.* . . . It is not passive but active, not from any other being, not from time, but from and in himself. . . . God has time, just because and while He has eternity. He has it not primarily on the basis of creation; since everything is from creation including time. He has for us the time of revelation, the time of Christ as well as the time of his patience; also the time of life, time of repentance and of faith. But it is actually He himself who has time for us. He himself is time for us, as surely as his revelation. As surely as Jesus Christ He himself actually is that time.[25]

Perhaps a bit shocking to some Barthians, here we see how Karl Barth has begun to shift away from an earlier transcendental view of divine immutability toward one less fearful of the element of change and time within eternity itself. Fundamentally, there is an element of time intrinsic to eternity itself. From the side of the eternal it suggests that Barth, somewhat like Berdyaev, has come to see the need of a dynamic eternity which can embrace time in some sense. While this time is solely God's time and not man's for Barth, it is significant that Barth should concede that it includes both duration and succession. In principle it calls to mind Berdyaev's doctrine of "celestial history," time which is of concern to God.

Seeing also that the sovereignty of the eternal implies not only unity but freedom, Barth, like Berdyaev, refuses to equate eternity with infinite time. This is a wholesome improvement over various rational ideas of eternity, which have long dominated theology. Yet Barth sees the unity of eternity involving pure *duration,* a duration however which he says is not sheer succession but *Gleichzeitigkeit* or simultaneity.[26] This seems to be a kind of flowing present and akin to the eternal now. Paradoxically, the beginning, present and end of God's time are one and the same to eternity. While much like Berdyaev's "celestial history" from a one-sided point of view, it is actually closer to Kierkegaard when viewed from the standpoint of man's time, or history. This is because Barth does not reconcile or even relate eternity to man's time with its kind of duration and succession. As denoted in the above quotations, he keeps eternity related only to its own kind of duration and succession. But immediately the stubborn question arises: What can such an eternity have to do with any kind of duration or succession if they have nothing in common with the time of man?

As suggested by *Gleichzeitigkeit*, a kind of homogeneity of time in eternity, Barth also has a doctrine of the eternal now, which we have seen important to existential thinkers like Augustine, Kierkegaard and Berdyaev. "God," says Barth, "is primarily now, for we are present only in relationship to Him." This version of the matter is Kierkegaardian and also means that, as Barth says, "We are not basically in the present but God is." [27] Here we see how Barth, like S. K., refuses to allow the reality of the temporal present in which men live. What then is there for eternity to relate itself to? we must ask. Only itself, would be the logical answer. Similarly, while Barth relates the character of eternity to a kind of eternal or celestial time, he does not do justice to what Berdyaev sees to be "celestial history" as correlative to "terrestrial history." Rather, for Barth eternity is the "pre-destination of time." [28] But this, again, is strictly God's time and disrelated from man's time. Barth asserts that eternity is "nonhistorical," even as revelation is "nonhistorical." [29] The historical refers to time as man knows it. This gives support to Barth's idea that the eternal Word is utterly transcendent of the historical Jesus, as enunciated in Barth's early work *Der Römerbrief*, an epochal Commentary on the Epistle to the Romans written back in 1918.

But the position taken here by Barth gives no revelatory significance to the personality, work and temporal humanity of Jesus as expressive of, let alone indigenous to, the Word. It matches Kierkegaard's claim that "from history one can learn nothing about Christ," for "sacred history" is entirely "eternal history." [30] Again, man's time and history are utterly insignificant and unreal to Barth, something inconsequential to God and His revelation even as a means to His own ends. This makes *chronos* a fictitious matter and he treats it in the negative, Platonic sense quite as Kierkegaard does. But even a dynamic eternity, which is conceded by Barth, can now make no real *ekstasis* of the Word on that basis and can provide no *kairos* of relevance to men of time. Therefore, Barth's transcendent dualism is much too stringent, keeping time and eternity too far apart. Barth, like Berdyaev, sees that eternity can be regarded neither as infinite time on the one hand, nor as timelessness on the other. With both Berdyaev and Kierkegaard he can say, "Eternity is not the before and after of infinitely prolonged time." [31] Such an eternity could account for no beginning or end of God's creation. While Barth, like Kierkegaard, negates the time of man and history in a somewhat Platonic manner, he does not negate *all* time, since he concedes a Godward time intrinsic to eternity, a time which, as we have seen, even includes duration and succession along with simultaneity.[32] It is the latter idea that moves Barth closer to Berdyaev than to S. K., since it allows for a dynamic eternity. In fact, Oscar Cullmann is in grave error when he accuses Barth of settling for a Platonic concept of a timeless eternity.[33] On the contrary, Barth keeps the only time he recognizes *within* eternity. Unlike Berdyaev, Barth has taken a theocentric rather than a Christocentric view of the problem, thus failing to relate eternity to the time of men. He keeps time strictly within the eternal Subject, God, but removes it altogether from the existential subject, man. Thus logically, this implies that in the moment of faith the man of existence is really lifted out of his time. Is this to the credit of a mature Christian doctrine of redemption? We have our doubts.

Yet we must credit Barth, like Berdyaev, for embracing a dynamic view of eternity and, like both Kierkegaard and Berdyaev, for keeping eternity qualitatively different from common time. Nevertheless, the rigid Barthian dualism of eternity and time is treated almost as a Manichean dichotomy in one sense, while really a monophysite monism in another, since it recognizes only one kind of reality, the eternal over against which all else stands as an evil temporal illusion. The defectiveness of Barth's position here is that it yields no significance whatever to human history and existence *per se,* just as it leaves Christian revelation, Christology and eschatology utterly transcendent. When revelation involves history, history *per se* contributes nothing to the revelation.[34] This matches Barth's earlier Nestorian Christology, and more qualifications of it will be required if his total doctrine of redemption is to have ethical and eschatological significance for this world of time.

Our criticism is that Barth allows no vital relation between eternity and history so as even to justify the divine use of history as a divine *means* or agency. In the legitimate interest of breaking a nineteenth-century quasi-equation of the eternal and the historical, which we see in the immanental thinking of theologians like Schleiermacher, Ritschl, Troeltsch and Harnack, basically Barth has destroyed even their relation.

Barth is bold enough to say that the Christian revelation pertains to "the eternal God who deals with man and who therefore acts in time." [35] But this acting in time and history is not one whereby time and history in any way can reflect or convey the eternal Word even in a refracted sense. The revelatory act is to a degree related to history but is not historical. Revelation is such for Barth that God grants man the perception of what is revealed irrespective of fallen man's relative capacities. Thus, any refractions of history are overcome since they are completely transcended.

Revelation, then, is not a real confrontation with the existing man of time and history, though it appears to be. It is an address which conveys no communication, let alone conversation, for it is a divine monologue. The defense of this is that the revelation is claimed by Barth to be *Urgeschichte,* primal or prehistory or, better, ultimate suprahistory of a kind which keeps it a complete *Geheimnis* or mystery.[36] It is so much of a mystery, in fact, that it has no intelligibility, critically speaking. Barth wants no *Anknüpfungspunkt,* no point of contact between God and fallen man's intelligence. Here is where Emil Brunner takes issue with him.[37] We must ask: If eternity is immune to human history and the Word is utterly "nonhistorical," how and why should God act in time, use time or become incarnate in temporal manhood in *any* sense? It could not be genuine if it is an eternal Word oblivious to man's time; it would not be a "word," the very meaning of which is communicative, mediatorial and relational. How can the revelation as a divine act be genuine or complete when it is claimed to occur only in God's time? Furthermore, what need has God of a transcendent type of time unless his eternality be a schizophrenic sort of being? Must not time be a matter of anthropological setting primarily, though we must protect its relevance to God and its possibility as well? Does not the man of faith who, according to Barth, exists in God's time presuppose a relation within the context of man's time and a revelation to a man who is still in his own time, a time from which he cannot extricate himself or be fully extricated on the mortal side of eternity? Is not the dialectical issue a both/and tension rather than an either/or dichotomy?

Barth says with candor, "That eternity meets us in time, is not a matter of course but a miracle . . ." [38] Well and good, we say, but only if that time is as much man's as God's and in a very real sense real in itself, i.e., real outside of eternity as well as within. Otherwise, it is neither "miracle" nor of redemptive significance for God to "act in time." Nor does it become consequential that Barth should say, as he does, that in Christ "eternity became time," [39] unless he concedes that the nature and character of eternity allows it to embrace more than its own kind of succession and intrinsic duration. A dynamic and redemptive eternity must deal with the successive and durational time of man as man knows and engenders it. Such is the true accommodation of a divine God-manhood.

Edwin Lewis, who is a strong dualist, but more of an empirical type, stoutly charges that "man can mean nothing to a God whose simultaneity is alien to linear time." [40] Here we see Lewis substantiating a basic principle we see in Berdyaev but not in Barth. Barth fails to be existential at the point of man as the knower and engenderer of time. Barth also misses the full redemptive capacity of eternity by keeping its activity so nonhistorical. The very time factor involved in divine revelation is strictly "another time than the one we know." [41] Obscuring the meaning of Incarnation, this gives little redemptive significance to the God-given "beginning, succession and end" [42] which Barth includes in the nature of an eternity which, while embracing the tenses in the unity of *Gleichzeitigkeit* on the one hand, transcends man's realistic time and history on the other. This is the way Barth keeps God utterly transcendent as the Totally Other.

Barth does not do justice to the Event of Christ through which God, while "Other," shows Himself not *wholly other* in an eschatological sense. In view of the foregoing, Barth jeopardizes the historical eventfulness of the biblical revelation. Even though we say he need not identify or synthesize the eternal Word with objective events *per se*, he cannot justifiably hold his position and retain either an eventful revelation or eventful divine act and spoken Word that is related to human time and history in *any* sense whatever. Barth's transcendentalism and concept of eternity disallow a truly revelatory incarnate event, because such an "event," while more than temporal, is packaged in the form of temporal events. Incarnation is meaningless apart from the connotation of "divine in-humanization" and intrinsic "temporalization." It demands that the divine substance of the Word was deliberately given human and temporal form of a kind which man can take seriously and which God takes seriously to the extent that he takes man seriously. It means that God sufficiently condescends to talk the language of man in historical and personal terms. Thus the infinite really accommodated the finite. Barth fears this accommodation. But without this there is no unique revelation, and Barth's total position should be placed alongside of transcendental mysticisms of a kind which see the temporal aspects of divine revelation as sheer symbolism and little more. While Barth would not yield to such a mysticism, he should be logically driven to it.

In his Christology Barth sees Christ as sharing "the fallen human nature" or "flesh" of men.[43] This is a bold but creative insight which theologians have long shied away from. Yet this very idea should make it all the more difficult for Barth's Nestorian dualistic Christology to warrant the Incarnation's revelatory role. While it differentiates the divine from the human and the eternal from the temporal, it all the more dichotomizes them so as to threaten even their relation, let alone necessary interrelation. Without a strong interrelation of the opposites, notwithstanding our objection to a rational synthesis, we do not have the paradox of genuine Incarnation. Furthermore, the eternal Word cannot legitimately be held to be "nonhistorical" when the Word-bearer assumed both manhood and, according to Barth, its "flesh."

From the standpoint of the problem of time and eternity, Barth's position makes not only for a Nestorian dualism but a peculiar combination of temporal Docetism and divine Monophysitism. This is a strange mixture. Barth's Christology is

Nestorian in that he retains the opposites involved and practically splits them apart in the process. It is monophysite in that the sole significance of Christ lies in the eternal Word which he brings. It is Docetic in that the temporal manhood which is involved is given no revelatory significance so as to interrelate the eternal Word with the Word-bearer of time. Again, speaking from this same standpoint, Barth does not guarantee the doctrine of "the Word made flesh." He has both elements, true enough, but they are not sufficiently related or paradoxically interrelated. Berdyaev does more to associate the Word with the God-man who related himself to time as men know it without succumbing to it. In this respect, the doctrine of eternity as held by Berdyaev is more dynamic and genuinely redemptive than that of Barth. It allows for more on both sides of God-manhood, both as the unique existential Event itself and as an Event of far-reaching eschatological implications for man in time and history.

Barth, however, speaks with existential insight when he says, "We cannot separate ourselves from *our* time." [44] But "our time" to which eternity chooses to relate itself in the coming of the Incarnate Christ, we maintain, must have sufficient relevance to the nature of the eternal to make the distinctive Event possible on the one hand, and feasible to a Christology true to both the New Testament *kerygma* and its temporal setting on the other. This calls for more than "God's time." It involves the time of the man Jesus and the time of the apostles who witnessed to the *kerygma,* even as it was, in turn, related directly or indirectly to the time of the Incarnate One as seen through "eyes of faith" from within history while above history.

It appears that for eternity to "act in time" and "become time," to use Barth's own terms with reference to the Incarnation, Barth should allow for a still more dynamic eternity, one not alien to any of the times concrete men know in terms we have previously set forth. Barth's idea of eternity is one which embraces its own kind of time in such a peculiar way as to keep the "eternal now" altogether transcendent of the now of "our time," a time which he himself has said we cannot escape. It does not even allow for Kierkegaard's idea of existential time as a type of eternity-in-time or Being-in-Becoming which at least allows for a touchstone of intersection. While Barth in his way

142

allows for an element of Becoming in eternal Being, he does not allow for the reverse of this as does Berdyaev, who finds his clue in the Christ Event. Barth seems to be looking into heaven, as it were, through something other than the Christ Event. Here he is theologically presumptuous.

What has been stated is of special significance when we note how Barth asserts that the Word became not only man but *a* man.[45] Christ not only assumed human form but concrete manhood of a fallen finitude, despite his actual sinlessness.[46] As suggested above, this supports the historical personality of Christ without its having relevance to the Word.[47] Yet, in keeping with the matter of "our time," Barth should concede that Christ, too, experienced such a time. Not denying the temporal conditions under which Christ appeared, Barth seems to contradict his own claim that the transcendent Word is identified with an eternity whose nature is disparate from time as men know it. Logically, it would appear that Barth's view of eternity should then disallow a revelatory Incarnate Event in historic time, one which actually incarnates the Word, providing it with a temporal channel and expression within historic time, even the "our time" which Jesus knew as other men did.

Barth really restricts the meaning of what we have discussed as existential time by lifting it out of our existence. Denying eternity a vital relationship with the time or times of men, while claiming to link the eternal revelation to an incarnation involving the time of men, he denies significance of said time as a channel or instrument of the revealed truth. This is not the tenable paradox it is claimed to be; it is untenable contradiction. Paradox is contradiction but not impossible contradiction! True paradox is a meeting of opposites in mutual tension and relevance. Just as there is a temporal Docetic element in Barth's Christology, there is an equivalent in the existential moment of faith.

Figuratively speaking, Barth makes the man of faith leap to the crossbar of the cross while being removed from the mucks of his own time. But we must not forget that the cross was stabbed into an earthen socket! We must not forget that the significance thereof was not only divine and eternal but expressed through what is human and temporal. We must not forget that the transcendent substance of the Word of Love was given a temporal *form*. Barth does not fully allow for a Jesus who *could* say, "He who seeth me seeth the Father" (John 14:9). While we concede that not all who saw Jesus saw the Father, those who did were not immune to the temporal conditions of the temporal form God chose to use. What does Barth really do to the moments of New Testament *kairos* or *kairoi*? Actually, he minimizes their significance and existentiality rather than "maximizes" them.

In view of this, Barth errs in having based his dualism of transcendence upon the Word rather than upon the Word-made-flesh, who as "flesh" dwelt as man among men. Barth keeps the Word in his eternality almost oblivious to man's kind of time, even that attributable to Christ's manhood. But does this keep the Act of the Word revelatory? Hardly. It keeps God speaking to Himself solely in terms of His own time. Revelation, then, remains a supratemporal monologue. Neither Barth's doctrine of eternity nor his basic Christology does justice to the time side of God-manhood. They restrict the redemptive power of the eternal side. Only in this sense, however, is Ulrich Simon right when he says, "Barth is committed to a non-anthropological theology." [48] Linear time, including that of Jesus' manhood, must be germane to the criticism, for Barth suppressed historic time's place in the dual role of Christ as Word and Word-bearer. This reflects Barth's Platonic to Kierkegaardian disdain for *chronos*.[49] To him it is utterly inimical to eternity.

However, we must recognize a second major adjustment in Barth's later thought, that involving Christ. At times in his later work Barth's transcendentalism is not so extreme. Earlier he said all polarity is done away with. "The eternal Moment can be compared with no moment in time." Neither the End nor *Heilsgeschichte* involves time, and the Resurrection is not an event among others. "Within history, Jesus as the Christ can be understood only as a Problem or Myth," said Barth.[50a] Later, Barth has come to concede that the Gospel centers in a once-for-all Act in both eternity and history.[50b] This does much to move Barth closer to our thesis. The great Act is said to be eschatological but only in the sense that it breaks off or ends history. Yet Barth crystallizes his second major adjustment when he says of Christ,

"The eternity in which He Himself is true time and the Creator of all time is revealed in the fact that, *although our time is that of sin and death, He can enter it and Himself be temporal in it, yet* without ceasing to be eternal, able rather to be Eternal in time." [51]

That this is a major concession should be recognized. But Barth still seems uneasy about it. He says of the Word made flesh, "The divine being does not suffer any change, and diminution, and transformation into something else, *any admixture with something else. . . .*" [52] The latter phrase particularly seems to undo Barth's important concession in support of his stubborn Nestorian Christology. Yet he concedes a paradox between divine eternality and a finite, human temporality when he asserts of God: "Who can question His right to make possible this impossibility?" [53]

Seeing the problem here Barth says, "He can be God and act as God in an absolute way and also a relative, in an infinite and also a finite . . . in a transcendent and also an immanent [way]. . . ." [54] While this agrees with his major concession, the question whether Barth's dialectics and total position are consistent with it is still legitimate. Paul Tillich said in a lecture [55] that he had conversed with Barth in August, 1958, when Barth as much as said that he saw the need to qualify much of his earlier, more reactionary claims.

We maintain that the concessions to which we point should be enlarged by Barth in favor of such an adjustment and likely will be, to some extent, in the later volumes of his *Dogmatik*. It appears that Barth has had to make a few concessions of this kind largely to offset the extremely non-historical existential position taken by Rudolf Bultmann. The latter's de-mythologizing of the New Testament *kerygma*, which we shall consider in Chapter VII, threatens to submerge and even negate the redemptive role of the Jesus of history, which Barth tries hard not to do despite the harsh duality of his Christology. What Barth is bent on avoiding is any point of contact between the divine and anything either ontological or anthropological, the real norm for which is Christ.[56] But can this extreme dichotomy be defended? we must ask. Even the faith encounter involves the self,.

hence no less than something subordinately anthropological, lest it be something other than an encounter.

Barth is not amiss when he says that the Christ who confronts us is not known historically.[57] To say that we are even indirectly related to him through his being remembered is to flee from the direct encounter, Barth claims, and displace the Christological by the anthropological.[58] While the Resurrection of Christ is not historical in the same way as the cross, Barth concedes it may have been an objective historical event, though it is not grasped historically.[59] Dogma and history meet in the Resurrection, but we cannot idealize, allegorize or symbolize it. Only *via* Pentecost does the faith community see the Christ and become the Church.[60] Why, then, do the Easter narratives "underline the concrete objectivity of the history there attested as against their evaporation into a history of the development of the Easter faith of the disciples"?[61] The answer is that they do not explain the Resurrection as historical fact so as to give faith "a this-worldly basis" without "hazard of trust and obedience."

Here is a strong point, we believe, yet Barth concedes that we cannot delete the temporal eventfulness behind the Easter stories. Seemingly unsure of himself here, Barth goes on to say of the Resurrection that the apostolic witnesses witnessed "an event similar to the cross in objectivity."[62] What does this demand but that Barth should take time and history more seriously than he has done in his basic claims of the time-eternity relationship? The same applies to the anthropological factor of human memory, especially in view of what Berdyaev has helped us to understand about memory as "an agent of eternity."

But, elsewhere in the same volume, while Barth says the cross and Resurrection share in a similar kind of historic eventfulness, he says they were not the same since they were not known with similar objectivity. He asserts that the Resurrection is *Urgeschichte*, that is, "prehistorical," or better, suprahistorical.[63] But on what grounds can both the cross and the Resurrection be said to be historical in any sense, unless known to be? Here Barth's dread of anything anthropological breaks down if for no other reason than that we are dependent upon the faith community of witnesses who witnessed in terms not only of their post-Easter faith encounter but in terms of what they remembered, though they, in turn, remembered somewhat selectively

146

in terms of what they encountered and believed existentially.

While Barth has come to see dangers in a Kierkegaardian indi-vidualistic "appropriation of salvation," [64] since the Church is ordained to the ministry of reconciliation, he sees that S. K. is right at the point that the Gospel must be existentially relevant to the self via "the *pro me* of faith." [65] With S. K. in mind Barth also says, "There have been many attempts to make the history of Jesus Christ coincident with that of the believer, and *vice versa*. The theology of the younger Luther (up to 1519) was nothing but a powerful move in this direction." [66] Rudolf Bult-mann in his way fosters this kind of individualism today. Barth, on the other hand, has come to see some of its weaknesses, though we see them not far removed from our main criticism of Barth's own weakness respecting the problem of time and history. Fur-thermore, it would appear that Barth remains fundamentally as extreme as ever respecting Christ as both the object and origin of faith, since he is held to be "without any identity between the redemptive act of God and faith as the free act of man." [67] This does not really blend with the assertion that a once-for-all divine act can be present to us only as we accept it from the apostolic witnesses.[68] Barth has not sufficiently re-lated the existential encounter to history and the historical aspect of the Church's faith-conditioned memory. Unless he tones down his transcendental emphasis he can never do so, we claim, in which case his view of transcendence will continue to spell serious error. Needed today is an adjustment akin to Berdyaev's rejection of both an exclusively transcendent view and a totally immanental one.

In view of Barth's over-all concept of eternity in relation to time it is important for us to question his Christology, especially since Christian thinkers of an existential perspective like Kierke-gaard and Berdyaev look to the Incarnation for the meaning of time, existence and the end. As seen above, Barth's predominant emphasis across the years has averred that the transcendent Word precludes the "realistic" time (*chronos*) of Christ's manhood, even as his historicity is irrelevant and revelation is "nonhis-torical." On the contrary, in view of our main argument, we have contended from a Berdyaev-like perspective that historical time is realistic *chronos*, and this applies to Jesus' own time even apart from the untenability of his biographical historicity in the scientific sense. Man's time *is* relevant, then, to the Word which became flesh. This means that Christ's manhood implies time *as men* know it in this world. It is not to say, however, that the measurements of time are to be equated with time, lest it fail to be a realistic time with which the Incarnation is involved.

Assuming we can trust the general New Testament faith portrait of Christ associated with the *kerygma* of the primitive *koinonia* with its concomitant but subordinate witness to the historical Jesus, we must put the question frankly and simply: Did not Jesus know the human anxiety of linear time in the wilderness, the creative innovation of it in the carpenter shop, **and anxiety's engendering of it in Gethsemane? Did he not know** the cyclic time of the cock's crow and the Sabbath's beginning and end, let alone the deadly deadlines of the calendar when Roman taxes had to be paid and Judaic rites observed? Did he not know the height of existential moments of prayerful communion with the Father, perhaps at its purest in a moment of Transfiguration, as well as the depth of existential moments of spiritual and psychosomatic suffering that issued in sanguine perspiration on one occasion and flowing lymph on another?

Without binding ourselves to a rationalistic orthodoxy on the one hand, or an objectified idealization of the historical Jesus on the other, this is to suggest that *if Christ as the Incarnate Son did not know time as men know it, as we know it, he has not revealed the God of redeeming* agape *who is great enough to be small enough to speak in terms that men understand!* And to say that revelation precludes this is to ignore the very need of a Christ who, while a prophet and more than a prophet, was and is the Eternal Word who "emptied Himself" to personify that Word of Love from within human existence so that our *chronos* in terms of which he, too, loved and spoke could be redeemed "in the fullness of time." It is our contention, in keeping with our basic thesis, that the *ekstasis* of the Eternal Word into *chronos* was the perfect *kairos*. Without a realistic common time or *chronos* with which to reckon, the *ekstasis* could not be revelatory, let alone be an occurrence of a kind which makes for the uncommon, redemptive time of *kairos*.

Donald M. Baillie says much in support of our observations here concerning the consequence of Barth's view of eternity in relation to time and the Incarnation. Referring to Barth, he

148

says, "He has reacted so violently against the 'Jesus of history' movement that he does not seem interested in the historical Jesus at all." [69] Barth's otherwise Nestorian Christology is in another sense in danger of being monophysite, Baillie also recognizes, as a result not simply of distinguishing but of *separating* the Jesus of history from the Christ of faith. We have seen this counterparted, if not centered, in Barth's separating eternity from man's time altogether, a weakness not fully overcome even by his later adjustments. Contrary to Barth, both the historical Jesus and the eternal Son are needed to express the ingression of eternity into time and give us a relevant *Heilsgeschichte* [70] as well as an atonement not simply potential in the eternal heart of God but revealed and shown actual in relation to men of time. Baillie suggests that merely to keep the Incarnation a symbol whose significance does not belong to the temporal manhood of Christ is to ignore what is implicit in the dogma symbolized.[71]

Much the same could be said of Paul Tillich and Rudolf Bultmann here, for their Christologies do not provide for an actual incarnate ingression of eternity into time but merely a symbolic one.[72] We stand closer to Baillie when he says, "Christology stands for a Christian interpretation of history, but it can stand for that only because it stands for the conviction that God became man in the historical person of Jesus. We must have a Christology in that sense or we have no Christology at all." [73] This we can accept in a balanced existential context which retains the primacy of the Christ of faith while recognizing the mediating but the subordinate function of the Jesus of history.

Relating this observation to our basic concern as focussed upon the central Existential Event, we would also cite the words of Rosenstock-Huessy, "Jesus embedded *all times, including his own,* in one supertime, one eternal present." [74] Yet it must be asserted that even should we be able to prove or accept the historicity of Jesus, a matter quite unacceptable from the standpoint of the "higher criticism" of the New Testament,[75] while not in terms of the New Testament *kerygma* itself, we maintain, it is another question whether we can establish objectively the historicity of the *Incarnation*. Accepting the Incarnation entails faith in more than either the Word on the one hand, or the actual historical Jesus on the other. The post-Easter perspective of the apostles united paradoxically the two factors of that to which the *kerygma* gives witness, the Living Lord and his historical sacrifice. Such is the paradox of the Christian revelation addressed to the paradox of man in his existential situation. Belief in the time event alone is not sufficient to give the believer a redemptive present. Needed is the Eternal Presence making present to him what was Present to that Event, namely the eternal Word. As Jesus was linked with the eternity of the Word and divine Sonship, we need the eternity of divine Grace to make his Word and Sonship illuminating to our lives in time. This calls for encounter *with the Word* in the existential Moment of faith. Only then do we realize our "contemporaneity" with Christ. As Angelius Silesius once said in *Cherubinischer Wundersmann,* Book I, 61-63, (cited by Barth in *Die Kirchliche Dogmatic* IV, 1, p. 287).

> Were Christ a thousand times to Bethlehem come.
> And yet not born in thee, 'twould spell thy doom.
> Golgotha's cross, it cannot save from sin,
> Except for thee that cross be raised within,
> I say, it helps thee not that Christ is risen,
> If thou thyself art still in death's dark prison.

Neither the historical Jesus nor the transcendent Word, respectively, can account for the full existentiality, personal relevance and vital faith in the Incarnate Son. A meeting of the two is required, while not subject to rational explanation so much as to a balanced existential interpretation.

In terms of a profound paradox, *the issue is neither an either/or alternative nor a rational synthesis but a both/and tension, existentially.* This is something which neither a malleable monism nor a recalcitrant dualism can adequately express lest time and eternity coalesce and obscure the *ekstasis* on the one hand, or be completely disparate and minimize the *ekstasis* and its full redemptive efficacy on the other. It is in view of this that we claim that *Berdyaev's bipolar metahistory* of unity-in-duality has rendered a great service in illuminating the factors involved in eternity's relation to time. *It keeps balanced, real, and in vital relation the two sides of existential time.* Once more we see how *Berdyaev brings together eternity and time without jeopardizing the reality of either.*

Baillie, we find, supports our fundamental argument here in repudiating any dualism or monism which claims to do justice to the paradox of the Incarnation. He concurs that it is a unique truth which cannot be conceptualized.[76] "It is impossible," says Baillie, "to do justice to the truth of the Incarnation without speaking of it as the coming into history of the eternally pre-existent Son of God." [77] This is not to imply that the human and divine natures of Christ are co-eternal, but it does imply that the human element of the Event belongs to a real order of linear time to which the eternal is not oblivious.[78] We interpret this to mean that the Incarnation is suprahistorical while involving the historical, for both realms are vital to it. Having Barth and Kierkegaard in mind, as well as Rudolf Bultmann whose position we shall subsequently consider, we note that there is grave danger in thinking that historic time or *chronos* is "an illusion from which God is free." Such an inference serves only to reduce the cross to an "accidental symbol of a timeless truth" [79] even as it minimizes the existentiality and revelatory significance of the Incarnate Event itself.

Despite our negative criticisms of Barth we reiterate his strong point. He has come to see that time is no longer to be regarded as an empty phenomenon. While eternity is not infinite time, neither is it totally averse to *all time.* Barth's main contribution here is that he preserves the dynamism of eternity, which at least embraces its own time, if not man's. Impregnated with eternity, existential time is the time that has "become new." While Berdyaev has seen the eschatological relation of this to the nature of both eternity and history more consistently than Barth, the "Bonn bomber" has seen it more astutely than "the melancholy Dane." Barth sees this "new time" related not only to eternity itself but even to the end related to it, as we shall see. With the problem of eternity clarified and that of the end looming large, we are now in a position to look directly into the meaning of the *eschaton.*

●　　●　　●　　●

Raising our sights, then, we will focus our lens more sharply upon that peak of Eschaton which stands both before and above us. Though it bespeaks the horizontal extremity of an insular ridge, it is far more than that, for we see it bedecked with a crystalline splendor which "cometh down from heaven." And without this eternal luminescence we could not see it at all, or if we could, little would it matter.

NOTES

1 Berdyaev, *Freedom and the Spirit*, pp. 189-193, 210.
2 *Slavery and Freedom*, p. 260.
3 *Freedom and the Spirit*, p. 190.
4 *The Beginning and the End*, p. 170. Cf. *Freedom and Spirit*, p. 127. "The freedom of spirit is not only freedom in God, but also freedom in relation to God." Cf. pp. 127-130. (Cf. Augustine's "freedom," both "major" and "minor.") For Berdyaev God is not object but subject and known by encounter and communion in the "I-Thou" relation of subjects or persons. As Karl Heim says in relation to Buber, an object is in the past, not present. (*Christian Faith and Natural Science*, p. 104.) There is no now "unless an ego is present" to say "this is my time."
5 *The Realm of Spirit and the Realm of Caesar*, p. 36.
6 Tillich, *Systematic Theology*, Vol. I, pp. 235f.
7 *The Meaning of History*, p. 63f.
8 *Ibid.*, p. 65f.
9 *Ibid.*, p. 66.
10 *Ibid.*, p. 67.
11 *Ibid.*, p. 67f.
12 *Ibid.*, pp. 52, 63ff. We take note here of Aquinas' awareness of the problem in his more rational theory of "aeviternity" which, he says, "differs from time, and from eternity, as the mean between them both," and "Aeviternity is simultaneously whole; yet it is not eternity, because before and after are compatible with it." (*Summa Theologica*, I, 10, 5, p. 80f). This shows the inadequacy of a rational time-eternity relationship which Berdyaev solves existentially, and to some extent Karl Barth, as we shall see.
13 *Ibid.*, pp. 66, 64.
14 *Solitude and Society*, p. 113. This contributes to the denial of eternity as infinite time, which is supported biblically by Edwin Lewis' reminder that "eternal" is not to be equated with "everlasting." Cf. his *Biblical Faith and Christian Freedom*, p. 34. As John Baillie says in *The Life Everlasting*, p. 244, 247ff, eternity is qualitative depth, not length. "The primary reference is not to time but to the quality . . . and it is a quality which may in part belong to the time that now is." p. 248f.
15 J. M. Spier in *Christianity and Existentialism*, p. 137, makes the following assertion: "To acquire a responsible view of time, philosophy cannot lack the light of divine revelation, for in this light not only is the temporality of all creation displayed, but our eyes are also opened to created reality which transcends the modal aspects of time in a religious sense."

[16] *Solitude and Society,* p. 191.

[17] Bertocci in his *Philosophy of Religion,* pp. 445-462, 549, sides with Berdyaev when he says the orthodox thesis goes too far in saying that nothing in God changes, though there must be a permanence in God, for a changelessness is lifelessness. Also, eternity implies a quality and creativeness similar to Berdyaev's dynamic idea. The quality of God's "function" does not change nor does his will to goodness, though his "psychic experience" implies a temporality akin to that of man, though higher.

[18] e.g., Ulrich Simon, *Theology of Crisis,* p .202.

[19] Berdyaev would take some exception to the concept of eternity held by F. H. Brabant, who in *Time and Eternity in Christian Thought,* p. 173 (Cf. p. 188), says, ". . . we may say that the Christian concept of eternity is the Greek idea of faultless perfection, moralized and deepened by the Christian sense of personality." Brabant errs by subordinating personality to a rational abstraction. God, he says, is object and subject. Goodness to a rational reality is also a person. But can a rationally objective being be personal? Needed here, Berdyaev would say, is a dynamic view of God's Being as Becoming, as person and Spirit. An eternity of abstract perfection is not a dynamic and personal eternity which can cope with time.

[20] *Truth and Revelation,* p. 97.

[21] *Ibid.,* p. 98f.

[22] *Ibid.,* pp. 46, 82-84. See our discussion above, pp. 95ff, 107ff. Karl Löwith in *Meaning in History* shows that *Heilsgeschehen* and *Weltgeschichte* are not to be confused. While concurring, Berdyaev helps us see that neither should they be dichotomized.

[23] Barth, *Die Kirchliche Dogmatik,* Band III, 2, 47, 2, p. 635. We are treating Barth as an "existentialist" largely on the basis that he sees the paradoxical nature of eternity's relation to time, though in an entirely different way from S. K. or Berdyaev.

[24] *Ibid.,* p. 636. This point is Augustinian. Infra p. 183.

[25] Barth, *Die Kirchliche Dogmatik,* Band II, 1, p. 689.

[26] *Ibid,* p. 686.

[27] *Op. cit.,* Band III, 2, 47, 2, p. 638.

[28] *Op. cit.,* Band II, 1, p. 689.

[29] Barth, *The Epistle to the Romans,* p. 145f. Cf. pp. 2, 57, 249 (1957 ed.) .

[30] S. K., *Training in Christianity,* pp. 26ff, 31, 33, 36, 60, 68, 216, 240.

[31] *Op. cit.,* Band II, 1, p. 686.

[32] *Ibid.,* pp. 688, 685.

[33] *Christ and Time,* pp. 62f, 66.

[34] Barth, *The Epistle to the Romans, op. cit.,* p. 145.

[35] Barth, *The Knowledge of God and the Service of God,* p. 70.

[36] *Ibid.* Cf. *The Epistle to the Romans,* 1957 ed., p. 237.

[37] Cf. Barth, *The Epistle to the Romans,* p. 145f; "Nein!" Barth's reply to Emil Brunner's *Nature and Grace,* also *The Word of God and the Word of Man* by Barth. Cf. Monsma, *Karl Barth's Idea of Revelation,* Chap. VI. Cornelius Van Til in the *New Modernism,* p. 357, says of Barth's monologue, "As only God can reveal himself, so only God can hear his own revelation. We hear that revelation only as we are partakers of the aseity of God."

[38] *The Knowledge of God . . .,* p. 71.

[39] *Die Kirchliche Dogmatik,* Band II, halbband 1, p. 694f.

[40] *The Creator and the Adversary,* pp. 161ff, 133f, 234, 103, 178.

[41] *Dogmatics in Outline,* p. 129.

[42] *Kirchliche Dogmatik, op. cit.,* p. 689, Cf. p. 705. Tillich, in *Systematic*

Theology, Vol. I, says in contrast to Barth and in support of our defense of Berdyaev's dialectic, p. 270, "If eternity is conceived in terms of creativity, the eternal includes past and future *without absorbing* their special character as modes of time. . . . The dissected moments of time are united in eternity." This involves man's "participation in the eternity of divine life" in the hope of eternal life. More than the "simultaneity" of eternity which erases the modes of time, as we have seen in S. K. and Barth, "Eternity is the transcendent unity," says Tillich, "of the dissected moments of existential time." (p. 774. Cf. p. 257). John S. Whale in *Christian Doctrine*, p. 58 misses this in denying past, present and future because of divine "simultaneity." While John Baillie in *The Life Everlasting*, p. 252ff, sees the quality of eternity, he allows it to so transcend time that it is alien to "the conditions of time." Successive time is altogether compressed into simultaneity, as it is for Whale. God is not in time though time is in Him, says Baillie.

43 *Die Kirchliche Dogmatik*, Band I, halbband 2, 1, pp. 167ff, 188.
44 *The Word of God and the Word of Man*, p. 143.
45 *Kirchliche Dogmatik*, Band I, halbband 2, 1, pp. 180, 165.
46 *Ibid*, pp. 167ff, 188.
47 *Ibid.*, p. 71, In contrast, Edwin Lewis in *The Biblical Faith and Christian Freedom* p. 154 says Christ means that God "broke into history." Cf. pp. 44, 61, 119 for other important insights.
48 Simon, *Theology of Crisis*, p .186.
49 Johannes Hohlenberg in *Soren Kierkegaard*, p. 284, says, "Later theologians, foremost of whom is Karl Barth, have, with their eye on Kierkegaard, constructed a concept of God which puts decisive and impassable gulfs between God and man. Even though support can be found for this in many isolated utterances of Kierkegaard, it is in fact not consonant with his real typical thought and spirit."
50 (a) *Epistle to Romans*, 1957 ed., p. 498 (Cf. pp. 109, 112, 336) ; pp. 57, 77, 500; p .114; p. 30 (Cf. p. 276f) for these respective statements and citations.
   (b) *Die Kirchliche Dogmatik*, Band III, 1, p. 6f.
51 *Ibid.*, p. 187f. Italics mine.
52 *Ibid.*, p. 179. Italics mine.
53 *Ibid.*, p. 183.
54 *Ibid.*, p. 187.
55 At the Univ. of Pennsylvania, Dec. 15, 1958.
56 *Die Kirchliche Dogmatik*, III, 1, p. 757.
57 *Ibid.*, p. 288.
58 *Ibid.*, p. 290ff.
59 *Ibid.*, p. 335f. Even this qualification should demand, faithwise, an existential both/and tension rather than an either/or, whereas Barth is right in refuting a rational synthesis or fusion.
61 *Ibid.*, p. 351.
62 *Ibid.*, pp. 352, 318.
63 *Ibid.*, p. 336.
64 *Die Kirchliche Dogmatik*, IV, 1, p. 150. Cf. pp. 689, 741.
65 *Ibid.*, p. 755f.
66 *Ibid.*, p. 767.
67 *Ibid.*, p. 767.
68 *Ibid.*, p. 287.
69 Baillie, *God Was in Christ*, p. 53.
70 *Ibid.*, pp. 113, 74.
71 *Ibid.*, p. 78.
72 We see this in much of both Vols. I and II of Tillich's *Systematic*

Theology as well as in his treatment of the resurrection. The latter is a matter of existential faith encounter made almost synonymous with regeneration. Cf. Tillich, *The New Being*, p. 24.

73 *Op.* cit., p. 79.
74 *The Christian Future*, p. 189. Italics mine.
75 Cf. Schweitzer, *The Quest of the Historical Jesus*, Chaps. IV, VIII, XIV, XIX. Cf. Harold Roberts, *Jesus and the Kingdom of God*, Chap. I.
76 Baillie, *op. cit.*, p. 119.
77 *Ibid.*, p. 150.
78 *Ibid.*, p. 190.
79 *Ibid.*, p. 190f. Though I would qualify, in view of our basic thesis, the use of the word "timeless" here in favor of "dynamic eternal."

CHAPTER VI

EXISTENTIAL TIME AND THE MEANING OF THE END

Having come to see that time demands more than a temporal source of meaning and how this calls for an eternity of dynamic character to qualify it, we may turn directly to the existential problems of the End. Weighing anchor we will view the dimensions of Kairos from another perspective. We will find that when aligned with her qualitative peak, the linear end of this island of time reflects an eternal sheen that outdazzles the foamy lace etching out her temporal shoreline. This is the eschatological dimension of existential time, the *eschaton* of *kairos*, the two ends of which, vertical and horizontal, are seen as one.

The eschatological problem of the End is another important matter which belongs to that of time and its meaning. Berdyaev makes this lucid in his existential interpretation of time. But before coming to grips with the explicit features of the End as seen by Berdyaev, it would be well to take note of what that End is *not*. This demands that we offset some of the features of the modern process philosophies of time with respect to the eschatological problems so as to make more significant to contemporary theology and religious philosophy the contributions of Berdyaev's existential eschatology to the meaning of time and its end. In so doing we shall seek to demonstrate how a philosophical teleology is inadequate as an interpretation of time and its end, even as it proves uncongenial to a theology seeking to do justice to New Testament eschatology.

The End in Modern Teleologies

The eschatological end given existential orientation by Berdyaev is not to be limited to the cosmic or teleological end arrived at by modern process philosophies. While it has been said by some that existentialism cannot do justice to cosmic time,[1] we are prone to think, on the contrary, that this criticism does not apply seriously to Berdyaev. Berdyaev has a place for cosmic time while recognizing its deficiency as a source of man's meaningful destiny. The criticism rather applies to thinkers like Kierkegaard and Barth who do not come to grips with the matter.

The discussion here undertaken will seek to demonstrate the deficiency of cosmic teleologies of time in view of the end and its place in the Christian interpretation of existence and history, and how Berdyaev accepts the reality of the cosmic *telos* while seeing its need of qualification in the light of eternity and the *eschaton*. Berdyaev has asserted the reality of cosmic time, as seen earlier in our discourse, but the significance of it is nil to him apart from its relation to the knower on the one hand, and its source of meaning in eternity on the other. Thus cosmic time, while acknowledged to be real, is meaningless to man and his destiny until enhanced by a supratemporal relevance and quality.

The basic distinction before us, then, is that of *telos* versus *eschaton*, the temporal end of the cosmos in contrast to the end as *both* temporal and eternal. This pertains to problems raised but left unsolved by certain outstanding evolutionary philosophers from Bergson through Whitehead to contemporary biological evolutionists. Putting certain ideas of time and the end as held by these teleologists in contrast to those of Berdyaev, we shall show how Berdyaev faces up to their problems, and upon designating them, we shall prognosticate certain features of his eschatological version of the end which help overcome the deficiencies of their theories of time and its end. Also, we shall see from another angle how *Berdyaev retains the reality of both eternity and time, in this case cyclic time, without jeopardizing the reality of either.* Upon demonstrating what the End is *not*, we shall move into a more explicit examination of Berdyaev's view of what it *is*. First, then, what the true End is *not*.

The End and Bergson's Creative Evolution

The French philosopher Henri Bergson was probably the most influential modern philosopher to construct a process philosophy of time. Fundamental to Bergson is the Heraclitean flux adapted to time as duration (*durée*) but not succession. Intrinsic to the natural process of the universe, time or *durée* is regarded as incessant Becoming.[2] From Berdyaev's standpoint, this is to be challenged for its failure to recognize the permanent element in the very nature of incessant change, a paradoxical matter we find not overlooked by Heraclitus in his *Cosmic Fragments* even with respect to the *Logos*. Bergson sees all as Becoming while not as Being. Consciousness, he claims, is the epitome of change.[3] Things do not change, yet all is change. Time is the universal changing duration and this universal consciousness is a kind of durational impetus or surge, the cosmic *élan vital*. Thus the universe is said to consist of conscious time.[4]

But the end or *telos* implied by this *élan vital* is kept potential by Bergson.[5] Somewhat as in the Hegelian System it is an unrealized *telos*. Bergson relates a hazy, unreal future to an impulsive present, making this relation the very principle of his evolutionary scheme.[6] The future, however, is little more than an illusion,[7] reminding us of Plato's illusory time and Locke's denial of its reality, as well as Kierkegaard's negation. But it is questionable whether the temporal *telos* could be real in any sense if the future is unreal in the sense of either horizontal or cosmic time. But Bergson's reply to this would be that the end is in the present moment of the *élan vital*. Here may we point out the similarity of Bergson's view, to a degree, with the Kierkegaardian idea of the future in the existential present.

But this hardly solves the problem of the end, for Bergson leaves it necessary on the one hand, and *only* potential on the other, while leaving it unrelated to succession. He keeps the end unrealizable. A strictly potential future or end is not a realistic future or end. While Bergson is right in rejecting a mathematical time line which equates time with its measure, from Berdyaev's standpoint he is wrong in rejecting the past and future as real in the horizontal sense of being successive, especially in view of his concern for the end of time, which to him is unfulfilled while ambiguously aimed at by the cosmic process. This being the case, the cosmos is in process of "fulfilling" an unfulfillable end, one which is potential but never actual. The universe like a gigantic dynamo is going but going "nowhere." While we must concede that little else can be expected from a cosmic philosophy, it may mean that philosophy is incapable of a better answer. It may mean that questions concerning the ultimate remain unanswerable until given a religious orientation. In this case what is teleological may have to become eschatological.

Berdyaev existentially resolves the problem of the future and the end by considering the end to be both temporal and eternal in the *Now,* something overlooked by both Kierkegaard as an existentialist and Bergson as an evolutionist. Kierkegaard missed it by failing to keep all tenses of common time real; Bergson missed it by failing to reckon with the eternal in relation to the present and the end.[8] In fact, he substitutes time for eternity or God as the key to the ultimate meaning of the cosmos.

Though Bergson relates his *élan vital* to a vague future, it has no realistic end, and is not comparable or even related to the eternal Now. In fact, time has no real succession since it is all at once. For the end to be real and consequential to man, who as the knower in existence can alone be concerned about it, the end, we maintain, must belong to a realistic linear future, not a hypothetical end or a potential future projected from, while restricted to, the present. This is especially true if the end is to be relevant to human history and destiny. Berdyaev's eschatological end resolves this conflict, as we shall see.

Bergson's idea of the end as an aspect of the evolutionary principle can effect the idea of progress but not destiny.[9] It sees the *telos* as an unfulfilled potentiality. It lacks the realistic end of chronos on the one hand, and the eternal dimension on the other, which is to be found only in the New Testament *eschaton,* seen by Berdyaev. But at least Bergson keeps the present *élan vital* in relation to the future, as he sees it. Barring their differences, this is something paralleled by Berdyaev's existential view. In this way Bergson leaves the door open to a mystery in the time process which he would substitute for eternity. But here is no forward movement, succession or progression and nothing that pertains to the origin and end of life. Likewise, here we see no design. Time simply *is,* and is a constant surging transition, while from nothing to nothing.

Had Bergson faced up to the significance of eternity's relation to time, he could have done much to enhance the relation between the moment and the end. His end is strictly temporal and potential in a merely hypothetical sense. This is inadequate if man's history, existence and destiny are to be meaningful and not swallowed up in a grandiose cosmic scheme. Furthermore, Bergson's "creative evolution" appears contradictory, since the temporal phenomenon of the *élan vital* is a deterministic process of nature which is not reconcilable to the freedom of man and the freedom implied by the idea of creation, which Bergson himself holds. Yet Bergson is to be credited with rejecting any mechanistic theory of the correlation of organic parts, since naturalistic evolution, he maintained, does not account for a *telos* which can, in turn, account for present correlations.[10] This idea is rejected, however, by such biological evolutionists of today as Alexis Carrel and Lecomte du Noüy, whose views we are about to consider. Bergson also rejected the idea of space-time, since space, he assterted, belongs to "the degraded realm of mathematical successive time".[11] In fact, Bergson refuted all scientific and rational philosophy,[12] something which Alexander, the next evolutionist to be considered, did not do.

The End and Alexander's Empirical Evolution

Attempting to combine a Hegelian monism with evolution, Samuel Alexander was both idealistic and naturalistic. Influenced by Minkowski, this forerunner of the theory of "relativity" developed a new realism which was adopted by Bertrand Russell and Alfred North Whitehead. This included an empirical method for understanding a nonempirical, *a priori* element known as "space-time." [13]

Space-time, Alexander asserted, is the basic stuff or *hulé* of the universe.[14] Alexander rejected the Kantian idea of time as a strictly *a priori* category as well as the Hegelian idea that only the eternal whole is real. These rejections lend some support to Berdyaev's position. Both object and subject are necessary to the knowledge of things, said Alexander.[15] But it appears that Alexander spatialized Bergson's *durée* [16] while giving it an intrinsic *nisus,* an inner impetus equivalent to Bergson's *élan vital.*[17] Unlike Bergson, however, Alexander attributes an element of succession within duration to time, while Alexander disallows the reality of time apart from space. Without space, time would be a perpetually renewed *now,* he claims. Events are "point-instants" and, similar to Bergson, Being is Becoming while in the form of "space-time," which is assumed to be infinite.[18]

Alexander admits that he does not raise "the thorny question of whether the mind is not also in space and time."[19] But, as earlier indicated with respect to Aristotle's dropping of the question of a soul or subject to know time and number, this is an existential matter which must not be ignored. In view of the subject as the knower and innovator of time, Alexander here rests content with the very presupposition of all scientific, materialistic approaches to knowledge, viz., the knower himself who, properly respected, must be seen to be the existential subject.

Identifying the emergent evolution of the universe with God, Alexander fuses it also with the cyclic process of cosmic time. God is the natural divine process of space-time, while so-called "deity" is the qualitative *telos* of this process. This is to say that God is the universe moving by its impetus toward its unfulfilled deity, the *telos*. Deity is to God what the *telos* is to the *nisus* of space-time.[20] Here we see that Being is a kind of Platonic Becoming. To a degree this parallels Berdyaev's mystical view of a dynamic eternity, save that it is a rational monism identified with cosmic time and therefore uncongenial to an existential eschatology which refuses to dissolve the paradox of time and eternity, as well as that of time and its end.

The unfulfilled deity of Alexander's scheme is an expression of temporal infinity; therefore, as the *telos* of the cosmic process, it remains an unfulfilled, remote end, which is akin to Bergson's end. Alexander denies any guidance of space-time from beyond itself. In this respect his scheme of the cosmic process is completely immanental and quite like Bergson's. Since Alexander identifies God with the space-time process, it is logical to say that his position caters to a notion of an eternity of infinite time. There is no transcendent or qualitative difference between eternity and time; eternity is simply a prolonged time. This scheme also keeps the process-God a universal embryo, an unfulfilled Being, which cannot embrace a real end.

The major deficiency here is the lack of a truly eschatological dimension of time. Alexander's teleology, somewhat like that of Bergson, lacks a supratemporal source of time's meaning. The end is a hypothetical temporal *telos*, somewhat like the Hegelian *telos*, while projected in such a way as not to be realizable. Here

161

we see a teleology based on a weak rational solution to what is really a suprarational, existential problem of eschatology. Let it be said, then, that such a cosmic *telos* cannot be substituted for, or adapted to, the New Testament *eschaton,* and any modern theology which assumes their immanental identity is running away from the problem of time and its relation to eternity.

The End and Whitehead's Emergent Evolution

Basing his philosophy largely upon Alexander's scheme, Whitehead maintains an infinite process of emergent evolution. In it he sees a new world constantly being born, a cosmic organism of Becoming in which space-time is basic.[21] The true *relata* are events rather than "bits of matter," [22] says Whitehead. All is in atomistic flux, while the universe is *also* a stable divine order. Being is Becoming, again, but with each atom in process of becoming or, more explicitly, "pre-hending" itself, and the whole universe accordingly. In this way the cosmos is moving toward its own end or ultimate fulfillment.

Whitehead's ideas of "prehension" and "creativity" are basically much the same as Alexander's *nisus* and Bergson's *élan vital,* while more applicable to a scientific perspective. Each atom is in process of prehending its potential self.[23] God as the ultimate goal or eternal object of the whole cosmos and its parts is basic to this as well as being the "repository" for the "ideas" of the cosmos. The latter points to a kind of Platonic to neo-Platonic idealism combined with a cosmic teleology.

God to Whitehead, as in Alexander's idea of deity, is the *telos* of the cosmic organism.[24] The temporal process needs eternal concepts or ideas to account for it. The process of Becoming, then, is one of atomistic events which meet with their Forms so that the actual is determined by the potential. This, again, combines a Platonic Absolute with the cosmic process. Real possibilities are always beyond the actual while very much related to the actual. Thus the permanence of God is seen intrinsic to the flux of nature and vice versa. While Whitehead's search for a nonstatic solution to the problem of permanence and change is commendable, he keeps it intrinsic to a necessitative, immanental process. God is the *telos* while also immanent to cosmic space-time. Both the end and the process belong to God and are interdependent for their self-fulfillment. But this does not do justice to such theistic ideas as a free Creator, a beginning of time, or an eternity transcendent of time.

Making God the necessary end and substance of infinite space-time leaves the idea of eternity temporal and God in servitude to creation. This cannot meet the requirements of the following provocative statement by Whitehead, which is really more congenial to Berdyaev's existential eschatology: "That religion," he said, "will conquer which can render clear to popular understanding some eternal greatness incarnate in the passage of temporal fact." [25] We see nothing supratemporal about an eternity which is immanent to a temporal process, and nothing which either demands or provides any incarnate truth when all is immanent. This is something which few thinkers in modern philosophy and theology have recognized but to which existentialists like Berdyaev have been sensitive.

While Whitehead sees history meaningless apart from a religious perspective, we suggest that it takes more than a temporal idealistic impulse to give eternal meaning to the events of history. A higher-than-evolutionary surge toward a projected temporal end is required. Needed is a communion with a supratemporal, transcendent eternity. This hints another basic difference between a cosmic teleology of time and a vital eschatology. Unless it is recognized, time fails to transcend itself and remains short of real meaning by lacking a close relation between the present moment and the end, an end which is more-than-temporal while also temporal. In short, such a time cannot be redeemed and hardly requires that it should be.

The End and Biological Evolution

The space-time theory, which actually goes back at least as far as John Locke,[26] is seriously questioned not only by Bergson but by Berdyaev. Rosenstock-Huessy brusquely says, "We have shaken off the prevalent superstition of our time that time and space can be lumped together as the two general frames of reference for all experience." [27] Perhaps of consternation to some theorists today, this reaction to a popular cosmic theory is given support by the distinguished British biologist Sir Joseph Needham. Referring to the space-time theory Needham says, "Is not this bondage our final evil?" [28] Space-time, he sees, is an artificial equation of space with an objectified, mathematical time.

But just as important to our present interest we note that Needham recognizes, as few scientific minds do, that the human experience of tragedy is *not* to be understood in terms of a naturalistic process related to time and change. Needham recognizes that the objective view of time, which readily lends itself to being spatialized, is too much of an assumption, and when combined with the naturalistic view of life and death, for instance, proves to be too superficial and ethically neutral.[29] Needham concurs with Berdyaev that horizontal time is arbitrary when reduced to a mere measurement used by the observer.[30] While appreciating Whitehead's preservation of both permanence and change,[31] a principle congenial also to Berdyaev, though on a more-than-cosmic-temporal basis, Needham makes the remarkable concession that we need an "eschatological" solution to the problem of time. Departing from what has been popular among process teleologists, Needham gropes for a supratemporal view of time, a solution which neither denies man's relation to the natural process nor limits the meaning of man to that process. Let it be said that this is a remarkable acknowledgment on the part of a contemporary thinker steeped in the biological approach to cosmic evolution. We venture to say that Needham's reading of Berdyaev has been of some influence upon his thinking at this point; in fact, at one stage in his thought Needham totally ignored the importance of time, as he himself has acknowledged, but eventually he came to the point where he could no longer avoid its crucial importance.

While Needham overtly accused Berdyaev of a pessimism with respect to human progress,[32] there is a strong sense in which this is not necessarily true. Berdyaev's eschatology is neither pessimistic nor superficially optimistic, as we shall see. The main point here is that Needham endeavors to combine "eschatology," a supratemporal view of the *telos,* with a process of natural evolution. While this is a big step closer to what we deem a more wholesome teleology of time, it still remains a deficient view of the end. This attempt to *identify* the cosmic process with eschtology is theologically counterparted, we find, in the theology of D. D. Williams.[33] From the perspective of an existential eschatology this is a grave inconsistency, if not a stark impossibility. The naturalistic view of cosmic time with its necessitative temporal end does not provide for a supratemporal factor in the end. The despair of real meaning that this implies for a thinker like Needham should help lead philosophers, surely theologians, to recognize the need of a higher source of time's meaning and end. Indirectly, we see this admission in Needham as well as Carrel, whose scheme we are about to consider. The Christian thinker must be extremely alert to what this entails and not dissolve the distinctiveness of his eschatology within a process teleology. As Kant admitted, the problems involving eternity belong to a transcendent theology.

Needham is looking to a cosmic *telos* while seeing the need, perhaps unwittingly, for something like the N.T. *eschaton*. His concession is commendable but his teleology falls short of it. While the *telos* gives design to the cosmic process, it fails to provide itself with a more-than-temporal meaning. Needham's evolutionary process provides a teleology but does not lend itself to a real eschatology. The dimension of eternity is not embraced from within this process philosophy of time, and in the truest sense cannot be. Theologians must be alert to this matter. Furthermore, Needham's profound respect for man's sense of the "numinous," which has kinship to Bergson's intuition and to some extent Berdyaev's regard for *gnosis,* is not accounted for by a necessitative process identified with cosmic time. The amoral, immanental cosmic process cannot yield spiritual insight into the eternal, as Needham himself seems to see. Yet, his recognition of the temporal problem of human tragedy and confessed need of a more-than-temporal *telos* are important pre-existential insights. To meet the demands of his search for the meaning of tragedy on the part of the man of concrete existence, Needham should embrace an eschatology which is not limited to a strictly temporal cosmology. A deeper look at Berdyaev and his eschatology should help inspire this.

The French biologist Alexis Carrel also seeks to show that there is a *telos* belonging to the organic process of the cosmos. An organism develops, he says, in accordance with "the present and future needs of the whole." [34] But here time is reduced to a cause. Referring to parts of the process Carrel says, "Time causes many changes in their appearance." [35] In this we see cosmic time linked with a horizontal notion of time in a series of causes and effects. Actually this is a notion which goes back to Aristotle's physical view of time. But this much is an objectivized view of time, one based on the pseudo measurements of time.

Yet Carrel recognizes that the self is linked with the future and is even pre-existent, biologically.[36] To a degree, these ideas are quite congenial or parallel to Berdyaev's view of the existential moment and of the pre-existence of man as a spirit. But in assuming time to be a cause Carrel does not have an answer to the problem of the past and the future. Berdyaev's position sees cause as a phenomenon of temporal existence. Cause is not time, and time is not cause; time is in man, not man in time. Despite the importance Carrel ascribes to the knowing self, in contrast to positivism and much superficial "scientism" of this age, he does not quite see this important point.

Though space and time are interrelated for Carrel on the level of the electronic, atomic and molecular structure of physical tissue, man's self is regarded as *above* space-time.[37] This is an important admission. While man is seen to be linked with the cosmic process, Carrel, quite like Needham, is concerned about man not being *bound* to that process. Thus he concedes with great insight,

> We must liberate man from the cosmos created by the genius of physicists and astronomers, that cosmos in which, since the Renaissance, he has been imprisoned. Despite its stupendous immensity, the world of matter is too narrow for him. Like his economic and social environment, it does not fit him. We cannot adhere to the faith in its exclusive reality. We know that we are not altogether comprised within its dimensions, *that we extend somewhere else, outside the physical continuum. . . . But he also belongs to another world.* A world which, although enclosed within himself, stretches beyond space and time.[38]

Assertions like this from biological evolutionists should give added inducement to the contemporary thinker to look beyond the *strictly* scientific approach to life and beyond process systems of cosmic time for the solution to man's temporal dilemma and the meaning of time and the end. Indirectly, this underlines the existential view of the self and reflects how man represents the paradoxical meeting of time and eternity, that he is a being on the frontier of two realms, as S. K. and Berdyaev have said, each in his own way. It also suggests that contemporary physical scientists like Carrel and Needham are, strange to say, even more congenial to the supratemporal meaning of time than are such rational teleologists as Whitehead and Alexander. Their admissions in behalf of the need for a supratemporal end, what we see revealed in the *eschaton*, lend themselves to the existential eschatology of Berdyaev, the details of which we are about to elaborate.

Carrel sees the place for more than an "extrinsic" time with an assumed "reality of its own." Besides this objective time there is what he calls a man's "inner time," a kind of time not limited to cosmic time. This, too, is a pre-existential insight similar to *Geschichte* and invites deeper consideration for time in the existential subject. "Memory," says Carrel, "is responsible for the passage of time."[39] Recognizing another principle congenial to Berdyaev's existentialism, he says that personality is associated with one's recollections. In addition, Carrel says, "We realize that we change, that we are not identical with our former self. But that we are the same being." [40] This supports Berdyaev's paradoxical idea of Being-in-Becoming and that a person is the seat of both change and permanence, and thereby the center of time with all its modes and tenses.

Like Needham, Alexis Carrel really gropes for an eschatological solution to the problem of time and the end.[41] While both thinkers have process philosophies which endeavor to combine a temporal process with a purposive teleology, Carrel, we believe, comes closer to the solution for which they yearn. This is essentially because he recognizes the reality of man's "inner time" or subjective time. This helps pave the way for an existential perspective which is more congenial to an effective eschatology and philosophy of time. Yet in Carrel's scheme this is not explicitly related to the end.

Another biological evolutionist who deals with the problem of "telefinalism." [42] as he calls it, is Lecomte du Noüy. Besides his objective approach to the biological processes of nature in relation to the *telos*, Du Noüy joins Carrel when he concedes that there is a kind of time which is not objective but subjective. Knowledge in general is subjective, he contends.[43] This shows respect for the role and uniqueness of the existing self. It calls to mind the admission of physicist Martin Johnson referred to in Chapter I.

Concentrating on the evolutionary process with its *telos,* Du Noüy sees God to be the intelligence and purpose behind the universe, but he fails to relate this end to the supratemporal aspects of what is meant by God. Asserting in one essay that God is "timeless," he also says, "He is in us." [44] But the God Who accounts for the temporal being of man and Who is even claimed to be "in" him can hardly be timeless, it seems. Du Noüy's "telefinalism" needs more light from the relation between the temporal end and the eternal. This calls for more than a *telos* which is "final," temporally speaking. The end of the cosmic process must somehow be related to the beginning. Whitehead saw this point. But in view of the deficiencies of each of the teleologists we have considered it becomes apparent that a higher dimension of time is needed, one which relates more closely the end, even cosmic *telos,* to the subject or knower of time in the present, the concrete man in existence. This in turn calls for an end which is not strictly teleological, again, but eschatological in the existential and biblical sense.

* * * *

We have seen how the process theories of cosmic time remain extremely deficient in their respective teleologies. Yet Carrel and Needham especially are to be credited with acknowledging in a pre-existential manner the need of a higher dimension of time and the meaning of the end. Both these thinkers, together with Du Noüy, also have conceded the importance of a subjective perspective of time. On the whole, however, we have described how process philosophy with its approach to the cosmos and the end, is inclined toward a deficient philosophy of time. The solution for which these teleologists grope together with a meaning of time and the end are better seen in the existential time-eternity relationship of Berdyaev's eschatology. *Something more than a strictly temporal telos is needed. There must be an end which is as eternal as it is temporal.* It is to a deeper and more explicit consideration of what this involves that we now turn. From the standpoint of the cosmos we have contemplated the end, but must shift our position so as to see its reflection of that eternal splendor which is not just its own. We must shift our attention now from what the true End is *not* to what it *is*.

The End In Existential Eschatology

We have seen the incapacity of process philosophies to give us the *meaning* of the end of time. We have also taken note of certain pre-existential concessions among them pertaining to the need of a supratemporal dimension of the end. This makes Berdyaev's version of the end all the more practical and worthy of our consideration today. What we have called his *"eschatological dimension" of existential time* becomes pertinent to this issue, for *it points us once more to the transcendent factor of eternity even as it preserves the temporal reality of the end.* Having seen to some extent what such an end is *not*, we can better uncover and appreciate what it *is*.

The end, for Berdyaev, is the very center of the problem and meaning of human destiny, just as the existential moment is the center of the problem and meaning of human existence. The two are interrelated, however, while not identical. The end is that aspect of the existential moment which gives it ultimate significance while also relating a realistic future of linear and cosmic time to a meaning-giving eternity. *Just as the present moment may be of eternal quality and intensity so that it is not simply* chronos *but* kairos, *so, too, the end may take on a supratemporal quality which makes it not simply* telos *but* eschaton. This, too, is fundamental to our basic contention, introduced in Chapter I, that time and eternity can be seen very much in relation while negating the reality of neither.

The Existential End and the Meaning of Destiny

Berdyaev saw that the end is essential to the attempt to find meaning in the tragic and prophetic aspects of an existence enmeshed with the problem of time. Time and existence, therefore, are fundamentally related to destiny. "The philosophy to which I would give expression," said Berdyaev, "is a dramatic philosophy of destiny, of existence which is in time and passes over into eternity, of time which presses on to an end, an end which is not death but transfiguration." [45] This statement epitomizes what we deem basic to our comparative study and developing argument.

It is noteworthy that here we see no desire to compress the future completely into the vertical or existential present as in Kierkegaard,[46] who, as we have seen, closes the accordion of successive time, thus squeezing out its significance even as a subordinate means to a divine end. Yet Berdyaev acknowledges the deficiency of horizontal time *per se*, while this deficiency is not its unreality or total insignificance. Here, again, the paradox of the time-eternity relationship is to be seen, for Berdyaev is an existentialist of a kind who refuses to allow the importance of either aspect of existential time to be depreciated altogether. The end of time, therefore, while a dimension of the present linked with the eternal now, represents a real destiny, a future fulfillment of existence in an existential moment pertinent to both historic men and the eternal God.

This *eschaton* is the hem of the Lord's eternal garment, which man is allowed to touch that his existence and history may have a special significance. It can be meaningful only to a spiritual being not lost in a cosmos understood exclusively as either a rational or empirical system. As Berdyaev's colleague Emmanuel Mounier has said, "No spiritualism founded on an impersonal spirit and no rationalism based on pure idea can have any real interest for the destiny of man." [47] This applies critically to the cosmologies of both Hegel and the teleologists treated above.

A meaningful end calls for the dynamic eternity upheld by Berdyaev, which alone can relate itself to time, including the future and future end, without embarrassment. The end, then, need not be lost in time nor dissolved by eternity. Linked with both, from the existential perspective, the end of time is such that it is transfigured by and in eternity. It is the relation of the eternal Now to the future end which accounts for this. For Berdyaev the eternal Now not only looks every direction at once, as does the Moment for Kierkegaard, but it embraces what it sees. Thus, for Berdyaev the end and the whole philosophy of time would needs be existential to be eschatological and eschatological to be existential. The prophetic character of time stems from its place for the future and end, while this must be seen from the perspective of the vertical present, a present with a depth dimension that to faith makes it not only temporally present but eternally present. One catches a glimpse of this when he realizes that the only time he lives is *now*, yet he cannot do so authentically without living to a future or a potential now. Yet what "future now" could possibly matter save as it is embraced by a "present now" to make it matter? And what now can this be save an eternal now neither defined, measured or identified by past and future? Such a Now must transcend the future even as it transfigures it without negating it.

This implies a "metahistory" which links the end to the beginning through the present. Were there no such possibility, all creation, including man, would be utterly remote to eternity, even to a faith perspective which is still man's after all, however inspired by God. Such an end can be seen only from the standpoint of the existential meeting of eternity and time in the faith-conditioned moment of *kairos*. In fact, the end is a type of *kairos*, while of a special dimension in that it belongs to a realistic future while it bespeaks a supratemporal, eternal quality. This is what we mean by the eschatological dimension of existential time as best expressed in terms of the New Testament *eschaton*. It is the divine-human end of existence, which looks up and ahead at the same time.

The plenitude of time lies principally in its positive existentiality, its relation to the eternal in the present. Events belong to the historical time series, while these remain empty until given meaning in terms of the end qualified accordingly.[48] This breaks up the notion of an all-inclusive, causal determinism. It challenges the rational objectification of both historic and cyclic time.[49] Time as intrinsic to human existence, especially that of the faith perspective, is too intensely personal to be so treated. The supreme example lies in the Christ who came "in the fullness of time" (Galatians 4:4; cf. Ephesians 1:10). While very much in the world of time, he was not of it; while involved in a temporal human existence, he was identified with an eternal Kingdom. Berdyaev states, "Thus the appearance of Jesus Christ is the meta-historical event *par excellence*. It took place in existential time but it broke through into the historical. . . ."[50]

171

In view of this temporal plenitude, a kind based upon faith in the God who disturbs and enters history, historical existence becomes both "conservative and revolutionary." Instead of negating history, Christ redeems it by revealing the God Who comes to man that man may return to God. The faith moments which see this belong to a "fullness" which spells out the redemption of time. Eternity thus qualifies *chronos* with the fullness which converts it into *kairos*. The eternity which accounts for this thereby entails not only time's alpha but also its omega. This links *kairos* not only with *chronos* in general, but with the *eschaton*. Berdyaev, therefore, can say, "It is possible for the world to enter into an eschatological era, into the times of the Paraclete." [51]

Thus, the *eschaton* implies a Kingdom which not only is present but is to be fulfilled. Linked with history, it transforms it as it transcends it. In this light Berdyaev can say, "Time does not contain history, yet . . . eternity moves out into time, and time moves out into eternity." [52] The so-called eschatological era to which Berdyaev gives frequent reference in his later works is a matter of special meaning to the faith community while also of temporal and cultural significance, for it is the terrestrial-temporal prelude, as it were, to the eternal fulfillment and transfiguration in the *eschaton*. This makes the End relevant to men of faith *now*, and in such a way as to inspire and direct the faithful on this side of eternity without condoning a mere "building of the Kingdom" on man's own idealistic terms. It calls for more than a utopian pattern for men to strive to fulfil, since is is based on the divine *ekstasis* essential to *kairos*. And what makes for the latter but the Spirit-with-spirit encounters conditioned by divine Grace and human freedom.

Berdyaev sees the prophetic character and plenitude of time, because he sees the relation of eternity to both the present and the future end. This is something which the sundry idealisms of history and the process teleologies we have considered could not allow. As one who sees both the temporal and supratemporal aspects of the end, Berdyaev vivifies our critique previously set forth of the teleologies of time when he states,

It is very important to establish the truth that there is an antithesis between teleology and eschatology as there is be-

172

tween teleology and creativeness. A consistent teleological view of the world recognizes a definite aim to which everything is subordinated, but it excludes an end, it makes an end unnecessary. The world ought to come to an end precisely because there is in the world no perfect conformity of purpose, in other words there is no complete conformity with the Kingdom of God.[53]

This is also an illustration of how Berdyaev stands between the philosopher and the theologian carrying on a conversation with both. The cross-fertilization of thought which this involves is very significant. As a religious philosopher he sees how theology must supply the answers to philosophy's ultimate questions, which it leaves unanswered. Berdyaev is a philosopher *qua* man and as such does not park his faith but sees how it is essential to his own existential situation. One could almost characterize his thought by saying that he deals with the realistic end of time, philosophically, while pointing to the eternal dimension of that end, theologically.

Yet this is not the whole truth, since Berdyaev sees the Bible protecting both the vertical and horizontal aspects of the end. This does much to keep the end to which he looks closely allied to the meaning of the existential present, which is the basic moment in which one lives. Existence is one's own existence, and one's very own existence persistently meets with the question of destiny. Kierkegaard saw the self asking such questions as: "Who am I? Where did I come from? Where am I going? Why wasn't I consulted?" [54] Authentic existence faces up to such questions and demands an answer of personal significance. This is something that objective theories including the cosmic teleologies of time cannot offer men. If anything, they tend to sweep the questioner aside or absorb him in their schemes.

As an existentialist of sorts Martin Heidegger is also sensitive to this subjective perspective, but his view is not one which chooses to deal with the eternal and eschatological dimensions of time. His view of destiny leaves him obsessed with the idea of death as the end, an idea not to be set aside to be sure. But for him death is a mere "nothingness" toward which all men are swept and which should be stoically accepted. Heidegger's thought is chronically steeped with the evil aspect of time, making the problems of anxiety and death the total significance of time. Man's *Dasein*, his "being there" in a concrete existence into which he has been thrown, is a matter of perennial despair. It moves only toward a deathly end, which proves itself the be-all and end-all of existence.[55] This end is solely the end of a person's own existence in linear time, and is seen to have no relationship to eternity. It is hardly attached in any way to a linear time of the world or a cyclic time of the cosmos, which for Berdyaev also pertains to the existing person-subject.

Heidegger portrays the basic alternative to any fideistic position which takes seriously an eternity significant to the problem of destiny and the end. This again calls to mind what Immanuel Kant said: Only a transcendent theology can give us eternity.[56] Berdyaev reckons with this without seeing eternity as though so transcendent that it is utterly remote. On the contrary, it becomes exceedingly pertinent to the "me" of existence who seeks the meaning of both his existence and destiny.

Existentially, then, Heidegger and Berdyaev pose the big alternative. "To exist is to choose," said Kierkegaard,[57] and this is as apropos to the fundamental interpretations of life as to many of its ethical and practical problems. The choice of faith which Berdyaev represents makes the end far more than either a *finis* or *telos*. For Heidegger the end is only the *finis* of death; for the teleologists it is the *telos* of a cosmic process. Neither has much room for a freedom of spirit for, unlike Berdyaev, they demand that man capitulate to necessity without a basic choice. While Berdyaev does not seek to escape this problem, he sees an eternal freedom qualifying a necessitated human existence. In fact, for Berdyaev the basic tension and duality of life is that of freedom versus necessity, the primary issue in all ethical and metaphysical thought.

The eschatological nature of time is enhanced by its powerful plenitude derived from the *kairoi* of faith, worship and related moral decisions and acts of creativeness which bring something new into the world. In such great moments the individual may be almost oblivious to the passing of a disintegrated, measured or binding time. The light of eternity pierces the darkness of all prosaic and rythmical time. Sheer *chronos,* while real to Berdyaev, neither defines nor exhausts such filled moments. Though time is a "decomposed eternity," it is not sheer non-Being. It is salvageable and can be transformed by an Eternity whose Spirit regenerates what man's sinful consciousness degenerates. *Chronos* belongs to man's Becoming and needs to be regenerated by the eternal as does the man whose time it is. "In a detached instant of time [*chronos*] man could never attain to the plenitude of experience and knowledge, the breadth of vision which would make him consciously assume responsibility for eternity." [58] Only the vibrant moments of *kairos*, which is as eternal as it is temporal, can redeem man's dull and enslaving *chronos* or salvage it from meaninglessness and relate it to the end so as to make for a destiny.

Paradoxically, the eschatological plenitude or intensity of time belongs to existential moments neither alien to, nor absorbed by eternity, but present with it.[59] In keeping with this, Berdyaev notes of the filled moments of creativity and decision that ". . . freedom which operates in historical time has its roots in existential time." [60] Here we begin to see one of the most basic factors in the eschatological orientation of ethical problems. While it is not our intent to expound this here, the matter of motives based upon a faith perspective in the eternal is of far-reaching consequence.

Only in this way, however, can a new era of religious virility be anticipated by the Church and a new era of cultural creativeness come about in a society which heeds her message. More than chronological on the one hand, and more than transcendental on the other, such an age presupposes these great moments of spiritual vitality related to, but also above, history or *chronos*, Berdyaev states, "The new aeon does not simply belong to the other world, to the other side of the grave. . . . It is also our world enlightened and transfigured and which has become creatively free." [61] It is such a revolutionary shift of emphasis, we believe, which can make more common time uncommon and put a much-needed eschatological stamp upon our culture and civilization, even as it demands that our theology be such that it makes this possible without secular over-accommodations.

In order to be meaningful, the future must be seen as something realistically deserving our anticipation while also related to the *eschaton*. From the standpoint of the present moment of *kairos*, such a future is highly relevant *now* while still a matter of an anticipated end. Faithwise such an end belongs now to

175

eternity, while experientially it has yet to be realized among men, even men of such faith. An unfulfilled destiny still implies an element of futurity, while this must be seen in relation to the *eternal now* to be of eschatological consequence. Simply to negate the reality of time, including the future, demands that we negate the man at the center of time, whose time it is. Nor is it enough to say with some contemporary theologians like Rudolf Bultmann, with a narrower existential perspective than that of Berdyaev, that the *end is now,* since that end belongs to the eternal God who is now.[62] As strong an insight as this may be, it must be realized that such an end to which we are privileged to be related by faith does not account for the unfulfilled aspect of the end even for the man of faith, whose faith does not remove him from existence but drives him back to it to live more authentically than he otherwise would.

There is a hopeful aspect to the present, which means that it pertains also to the future. This prevents the future from being altogether perverse simply because what the hope signifies is not fully actualized in the present. It is the existential moment which makes that hope real. Hope always involves the future from the perspective of the present. The end to which the Christian hope looks involves the present look upward as well as forward. Thus a present hope implies that the end is both temporal and eternal. The moment of *kairos,* then, includes a hope not only of eternal reality and potentiality but of an expected actuality in some form. This is to look to the *eschaton.* Berdyaev expresses the tension and basis for this most shrewdly when he states the following:

> The end is the conquest of both cosmic time and historical time. . . . But existential time, which has its roots in eternity, remains, and it is in existential time that the end of things takes place. This will be the entrance into a new aeon. This is not yet eternity, which men still try to objectivize. The sharp line which marks the frontier between the here and the beyond will be obliterated.[63]

Thus it is the existential *kairos* which implies genuine hope, for it is linked with *the eternal now,* to which the unfulfilled end of time is eschatologically relevant. It means hope not only in the world beyond but for this world, with the latter dependent upon the former.

The end amounts to a paradox, a spiritual mystery based upon a *kairos* not alien to future *chronos*.[64] This is the uniqueness of *eschaton*. It would not be the case, however, were history an endless stream absorbed by the cosmic process of *durée* and cyclic time. Historic time must be *given* significance not only from its future end but from its supratemporal end. The latter qualifies it and gives it a higher dimension, since the meaning of history or historic time is not immanent to itself.[65] "The paradox of time leads to this," says Berdyaev, "that the end of the world is always near. . . . And at the same time is projected upon the future and tells of the coming of an apocalyptic era." [66]

In speaking of an "apocalyptic era" Berdyaev essentially means what we have already set forth, but with the symbolic stress upon the need for the divine transfiguration as something from beyond man. Revealed truth and the complement of divine activity are essential to the paradox of the end and its relevance to human existence in this world. "The mystery of religious life remains inexplicable without the *coexistence of unity and duality,* without the meeting of the two natures and their fusion without *loss of distinction*." [67] This is fundamental to the whole time-eternity relationship and more specifically to the existential *kairos* and *eschaton*. Only a "symbolic language" limited to neither a monism nor a dualism of an ontological nature can express this. Not a rational theory, it might better be expressed as an existential dualism, while in its pneumatological connotations it has much in common with the neo-Platonic scheme discussed above.

"The relationship between man and God is paradoxical," Berdyaev stresses, "and cannot at all be expressed in concepts." [68] This is something which theological Scholasticisms and immanental "modernisms" have overlooked or resisted to great degrees. Paradoxically, man is not rationally a "synthesis of the finite and the infinite," as Kierkegaard also saw. He is a being living on the "frontier between two worlds." [69] But only as these contrasting factors of the time-eternity relation are recognized and interrelated accordingly, can men of concrete existence

177

know a meaningful destiny. The end, then, is both temporal and eternal, while in the highest ultimate sense, as we shall see, it belongs to eternity.

We would describe the paradox hailed by Berdyaev as a "both/ and tension" with similarity to, yet important difference from, Kierkegaard's "either/or." Dialectically, Kierkegaard represents an extreme Kantian reaction from the dialectical synthesis of Hegel, whereas the dialectics of Berdyaev might be characterized as between Kant and Hegel. Can either a rational synthesis or a stringent dualistic dichotomy represent a real tension? Can either reflect a true paradox? We think not. Berdyaev has the stronger dialectic and in this respect is more existential and descriptive than those of either extreme.

The Existential End and the Meaning of History

A new understanding of history is much needed today. If history is to have meaning, it cannot be self-contained. Since it fails also to gain real meaning from a process teleology, the only possibility is that of an eschatological perspective. A meaning for history must involve a destiny for men who are its subjects.

Inasmuch as the problem of destiny is attributable to human existence, it pertains also to history. We have seen how process philosophies and cosmic time with its necessitativeness cannot account for history and how the cosmic *telos* cannot do justice to the meaning of the end. For Berdyaev, however, the meaning of history does not stem from either the cosmic *telos* or historical *finis, per se,* but from existential time and its eschatological dimension or *eschaton,* the end of history linked not only with the cosmic end but with the End in eternity. Men cannot rise above the fatalism of cosmic time in favor of a destiny relevant to their moral freedom in existence without seeing the end of history related to eternity.[70] Only this awareness can provide an antidote to temporal frustrations and fears amplified by a necessitative cosmic rhythm.[71] Only as the end is seen to be the *eschaton* in which eternity has invested itself can this weakness be overcome. Christ is the Key to the Kingdom who unlocks in moments of *kairos* the meaning of the Kingdom's *eschaton* of hope for man's existence and destiny. As St. Paul says, "Christ is our hope" (I Timothy 1:1).

To say that history's end *is* the existential moment without relating it to the future is inadequate. This is the tendency among one-sided existential theologians like Rudolf Bultmann under the influence of Kierkegaard and Heidegger. An "open future" does not complete the meaning of history and human existence related to all the tenses of time, and the future is an important eschatological matter for both the meaning of destiny and the meaning of the Kingdom. The *eschaton* is a supratemporal goal belonging to the eternal now, but not without relation to its temporal medium and consequence, including the temporal *finis* or *telos* of time. "Time must have a stop," said Shakepeare's Hotspur.[72] To be existential such a halt must be *at* while *above* history's *finis*. Thus history ends as *Historie* but is consummated through a fulfilled Kingdom terrestrially as well as celestially and taken up into eternity in the *eschaton*. History will have a realistic end, while simultaneously being transfigured into the ultimate end of eternity.

But a problem arises right here. Berdyaev provides for the end of time in a way that makes it clear that it ends for man. But does time end for God? At this point Berdyaev is not clear, if he raises and reckons with the question at all. While we see a latent answer in his provocative doctrine of "celestial time," Berdyaev errs in failing to see or failing to express it overtly. Logically, Berdyaev should say that time *ends* as sheer linear *chronos* but upon being transfigured in the *eschaton* amounts to a kind of *kairos*-within-eternity, that is, "God's time" or time as relevant to Him from the standpoint of its fulfillment and redemption. This follows through on celestial history's dynamic capacity to cope with man's time. A parallel is seen in Karl Barth's view of time within eternity as discussed in the previous chapter, save for the fact that Barth will not concede that the time of concern to God is in any way man's time.

Berdyaev allows for the eschatological resolution, consummation and transfiguration of time and history in their "return" to eternity at the end of the world and the close of the Christian interim between the revealing of the End in the Christ Event and its actual fulfillment in the transfiguring End. A strong factor here is that through the transfiguration of time and its eternal counterpart in "celestial history," Berdyaev retains the identity of men in the mystical "return" to eternal communion with

God. The unity-in-duality seen in the End as well as in the dynamic character of eternity prevents Berdyaev's mysticism from being a Greek concept of immortality, a loss of individuality in an everlasting "blur." It preserves the element of communion.

History gains meaning through the *kairos*, its core of eternal and redemptive significance, and from the *eschaton*, its ultimate goal. The latter implies that the end is not just *finis* or *telos*, as we have seen, but purposive consummation and goal. This gives the man of faith a higher sense of vocation in life. Destiny and vocation are now interrelated. This in turn affects history as it affects men whose history it is. Berdyaev could say with eschatological depth, "The philosophy of history is above all a philosophy of time." [73] A philosophy which neglects this is in error, as is a theology which is too transcendent to do justice to the problem of time.

But history's meaning, for Berdyaev, stems from a sacred history which is profoundly eschatological. Without common "history" we cannot speak intelligibly of a "sacred history" unless it be a kind of "celestial history" oblivious to *chronos*, which Berdyaev does not subscribe to, since *kairos* and *eschaton* are not altogether removed from it. Contemporary theologians who speak of *Heilsgeschichte* as the biblical basis for redemption should remember this. If *Heilsgeschichte* is held to have no connection with *Historie* through a vital Spirit-filled and faith-qualified *Geschichte*, they debilitate the meaning and redemptive significance of the *Heilsgeschichte* to which they look. They might just as well identify it with a celestial history of the kind which, for Karl Barth, is strictly God's time and, therefore, alien to man *qua* man of concrete temporal existence.

But, from Berdyaev's standpoint, unless the linear time factor of history is retained, however deficient it is, the dynamic present of the existential moment would be strictly the eternal Now of God with no relation to men and history as men know it. Such a weakness is seen in the Kierkegaardian version of existential time, which has left its deep-seated imprint on Barthian thought. James D. Collins lends support to our observation here when he says,

By distinguishing so sharply between ordinary historical events and the unique paradoxical event, Kierkegaard establishes a cleavage at the heart of history which he does not attempt to bridge and which, perhaps, he thinks neither can nor ought to be bridged. . . . The contemporaneity of each individual believer with Christ tends to cancel out the ordinary historical process and abandon to meaningless triviality the secular generations and their travail. The Incarnation does not become for Kierkegaard, as it did for Augustine, the central reality in and for all history, lending it sense and direction and a motive principle.[74]

This goes back to S. K.'s failure to keep both eternity and history real while existentially related. Berdyaev improves upon this by keeping the two in relation without jeopardizing the reality and role of either. This again points to our claim that Berdyaev's existentialism is superior.

In a certain sense Porret is right in describing Berdyaev's view of history as "an interior epoch of eternity," [75] but it is only as eternity breaks through existentially to qualify history and its end.[76] This challenges the notion of the historic end seen earlier in our examination of Hegel's theory of "the eternal now" in which only the eternal whole is real and, consequently, successive time and history lost or obscured in the universal and immanent process of attainment. Hegel's rational end, while teleological, is not truly eschatological. It fails to keep the end, history and eternity, both real and in vital relation.[77] Such a deficiency is to be expected of an ontological monism of ultra-rational dialectic and scope. But, should such be expected of an existential dualism adapted to the expression of the Christian revelation?

At this point S. K.'s dialectic is closer to Hegel's than is readily perceived, inasmuch as he, too, leaves us with an unreal *chronos*, even as he accentuates the "eternal now" unto the near abrogation of time. Yet we have seen similar defects, to varying degrees, in the positions assumed by Plato, Aquinas, Kant and Barth. Either of these ontologies, dualistic or monistic, comes up with something seriously defective in the time-eternity relationship.[78] But Berdyaev allows us to capitulate to neither the Hegelian nor Kierkegaardian extreme. He sees that to dissolve the tenses is to deny the reality of history, let alone a meaningful history and its end.

181

Berdyaev, while stressing the existentiality of the present moment under the eternal Now, safeguards the realistic past and future, history and its end, in relation thereto. He says that history is a struggle which existentially includes a dialogue between man and God. While much of history is inauthentic, unexistential and enslaved to pseudo time,[79] there are momentous existential events which interrupt the historical series to give it rich meaning and destiny-making significance.[80] The coming of Christ, we might say, was the supreme such event which even caused Western history to turn a corner. While this is of subordinate significance to Christ's eschatological message and redemptive role, Jean Paul Richter, a Swiss writer, was not altogether wrong when he said of Christ: "He lifted the doors of history from their hinges and turned the course of history into new channels."

We cannot be blind to this. But it was because Christ himself was the true "hinge of history" that his followers were accused of "turning the world upside down" (Acts 17:6). [81a] A realistic, chronological history takes on a new and higher dimension because of the unique Christ Event. Sacred history qualifies the secular as it uses it. The Church, despite its many historic faults, has helped realize this through its distinctive message, fellowship and vocation. Thus we see the strength of Berdyaev's position, for it retains the reality and role of historic time while related to a dynamic eternity. This is fundamental, we believe, to a mature Christian philosophy of history. To be Christian it must be eschatological, and this implies the Christ who *relates* eternity to time in order to redeem it.

Napoleon was wrong in saying that history is but "a fable agreed upon," and Henry Ford in calling it "bunk." Berdyaev helps us see it can have meaning, purpose, direction, goal. While he concedes that the cyclic factor of cosmic time is apparent in history, it need not be interpreted fatalistically. This challenges the pessimistic view of history held by Otto Spengler, whose biological view of cyclic rhythm is fatalism at its worst. History for Berdyaev is a drama moving toward a climax, with man a free spirit at the heart of its tragedy and comedy.[81b] Yet there is a rhythm of cultural development recognizable in history, and no culture is "immune from decadence." [82] Though Berdyaev sees, with Spengler, certain "biological stages" of development, he does not regard them to be necessitative or fatalistic in the manner of Spengler. Spiritual transfiguration in terms of existential moments looking to the End can give new birth to the creative freedom of human culture; therefore, Berdyaev rightly maintains that Spengler's pessimism is not the last word about civilization and history.

While men exist in relation to cosmic time they can rise above it.[83] It need not spell sheer fate or doom. Berdyaev says that a civilization must sometimes die to be reborn,[84] but a cultural recrudescence based on a spiritual and eschatological outlook is essential to this cultural resurrection.[85] Only as history is seen to have a meaningful end can it experience "its denouement and catharsis." [86] It was Hebrew Messianism rather than Greek logic which gave men a spiritual *Weltanschauung* that made possible the very philosophy of history.[87] A scientific view of history is inadequate,[88] even as objectified ideas of the future adapted to the evolutionary principle become perversions of the end, as reflected in Marxism.[89] Inevitable decadence on the one hand, and inevitable progress on the other, are both deficient notions. One generation is neither the "assassin" of the next nor its "fertilizer" by necessity.

The outcome of terrestrial history need not be limited to the conditions of common time when seen to be reintegrated with celestial history. Its tragedy, wherein man is enslaved to common time and its measurements, can be redirected through a spiritual "catharsis." [90] This is basic to the "new aeon of the spirit." As Berdyaev states,

> We must admit within the hermetic circle of history the super-historical energy, the irruption within the relations of terrestrial phenomena of the celestial noumenon—the future coming of Christ. This concept of the ineluctable end of history is at once the final conclusion and fundamental premise of the metaphysics of history.[91]

Again, existential time or *kairos* is essential to the eschatological meaning of history, for it is the "irruption of eternity into time, an irruption in cosmic and historic time," which makes for what Berdyaev describes as "an addition to and fulfillment of time." [92] This makes history meaningful upon becoming more than evo-

183

lutionary or necessitative. While it ties *Historie* to an intensely personal *Geschichte,* it is a *Heilsgeschichte* which includes eternal destiny. The clue here is the Christ of the End, who is the Christ of the present to men of history committed to his eternal Presence, which embraces the past as well as the future.

The Existential End and the Meaning of Progress

Berdyaev saw that the modern idea of progress has been borrowed from Judaeo-Christian eschatology.[93] The latter was secularized and de-existentialized, as it were, as Western man's Hellenic logic became hog-tied to the common time of history and especially the cyclic time of nature. This sterilized the biblical view of time's meaning in eternity. But the Greek concept of cyclic time adapted to evolutionary theories in modern process philosophy and positivism can account for neither progress nor history itself.[94] Blind, amoral cosmic forces of nature are oblivious to a goal.[95] While the linear view of progress adhered to by humanism, Spencerian optimism and "progressive religion" is closer to history than evolutionary views of process philosophy, it, too, is deficient, for it keeps the end strictly–within common history.

If progress is to be a tenable idea it must mean that "development implies potential existence." [96] Progress relates the present to the future, but Berdyaev also shows that it includes a creative development of culture subsumed under a supratemporal End which is also intratemporal. The moral and spiritual development of man is by no means a cosmic necessity, while neither is it mere secular history. This again challenges any attempt to adapt eschatology to a process teleology such as undertaken by D. D. Williams in his work *God's Grace and Man's Hope.*[97] Cultural progress under spiritual inspiration rather implies "a transcendent principle of intervention," a matter of transfiguration[98] stemming from *kairos* and *eschaton,* not mere *telos.* This marks the main difference between culture and civilization.[99] It also demands a "transvaluation of values" [100] in view of a purpose and end from above history. A naive futurism is inadequate; thus linear idea of progress is condemned by Berdyaev along with an evolutionary optimism. Arnold Toynbee joins Berdyaev at this point, saying that real progress is spiritual and looks beyond cyclic and linear time.[101] While not accounting for it religiously, Pitirim Sorokin, the Harvard sociologist, acknowledges the need of the spiritual factor in his sociological formula of the cultural rhythm of civilization. He sees it as: Crisis—Ordeal—Catharsis—Charisma—Resurrection.[102]

The evolutionary notion of progress is often adapted to the idea of a terrestrial Utopia as in Marxism. But Berdyaev sees a perfect existence impossible within common time and history; it demands the end of history. While Berdyaev is accused of pessimism because of this,[103] he sees real pessimism to be the sequel to the false assumption that perfection is immanent to human imperfection.[104] Ironically, despair is really written into a superficial optimism. Berdyaev condemns the false secular ideas of progress, but he does not say there has been no progress in civilization.[105] To be genuine, however, progress demands an eschatological orientation, something superior to either a natural or idealistic *telos*. An unending history is meaningless.[106] This does not mean that Berdyaev renounces this world, as F. H. Heinemann erroneously claims,[107] but would see it transfigured, culturally reborn and eschatologically fulfilled from above itself. *The co-inherence of history and eternity*[108] *are needed to inspire creative acts which make for a true cultural progress linked with destiny.*

All this calls for faith in a divine edification, not just in moral acts. "Modern 'activism' is a negation of the eternal," says Berdyaev, "the enslavement of man to the temporal. The moment is not of value having relationship to eternity or God." [109] But if men look to a higher time and a higher end, even "technics can be oriented to the service of God. . . ." [110] But a profane, impersonal mechanization of life does not spell true progress.[111] An axiological quality of culture must come from beyond civilization's timestream or nature's rhythmic process and man's expediencies. This demands an active, creative eschatology, not a mere struggle in linear time or surrender to an evolutionary process, lest all human existence be transitory and meaningless.[112] Here Berdyaev thinks as a real prophet should.

Berdyaev is neither a pessimist nor an optimist.[113] We ask: Should a mature Christian view of life ever be either? Should it not be what Paul Tillich calls a "belief-ful realism," [114] an ability to face existence as it is while drawing hope from a trans-

185

cendence which makes itself relevant to all of life and culture? While Harold Laski accepts Berdyaev's idea of the contemporary turning-point in Western history, he labels him an "escapist." [115] But, unlike Berdyaev, Laski, a Marxian, fails to see the logical despair implicit in a futuristic optimism. Actually, Berdyaev does not abandon the world nor its history, as we have come to see, but accepts them and points them to their eschatological source of significance and redemption, a matter highly relevant to a religiously orientated culture. Laski does not see how the Hegelian dialectic adapted to the Marxian materialism leaves much to be desired. Basically, it leaves the existing man, as Bobbio puts it, "a speck of dust in the whirlwind of Universal History." [116]

Berdyaev's view faces up to the tragedy within history while keeping existence hopeful in more than materialistic terms. His case is intellectually justified. Today it is really the humanistic, evolutionary optimist who has come to despair. H. G. Wells is an example of this. Without seeing any real meaning to history [117] he was for many years very optimistic about modern man's future. [118] But at the age of 65 he came to say, "The human story has already come to an end. . . ." [119] George Bernard Shaw is another such example. Shaw has at least confessed that men of this age might well go back and listen to one Jesus of Nazareth. Would that they would if they could! As W. Macneile Dixon has stated in his Gifford Lectureship, "Even the believers in unlimited progress, that childlike and charming nineteenth-century creed, are beginning to have their doubts." [120] Indeed, they have failed to see that history is more than so many passing events. To be of meaning history must be seen belonging to "History!" It lacks meaning without a meaning-giving End that is as eternal as it is temporal.

In looking at the contemporary world crisis, Berdyaev sees rightly that " a whole historical epoch is closing and a new epoch is beginning." [121] The crisis centers in the depletion of a humanistic time-enslaved culture and secularized idea of progress. Renaissance humanism has begun to destroy itself by its own dialectic, severing man from the supratemporal source of his dignity, a dignity which it borrowed from revealed religion only to derogate it. This, we believe, is the very locus of the contemporary Western crisis. Failure to see time having a meaning which relates the past and future in the present is also basic to this crisis. A meaningful time is needed if progress is to be more than a fictitious dream. It must be returned to its original orientation in eschatology. In view of the New Testament principles of time and its end, the yoke of natural necessity must be thrown off together with modern man's optimistic halo of self-sufficiency. Humanism has severed itself from the source of freedom and dignity recovered through the Reformation and Renaissance. Its notion of inevitable progress has burst like a soap bubble. As one scientist is known to have said, "The superman built the airplane, but the ape-man got ahold of it!" Yet, if modern man returns by faith to the center of history's meaning, Berdyaev believes, he can experience a "new middle ages," i.e., a new era of spiritual life and cultural resurgence.[122]

But in saying this Berdyaev risks being misunderstood. He does not mean a new age of ecclesiastical domination, a dream of Roman Catholicism, but an age of faith-guided culture. Even so, it calls for a spiritual "aristocracy" to lead the way, an idea comparable to that of Plato in his *Republic*. This calls for an eschatological perspective on all things, a profound regard for the meaning of time and the end of history. *At the center of life must be a spiritual* Weltanschauung *based on existential time and its end.*[123] The revealed eternal end must qualify the temporal means. This is not an escapism, but the very clue to the meaning of man's existence, destiny and true progress. Without it the sacred elements of culture are not born to direct and redeem a secular civilization, the one being qualitative, the other quantitative.[124] A time of crisis—such a time as this—is the opportune time for men to reappraise these matters unto the possible rebirth of spiritual culture and the recovery of the eschatological meaning of history and progress.

The End and the Meaning of Eschatology

From various angles we have come to see through the religious philosophy of Berdyaev that *existential time has an eschatological dimension which gives an eternal quality to the end while not refuting either the reality of history and time related thereto or reducing the redemptive dynamic of eternity itself.* Just as *kairos* embraces a realistic *chronos*, redemptively, so

187

eschaton embraces a realistic *finis* and *telos*. This is fundamental to time's eschatological dimension. It is germane to our thesis that, more than other existential theories, Berdyaev's view keeps both time and eternity real while in vital relation. This is a relation belonging to the tension and paradox of existence. It is because of this that Berdyaev sees the importance of "historical Christianity" yielding to "eschatological Christianity." [125] Needing symbolic expression, just as the symbol of *kairos* is found in the Incarnation, the symbol of *eschaton* is to be seen in the Apocalypse.

Paul Tillich joins Berdyaev in accentuating the importance of existential time as the seat of history's meaning. It is what he calls "qualitatively fulfilled time." It is *kairos*, "fullness of time" or "decisive time" as found in the N. T., and is opposed to a Platonic "timeless *Logos.*" *Kairos*, Tillich says, is "time disturbed by eternity"; it reveals the *Logos* to *chronos*.[126] The *eschaton* is "the ultimate" or "the transcendent meaning implied in history." Tillich also points out that history in this sense does not necessarily mean "development," while it may do so. Like Berdyaev, Tillich rejects the ideas of humanistic progress and Utopia, since they locate the meaning of history within secular history itself. He stands again with Berdyaev in rejecting the idea that a mythological end, what to Berdyaev is the symbol of the Apocalypse, can be left unrelated to history itself. Like Berdyaev he sees the past and the future to be realities immanent in the present, existentially, through a person's remembrance and expectation of events. Eschatologically, every event is related to an ultimate fulfillment.[127] "There is nothing in the ultimate," says Tillich, "which is not in history. *In the ultimate there is no fulfillment that is not intended in history.*" [128] While perhaps a bit intemperate in its omniscient manner of expression, this supports Berdyaev's idea that the end is both future and eternal in the *eschaton,* while the completely fulfilled end is in eternity.[129] History both ends and is fulfilled.

In contrast to the view of Oscar Cullmann who places Christ at the center of horizontal history as the Messianic mark of the BC—AD division,[130] Tillich further stands with Berdyaev when he states, "The center of history is the place where the meaning-giving principle of history is seen." [131] From this center the beginning and the end are determined and correlated. The event of eternity's invasion into time, Berdyaev maintains, is the center of meaningful time, and Tillich concurs that the end is "the goal" of that for which the distinctive event is the center. For the Christian, Christ is "the center of history in which beginning and end, meaning and purpose of history are constituted." [132]

But this "center" is not simply in common history as it is for Oscar Cullmann. It comes alive in the existential moment for the person committed to Christ by faith, even as the great Event to which it looks was a person committed to the eternal source of truth. Thus Christ as the center is the "unconditioned condition within history." The significance of this for eschatology and history's meaning is that history is "sacramental," since Christ *has come*; and *now* history is prophetic since Christ as the end *is coming*.[133] Tillich also says that history has "a suprahistorical end," the *Parousia*, and an "inter-historical end," which allows for a victory over evil in time through the reign of Christ. This blends with Berdyaev's position. By this Tillich means to retain the reality of time in the *eschaton* so that, in a manner similar to the position taken by Berdyaev, world history can be "the fragmentary actualization of salvation." [134] To Berdyaev this is the "terrestrial" Kingdom at the end of history or what he speaks of symbolically as Christ's Second Coming.[135]

Unless the future end is regarded as a moment of linear, historical time the idea of existential time as *kairos* is of little significance to the Christian idea of *eschaton*. The one belongs to the present, epistemologically, the other to the future. Though deficient as time, the end is related to a redeeming eternity. Were there no real time side to the end, today's man of faith would be living this very moment in the End identified with Christ and his Kingdom, actually and terrestrially, mind you, not just potentially.[136] This should be the case, it seems, if the more one-sided existential time of Kierkegaard and the concept of eternity held by Barth were correct.

While the Christian lives by faith in the eternal Now, there is a temporal problem here which cannot be bypassed. We see it also in the New Testament itself among the Synoptists and St. Paul, who struggle to express and reconcile the present and future aspects of the Kingdom.[137] The future aspect of the end is not to be dismissed or minimized, we deduce, so long as redeemed men do not live fully in the end, i.e., in its purely eternal aspect. Otherwise, references to the end of time are opaque. The *finis* or *telos* of time is consequential to eschatology, and will be until its transfiguration into the very bosom of eternity. While the Christian is by faith living in relation to the "eternal now" of God, he does not live in the bosom of eternity, actually, but "gracefully," so to speak. He believes with St. Paul in the "age to come" but he lives primarily in the "present age." [138] The latter is faithwise the "new age," but unfulfilled. This is the tension which is even reflected in a Christian's existence and is not resolved this side of his eternal immortality. While the eternal now is real and vital to him, so is the time to which his existential moments pertain. If not, he should be at the portals of heaven now!

While the Fourth Gospel sees the *presence* of eternal life, it bespeaks John's Platonic form of theology that he should tone down the time side of the eschatological problem, which is so basic to the earlier written Synoptics and the epistles of Paul.[139] Rudolf Bultmann has catered to Johannine eschatology while being prone to remove the Christian's faith from this very tension of time and eternity.[140] But this may be too extreme. Berdyaev sees that the end that is present to eternity is not altogether extrinsic to the end that is future time. The refusal to acknowledge this may be an evasion of New Testament eschatology rather than its witness and vindication. Only as time is real even to the End is it redeemable to any eternal avail. Berdyaev projects this in *his existential view of the End, which sees it transcending history while also associated with it.*[141] The *eschaton* is the perfect existential moment at history's end, while taken up into eternity. This is the dynamic paradox of the time-eternity relationship which, we contend, keeps both elements significant and real while very much in relation.

The dynamic relation of the *ekstasis* and *kairos* to *eschaton* may be said to be the basis for Berdyaev's entire eschatology. Since it pertains not only to the redemption of history but also to the cosmos, the cosmic process is itself eschatological. It is regarded as *theosis*,[142] designating the ultimate return of all things of all time to God in eternity. Its symbol is Apocalypse.[143] While the first advent of Christ reveals time's meaning, the second advent symbolizes its fulfillment in "terrestrial history," the historical side of the Apocalyptic End.[144] These symbols are necessary to express the paradox and tension of the time-eternity relationship.[145]

In keeping with the idea of *theosis* Berdyaev, who, as we have seen rejects both monistic and dualistic ontology in favor of an ethical dualism of freedom *versus* necessity, does not hesitate to interpret the End as an *ultimate* monism, eschatologically speaking.[146] No rational or idealistic theory can handle the paradox involved in "the social and cosmic transfiguration and resurrection" [147] belonging to *eschaton* and the cosmic *theosis*. Here it is noteworthy that, despite his rigid dualism, Karl Barth holds a somewhat similar position. He concurs that eschatology calls for an *ultimate* monism.[148] This would appear essential to a monotheistic redemption. While Barth's metaphysical dualism may be said to apply to history [149] between the revealed and fulfilled end, he, like Berdyaev, sees a monism implied in the fulfilled end, where the act and purpose of God is executed and vindicated.

But we must assert that Barth can have an eschatological monism only because he peculiarly refuses to allow time to have any significance within man's historical existence; time belongs only to eternity. So if eschatology is ever regarded as a form of "escapism," it would be more easily ascribed to Barth than Berdyaev. Barth's eschatology is an artificial solution to his dualism. as we shall see, if it is any solution at all. It does not entail a transfiguration of history but removes itself from history. Berdyaev has in mind Thomism when he makes the following statement, but it would apply equally well, and even more so, to Barthian theology today:

> The conservative element in Christianity cannot tolerate even the idea of a potential creative energy, because, so far as it is concerned, everything has been finally actualized, and it almost looks as if men wanted to limit it for fear of its possibilities.[150]

This weakness is overcome by Berdyaev in his more dynamic type of eschatology, one which gives man, the redeemed man especially, an active and responsible role under the Grace of God and the influence of His Spirit.

But before closing this phase of our comparative study it is necessary to point to another defect in Berdyaev's own eschatology and view of time. It is this: In relating *theosis* to the End, it is questionable whether Berdyaev demonstrates *how* the cosmic *telos* is to be "transfigured" so as to be "theosized" into eternity *per se*. While Berdyaev asserts it, he does not clearly demonstrate what is involved. He is quite clear respecting what is involved in the relation of history to the *eschaton* but not so clear respecting what is involved in the relation of the cosmic process, with its cyclic time and *telos*, as pertaining to the *eschaton*. It would seem that the existential perspective is not applied satisfactorily here, though it is made clear that it includes the relevance of cyclic time to the concrete man. In view of Berdyaev's idea of a "fallen cosmos" besides a fallen man, something tantamount to the existential transfiguration of cosmic time and its *telos*, would very much be in order to complete his distinction between teleology and eschatology.

But how does a necessitative teleological rhythm enter into a moral and spiritual relation with the redemptive and dynamic *eschaton*? How is the cosmic process related to a spiritual redemption? Cosmically, where lies the transfiguring relationship? Does it center in man, since he is the seat of the existential perspective? Not entirely, it would appear, since God-manhood is the basic clue to eschatological transfiguration for Berdyaev. What is involved in the God-manhood of the symbolic Second Coming, then? Would it not have to imply a cosmic event, whatever else it is? Just what is the cosmic significance of a redemptive God-manhood in relation to the *eschaton* and *telos*? These questions remain unanswered. On the other hand, is it possible the questions are too rational in perspective?—thus constraining the eschatological answers which must remain mystical after all, quite like the basic meaning and understanding of the Incarnation and the work of the Holy Spirit? To answer the questions may be the counterpart to solving the mystery of divine creation and its relation to the cosmic process.

*   *   *   *

In this chapter we have come to see how modern process teleologies fall short of a meaningful *telos*. Needed is a suprarational dimension thereof, one which Berdyaev holds to by relating, in principle, the cosmic *telos* to the *eschaton*. Also, history is seen to have meaning through its eschatological tie with destiny. Progress likewise lacks a self-contained meaning. It must look to the end, an end which is not immanental while not totally transcendental either. The *eschaton* is a paradox which preserves the tension of existence even as it draws upon the paradox of revealed truth to both enunciate and resolve it. This keeps the understanding of time and history dependent upon eternity, while it is not obscured by it. It is superior to Barth's position, which only resolves the problem and meaning of time in heaven, as it were, and not on earth. Berdyaev powerfully shows how history is involved in the redemptive action of God, lest the purpose of creation be lost as focused in man. There is an end which is not sheer *finis* but purposive goal, and only as it is attained under God does time *per se* come to a *finis*.

We have seen how Kairos is a wondrous isle of destiny as well as salvation. Having kept our perspective aligned with both her horizontal and vertical extremities, we have found them to be as two-in-one, not identical but interrelated. Cross-like, this meeting point is her distinctive eschatological dimension. Since we learn of it in terms of revealed symbols, we can move closer to her Apocalyptic apex to discover that what adorns Kairos is an eternal sheen reflecting a Kingdom from above. It reminds us of Christ's Mount of Transfiguration, a sublime revelatory moment not unrelated to his mission and kingly End.

NOTES

1 Spier, *Christianity and Existentialism*, p. 137.
2 Bergson, *Creative Evolution*, p. 2.
3 *Ibid.*, p. 5. "Consciousness cannot go through the same state twice."
4 *Ibid.*, p. 10. Cf. pp. 9, 21. Cf. *Time and Free Will*, pp. 114, 12, 152 and *Two Sources of Morality*, pp. 180, 220, 214f.

5 Bergson, *Time and Free Will*, p. 224.
6 *Creative Evolution*, pp. 15, 22.
7 *Ibid.*, p. 342.
8 *Ibid.*, p. 96. While the typical philosopher may not accept revelation, Bergson, not being rationalistic or materialistic, might have been more amenable to its place in his philosophy at this point. Berdyaev saw the need of revelation in philosophy even as "a trancendent event which philosophy can transform into an imminent datum." *Solitude and Society*, p. 5. Faith pertains to all knowledge. Cf. Lampert, *Christian Revolutionaries*, p. 335.
9 Berdyaev recognizes this also in *Solitude and Society*, p. 115.
10 *Creative Evolution*, pp. 23, 88.
11 *Time and Free Will*, pp. 181, 190, 221f, 232.
12 Cf. Berdyaev, *Der Sinn Des Schaffens*, pp. 32-34.
13 *Space-Time and Deity*, Vol. I, pp. 1-5. Cf. p. 345. Cf. Metz, *A Hundred Years of British Philosophy*, pp. 622-625.
14 *Ibid.*, p. 8.
15 *Ibid.*, pp. 10-20.
16 *Ibid.*, p. 35.
17 *Space-Time and Deity*, Vol. II, p. 357.
18 *Op. cit.*, Vol. I, pp. 336-339.
19 Alexander, "Space-Time," *Aristotelian Society Proceedings*, 1917-18, Vol. XVIII, pp. 410-418.
20 *Op. cit.* Vol. II, pp. 353, 343, 365. How strange that Alexander could postulate an abstract *a priori* like space-time, and yet refuse to postulate the God of creative spirit behind the universe! How audacious to postulate a *hula* which is even basic to God himself! Cf. Edwin Lewis, *God and Ourselves*, p. 58.
21 Whitehead, *Process and Reality*, Chap. II. May the writer add here a word of acknowledgement to Dr. Eric Mascall of Christ Church College, Oxford, for certain clarifications received from his 1949-50 lectureship on Whitehead's philosophy.
22 Whitehead, *The Concept of Nature*, p. 48ff. This is also fundamental to Einstein's theory of relativity. Cf. Whitehead, *Modes of Thought*, Pt. I, Lecture I.
23 *Process and Reality*, pp. 15-18.
24 *Modes of Thought*, Pt. II, Lecture II.
25 *Adventure of Ideas*, p. 141, quoted also in our Foreword, p. v.
26 Locke, *Essay Concerning Human Understanding*, Ch. XV, p. 91. "To conclude, expansion and duration do mutually embrace and comprehend each other . . ."
27 Rosenstock-Huessy, *The Christian Future*, p. 166. Cf. p. 173: "From Thales to Hegel all philosophy began its thinking with the world of space or the knowing mind and a corresponding logic of timeless abstractions, and time appeared consequently in foreshortened perspective, being considered primarily from a spatial point of view." As the offspring of philosophy, science followed suit.
28 Needham, *Time: The Refreshing River*, p. 240.
29 *Ibid.*, pp. 65, 71.
30 *Ibid.*, p. 73.
31 *Ibid.*, pp. 199, 184-200.
32 *Ibid.*, p. 240ff.
33 D. D. Williams in trying to communicate theologically rather over-accommodates process philosophy. He remains bogged down by his attempt to adapt his eschatology to an evolutionary process metaphysics. He fails to do justice to the supratemporal factor in eternity and the *ekstasis* in

Christ and the *eschaton*. Yet he sees with Berdyaev that God enters into relation with man in time. *God's Grace and Man's Hope,* pp. 116, 134f. See below, Chapter IX, p. 265f.

34 Carrel, *Man, the Unknown,* p. 197.
35 *Ibid.,* p. 237.
36 *Ibid.,* p. 262f.
37 *Ibid.,* p. 266. Cf. Carrel, *Prayer,* p. 50.
38 *Ibid.,* p. 320.
39 *Ibid.,* p. 176, Cf. pp. 163-177.
40 *Ibid.,* p. 177.
41 *Ibid.,* p. 187.
42 DuNoüy, *Human Destiny,* pp. 52, 43.
43 *Ibid.,* p. 26ff and Chapter II.
44 *Is God Out of Date?* pp. 23, 29, 33, and *Human Destiny,* p. 200.
45 *The Divine and the Human,* p. v.
46 Cf. note 74. Berdyaev saw the present as both temporal and eternal in existential time while shedding meaning on all time from that "Moment."
47 Mounier, *A Personalist Manifesto,* p. 70.
48 *The Beginning and End,* p. 206.
49 *Ibid.,* p. 166. Berdyaev allows for eternity's relation even to cosmic time. Cf. *Slavery and Freedom,* p. 260, but we are not shown just *how* this is done.
50 *Ibid.,* p. 167. Cf. p. 211.
51 *Ibid.*
52 *Ibid.,* p. 230. Cf. *Destiny of Man,* p. 289.
53 *Ibid.,* p. 185f.
54 Cf. S. Kierkegaard, *Repetition,* p. 114.
55 Heidegger, *Existence and Being,* pp. 25-31, 355-392, 40-66, 80-100. Heidegger overworks the evil aspect of time as born of anxiety, something also realized by Berdyaev but not restricted to that due to a person's innovation of time by creative activity as well. Cf. Berdyaev, *Destiny of Man,* pp. 145f, 147; *Solitude and Society,* pp. 98, 115, 120f, 133. Heidegger sees existence solely as a temporal *Dasein,* constant anxiety moving toward a meaningless end which spells only death. Erecting an ontology of the *is* of existence, he makes Being synonymous with a meaningless existence vitiated by evil time and nothingness. *Dasein* includes the dread of the cold fate of being-in-the-world, and the impersonal *Das Man* of being one-like-so-many together with the *Verfallen* of a fallen corrupt cosmos. But we might ask: From what is existence fallen, if there is no eternal order from which to fall? What matters the anxiety if the man who experiences it is of no more than temporal significance? Heidegger refuses to look beyond the muck of evil time and, being psychopathically obsessed with it, he fails to account for the source and the place of his own philosophical creativeness.
56 *Critique of Pure Reason,* p. 531.
57 Kierkegaard, *Either/Or,* Vol. II, pp. 150, 177, 194, 210, 216. (See above p. 110f.)
58 *Solitude and Society,* p. 111.
59 *Ibid.,* p. 112.
60 *Truth and Revelation,* p. 86.
61 *Ibid.,* p. 153.
62 Cf. Bultmann, *Jesus Christ and Mythology,* pp. 62, 64f, 69, 71f, 74, 77ff.
63 *The Divine and the Human,* p. 197.
64 *Spirit and Reality,* p. 163.
65 *The Divine and Human,* p. 168.
66 *The Beginning and End,* p. 233.

67 *Freedom and Spirit*, p. 189.
68 *The Realm of Spirit and the Realm of Caesar*, p. 36f. Cf. p. 190. *Truth and Revelation*, p. 82 and *Freedom and Spirit*, p. 189.
69 *Truth and Revelation*, p. 16.
70 Cf. Stanley R. Hopper, *The Crisis of Faith*, p. 302.
71 Berdyaev, "Fatality of Faith," *Christian Century*, Vol. 56, May 10, 1939, p. 603f.
72 Shakespeare, *King Henry IV*, Part 1, Act II, Scene 4. Aldous Huxley employs this as his theme in *Time Must Have a Stop*, p. 296f. Despite his "perennialism" we maintain that Huxley has some balanced pre-existential insights. He states, ". . . time must have a stop. And not only *must* as an ethical imperative and an eschatological hope, but also does have a stop in the indicative tense, as a matter of brute experience. It is only by taking the fact of eternity into account that we can deliver thought from its slavery to life. And it is only by deliberately paying our attention and our primary allegiance to eternity that we can prevent time from turning our lives into a pointless or diabolic foolery." *Op. cit.*, p. 297. Cf. p. 115f. While Huxley fails to acknowledge the existential clue of the Incarnate God-man and the meaning of the *ekstasis*, he sees eternity as the "eternal divine now," pp. 194, 190, 200.
73 *The Beginning and the End*, p. 205.
74 Collins, *The Mind of Kierkegaard*, p. 173. Cf. David F. Swenson, *Something About Kierkegaard*, p. 109. Swenson says that to Kierkegaard the Hegelian view of history was congenial to the extent that it apprehended history ". . . as if it had never been present or future; it interprets the heroes of the past as if they had never been alive . . ."
75 Porret, *La Philosophie Chrétienne en Russie*, p. 137.
76 *Truth and Revelation*, pp. 54, 88, 144. Cf. *Slavery and Freedom*, pp. 255, 260.
77 Hegel, "Introduction to the Philosophy of History," *Selections*, pp. 442, 440, 349-354. Cf. pp. 354-359.
78 Cf. Berdyaev, *Truth and Revelation*, p. 88; *Freedom and Spirit*, p. 190.
79 *Slavery and Freedom*, p. 256.
80 *Beginning and the End*, p. 166.
81a Richter reflected a nineteenth-century desire for a historical, hence secular, security concerning Christianity. Our position does not succumb to this, nor does it stand completely with Carl Michalson whose provocative work, *The Hinge of History*, is close to Bultmann's existential perspective. We maintain that the hinge is linked with its lapels or collars of *Historie* without being identified fully.
81b *The Meaning of History*, p. 28.
82 *Ibid.*, p. 194.
83 Cf. Berdyaev, *Leontiev*, pp. viii, 80-82. Leontiev also saw three stages in cultural development: (1) the stage of primary simplicity, (2) the stage of flowering complexity, (3) the secondary stage of confused simplification. His was also an amoral aesthetic interpretation with a Hegelian formula of synthesis through "unity in variety." Cf. Munzer, "East and West," *Commonweal*, Vol. 41, Dec. 8, 1944, p. 202. For a good digest of Spengler's view see G. O. Griffith, *Interpreters of Man*, Chap. XII.
84 Berdyaev's work, *The End of Our Time*, does much to illuminate this point.
85 As for cultural "resurrection" we have used the term in view of Pitirim Sorokin's formula in *The Crisis of Our Age*, p. 321. Sorokin also uses the term "catharsis" in relation to the next quoted phrase.
86 *Meaning of History*, p. 28. Cf. *End of Our Time*, p. 153.
87 *Ibid.*, pp. 30-33. Cf. *Essai de Métaphysique Eschatologique*, pp. 223ff, 124.

[88] This, too, is seen by Sorokin, *The Crisis of Our Age*, which analyzes the trend of Western civilization.

[89] *Meaning of History*, pp. 10-12, 191, 195.

[90] Sorokin's formula included "catharsis" but with no explanation for it. Cf. p. 230 below.

[91] *Meaning of History*, p. 195.

[92] *Slavery and Freedom*, p. 260.

[93] Cf. Reinhold Niebuhr, *The Nature and Destiny of Man*, Vol. II, p. 24. Niebuhr and Berdyaev concur at this important point.

[94] Berdyaev, *Freedom and the Spirit*, p. 303ff; *The Divine and the Human*, p. 58. Cf. Jacques Maritain's three essays on progress in *The Freedom of the Intellect*, in which he brings forth similar arguments in relation to the modern idea of necessary progress, which he deems a false social myth, quite in keeping with Berdyaev.

[95] Baron F. Von Hügel both in his *Essays and Addresses on Philosophy of Religion* and *Letters* reflects this. L. V. Lester-Garland comments in *The Religious Philosophy of Baron F. Von Hügel*, Chap. II, that in history there "is the operative presence of some original, teleological interrelation" or pre-existing harmony. This end, however, appears too necessitative from a Berdyaevian perspective. Lecomte du Noüy in *Human Destiny* tones down the idea of evolutionary necessity by showing that it involves retrogression as well as progression.

[96] *Freedom and Spirit*, pp. 307, 314.

[97] Cf. note 33, above.

[98] *Freedom and Spirit*, p. 315. See *Der Sinn des Schaffens*, Chap I, for the inner meaning of spiritual transfiguration. Cf. Pfleger, *Wrestlers with Christ*, pp. 269, 271, 286, 294.

[99] See Berdyaev, "Le Destin de la culture," *Chroniques*, p. 73ff. Cf. "Lettre à mes ennemis de la culture," *La Nef*, October, 1948, Paris, p. 43f. Civilization is struggle against nature; culture is symbolic and based on spiritual motivation. Cf. note 117, below.

[100] *Slavery and Freedom*, preface, adapted from Nietzsche. Arnold Toynbee says much in support of Berdyaev in many places throughout his work. In his *Civilization on Trial*, Chaps. 8 and 13, he even says there is but one "savior" which can give birth to a new civilization; it is "spiritual transfiguration" relating this world to the eternal Kingdom.

[101] *A Study of History*, p. 38f. (Cf. footnote 100 above.)

[102] *The Crisis of Our Age*, p. 321. Cf. 160d, 165, 313. Sorokin and Berdyaev concur that today marks the end of an epoch and culture needs fresh creativeness and revaluation (p. 17). Also, though cyclic tendencies in history are real, neither optimism nor pessimism is right, for Western culture need not die (pp. 13ff, 24f, 32). Sorokin has come, however, to see the need of eternal values and "the transcendental." Cf. "Your Family—The Key to Happiness," *Redbook*, 1951. Cf. *Social Philosophies of an Age of Crisis*, pp. 139ff, 266f, 318. More on the "catharsis" and "charisma" is suggested in *S.O.S.: The Meaning of Our Crisis*, Chap. III. Cf. pp. 69-71. R. W. Flewelling, in *The Survival of Western Culture*, provides some important correctives for culture (Chapters XV-XXVI, especially), but he fails to relate the ethical to the "transcendental" dynamic.

[103] Cf. footnotes 113, 115.

[104] *The Meaning of History*, pp. 191-193, 196ff. Cf. D. R. Davies, *Secular Illusion or Christian Realism?*, pp. 8ff, 42ff.

[105] *Ibid.*, p. 34.

[106] *Dream and Reality*, p. 296.

[107] *Existentialism and the Modern Predicament*, p. 77.

108 Cf. Charles Williams, *The Descent of the Dove,* pp. 84, 10, 103, 217, 235.
109 *De l'Esprit Bourgeois,* p. 87.
110 *Ibid.,* p. 78.
111 *Ibid.*
112 *Métaphysique Eschatologique,* p. 189. Cf. *Towards a New Epoch,* p. 75. This is the very theme of the book.
113 Berdyaev, *Spirit and Reality,* p. 125f, 103. Cf. "Christian Optimism and Pessimism," *Christendom, Spring,* 1936, No. 3, Vol. I, p. 426f. C. H. Moehlman, in *Religion in the Twentieth Century,* editor V. Ferm, p. 266f., wrongly accuses Berdyaev of "pessimism" as a bedfellow of Karl Barth under "philosophical totalitarianism." Emil Brunner in *The Mediator* is closer to pessimism than Berdyaev, asserting that man has no ethical relation to history save Christ. Brunner says here, "The Christian does not believe in 'progress' in this world. But he believes in the Kingdom of God. . . ." (p. 615). Cf. Brunner, *The Eternal Hope,* pp. 21ff, 67ff.
114 Tillich, *The Religious Situation,* pp. 176, 218f.
115 Harold J. Laski, "Religion and Communism," *The New Statesman and Nation,* Oct. 14, 1933, p. 460.
116 *A Philosophy of Decadentism,* p. 2. Cf. Hegel's "Philosophy of History," *Selections,* p. 361.
117 H. G. Wells, *Outline of History,* Vol. III, pp. 1, 196.
118 Cf. *Wells, The Salvaging of Civilization,* an optimistic view of democracy.
119 Cited by Luccock, *Communicating the Gospel,* p. 52, "end" here being "finis" in intent.
120 *The Human Situation,* p. 34.
121 Berdyaev, "The Crisis of Man in the Modern World," *International Affairs,* Vol. 24, Jan. 1948, p. 100.
122 *The Fate of Man in the Modern World,* pp. 9, 21. Cf. *Meaning of History,* p. 90.
123 *Spirit and Reality,* p. 163.
124 *Ibid.,* pp. 90. Cf. Berdyaev. "Le Destin de la culture," *Chroniques,* deuxième numero, Paris 1926, p. 75.
125 *The Divine and the Human,* pp. 1, 18f.
126 Tillich, *The Kingdom of God and History,* p. 174, *The Religious Situation,* pp. 176, 18f.
127 Tillich, *The Interpretation of History,* pp. 270-278.
128 *Ibid.,* p. 279f. Italics mine.
129 *Ibid.,* p. 280.
130 Cullmann, *Christ and Time,* pp. 19-25, 44, 32, 54ff, 100, 147.
131 Tillich, *The Interpretation of History,* p. 250.
132 *Ibid.,* p. 251.
133 *Ibid.,* p. 264, Cf. p. 262ff.
134 *The Kingdom of God and History,* p. 126f.
135 Berdyaev, *The Meaning of History,* p. 198. Cf. *Divine and the Human,* p. 174.
136 Cf. Berdyaev, *The Destiny of Man,* p. 289.
137 Cf. Moffatt, *The Theology of the Gospels,* Chap. II; also Stewart, *A Man in Christ,* pp. 260ff, 293. Cf. Hebrews 12:22-24 where the future is expressed in the present.
138 Ephesians 2:7. Cf. Romans 8:18, 11:5; Galatians 1:4; II Tim. 4:10.
139 Cf. Moffatt, *op. cit.,* pp. 24ff, 204ff.
140 Bultmann, *The Theology of the New Testament,* Vol. I, pp. 274f, p. 324f; p. 75f.
141 *The Beginning and the End,* pp. 234, 207.
142 We note here how *theosis* pertains to the *eschaton* in a cosmic sense. In

fact, Berdyaev sees the Incarnation of Spirit as *"theosis"* or as becoming a "world process," a completely new cosmology based on transfiguration. In this he also defends the view of S. Bulgakov. Cf. Berdyaev, "Der Geist des Grossinquisitore," *Orient und Occident*, Heft 1, March 1936, pp. 35, 38; also *Truth and Revelation*, pp. 65, 144. Noteworthy here are such N. T. passages as Rom. 8:38; Eph. 1:21, 6:12; Col. 2:10, 15; Rev. 21:1, 5; I Cor. 15:25-28.

143 *The Destiny of Man*, p. 289.
144 *Spirit and Reality*, p. 197.
145 *Solitude and Society*, pp. 114, 117. *Truth and Revelation*, pp. 13, 46f, 82; *Freedom and Spirit*, p. 190.
146 Berdyaev, *The Realm of Spirit and the Realm of Caesar*, Chap. X and Chap. XI. We take note that Berdyaev's use of the term 'monism' is distinctively eschatological, while his philosophy in general is an ethical, not ontological, dualism of freedom of spirit *versus* necessity of nature and temporal enslavement.
147 *Truth and Revelation*, p. 125; *Beginning and End*, p. 164.
148 Cf. G. O. Griffith, *Interpreters of Man*, p. 215. Cf. p. 214ff.
149 Note what we say below about Barth's treatment of the "interim," p. 247f.
150 *Freedom and the Spirit*, p. 313.

CHAPTER VII

EXISTENTIAL TIME AND THE KINGDOM

The existential interpretation of time, eternity and the end as proffered us by Nicholas Berdyaev helps clarify and, to some extent, resolve the basic tension seen today in New Testament eschatology. We have seen where existential time lends itself to a balanced Christology, whereas our main concern is its relation to eschatology. The fundamental biblical problem in this regard is that of the tenses of the Kingdom and its interpretation. It would appear that a basic need in theology today is for a new understanding of time and history, one which will allow for the retention of both the present and future aspects of the doctrine of the Kingdom, while kept dependent upon the supratemporal source of its meaning in the eternal now and *eschaton*. That for which we contend helps to meet this need.

Before examining some of the cardinal contributions to New Testament eschatology in recent decades, so that the issues involved may be illuminated by our basic contention and comparative study, it would be well to crystallize Berdyaev's view of the Kingdom in the light of the principles discussed in the previous chapters. Together they shed a special light on the problem of eschatology, indeed a midnight sun for this phase of our expedition whereby we might see what is not always seen even on the Isle of Kairos.

The Meaning of the Kingdom's Coming — Berdyaev

Berdyaev states, "The good news of the approach of the Kingdom of God is set in opposition to the world order. It means the end of the false harmony which is founded upon the realm of the common." [1] This implies that God in his eternality chooses to unveil Himself sufficiently to judge, yet redeem, a real but fallen *chronos* and history. It is to be understood that the reign of God comes about through His willful love and sacrifice in which He strives with men against the falsity of a temporal world. This can be seen best through Christ, and no more clearly than from a *balanced* existential perspective.

"The Kingdom of God denotes not only redemption from sin and a return to original purity, but the creation of a new world." [2] Thus the Kingdom both *is* and is *to be.* Not just symbolic, while it is that, too, the Kingdom is spiritually real and relates the eternal to the temporal. "It is not only the other world, it is this world transfigured," says Berdyaev. The Kingdom, quite like the eternal God Whose Kingdom it is, is not a static principle or ideal but a dynamic, creative, pneumatic reality. As the eternal makes its incursion into moments of time seen through faith and expressed in moments of worship, ecstatic creativeness and ethical responsibility, it means a new spiritual epoch has dawned. This, in turn, means a new light in the darkness, hence a fresh struggle, a new emergence of a God-endowed good over an evil and empty, fallen time.[3] While Berdyaev is in danger of overplaying the role of man's *gnosis* or spiritual affinity with the Kingdom, his regard for the meaning of divine Grace rescues it from an otherwise faulty anthropocentricism. Godmanhood is still central. He overtly states, "Eschatology must be freed from every sort of naturalism and must be expressed in terms of the spiritual life." [4] The Kingdom is Spirit and Freedom.

Not identified with it but represented by the Church, the Kingdom is an interrelation of the past, present and future in the oneness of eternity without the loss of time's particularity. Berdyaev says, "The primitive Christian lived in an atmosphere of eschatology in expectation of the Second Coming of Christ and the advent of the Kingdom of God. . . ." [5] The Church was institutionally established only in view of the historical interim ahead, the moment of the Kingdom's actualized fulfillment not having arrived. "But the Church on earth must never be confused with the Kingdom of God, still less identified with it, for the Church is only the means whereby we are brought to the Kingdom." [6] The Kingdom is of the invisible and eternal, not the visible and historical *per se*. Never should the Kingdom of God and the Kingdom of Caesar be confused as in an ecclesiastical monarchy of "Papo-caesarism." The Kingdom is not a "hierocracy" but a transfiguring power-in-operation. Nor is it a Platonic image or mere symbol of the eternal. Functioning in relation to time, it ends time only upon redeeming it unto its true fulfillment. But sometimes the Church stifles this eschatological principle and fails to expect such a transfiguration and end of time.[7] It must be realized that such an expectation is germane and complementary to a faith which sees the Resurrection of Christ at its center.

In view of Berdyaev's strong emphasis upon the meaning of history as eschatological in anticipation of a transfigured world, "a new heaven and a new earth," it is necessary to see the importance of man's creative role in the interim of history. For Berdyaev the creative acts of men are significant in helping to prepare for the end seen from the temporal side, just as "the new aeon" of the spirit is a condition of the end.[8] Figuratively, just as John the Baptizer was the harbinger of Christ in the advent, it would seem that the *koinonia* in particular, and creative personalities in general, become harbingers of Christ in his second advent. But Berdyaev is rather vague at the point of the difference between a man's creative acts and his Spirit-inspired creative acts of faith; nevertheless, he says, "The apocalypse of the religion of the Spirit depicts the final destinies of mankind as a divine-human act, as a work achieved by the collaboration of God and man." [9]

Like eternity and time, both *agape* and *eros* have a role to play in the religion of the end.[10] This calls to mind Augustine's *Caritas,* a two-way interpretation of love in the God-man relationship. But Berdyaev's way of relating the two kinds of love is not really clear. To be consistent, he should enunciate a paradoxical regeneration of *eros* by *agape* comparable to eternity's regeneration of time in the *kairos.* This would support the idea of a spiritual creativity as well as ethics serving an eschatological end.

A passive waiting for the end as seen in the eschatology of the Russian thinker Solovyov, for instance, is not adequate.[11] It smacks of a pre-millennial fundamentalism. Countering this Berdyaev says, "The Second Coming of Christ and the Kingdom of God, are also being prepared by human activity and human creativeness. The end of the world is man's responsibility as well as God's." [12] This is feasible only where the Kingdom is regarded as "belonging both to the here and the now and to the world beyond. . . ."[13] It is to this that the idea of progress and its relation to human creativity must always be subsumed. "Creative power fixes its gaze upon eternity, upon that which lies outside time."[14] It is because of this that history can be pregnant with a newness related to man's spiritual communion with the end of history and reflect thereby "a pull towards an end by which everything is resolved."[15] Thus creative acts are prophetic acts looking to the *eschaton*, with its future and supratemporal meanings. Not ending the world in themselves, such acts give man an eschatological vocation, for they help prepare for the End from the time side. This keeps eschatology as active as it is passive, while by no means bound to either linear or cyclic time *per se*.

In this respect Berdyaev could say, "The Kingdom of God is not merely a matter of expectation, it is *being founded*, its creation is beginning already here and now upon earth." This is of marked significance to the existing person, particularly the committed Christian. As Berdyaev says, "Every man has to live his inner Apocalypse, which is based on the fundamental paradox of time and eternity. . . ."[16] Seeing the socio-ecclesiastical aspects of it, Berdyaev could even say, "Ecumenical religion is the religion of Spirit purified from enslaving elements. . . ."[17] This is to be seen in contradistinction to a "progressive" religion which projects world harmony merely into an assumed future.[18]

The church must look to the vertical, not simply to the horizontal,[19] for the Kingdom is existentially in every moment.[20] Only in this context can it be understood that "The Kingdom of God is within you" (Luke 17:12). Berdyaev brings the matter to a head when he says, "But the Kingdom of God . . . must be regarded as belonging both to the here and now, and to the world beyond, as at the same time earthly and heavenly."[21] The eternal and divine are not continuous with history; there are only "inrushes" of it into history. This is the leaven which changes the world of time through a victory over time. Only by this can positive, creative and good acts have relevance to the Kingdom of God and eternity. Now *kairos* and *eschaton* are to be seen mutually related from a bifocal existential perspective of the present.

If this is the main principle of the Kingdom consistent with the existential time-eternity relationship in Berdyaev's thought, how might it shed light on the problem of New Testament eschatology in view of the varying positions taken by contemporary biblical scholars? Anticipating enlargements of Berdyaev's regard for the End and the interim in the next chapter, we turn to a comparative examination of outstanding interpretations of the New Testament doctrine of the Kingdom.

The Problem of the Kingdom's Coming—Schweitzer and Dodd

Whereas Albert Schweitzer, near the turn of this century, stressed the anticipation of a *future* cataclysmic coming of the Kingdom based upon the Synoptic accounts of Jesus and his teachings,[22] the work of C. H. Dodd has stressed, quite to the contrary, the historical *presence* of the Kingdom in his theory of "realized eschatology." [23] We are persuaded that the contradictory positions which these exegetical theories represent cannot be resolved by accepting one or the other *in toto*. Both point to factors which must be respected if theology is to be truly eschatological and at the same time communicative. Only a *balanced existential perspective* of human existence and destiny can provide for this. Here we find Berdyaev's existential eschatology illuminating and germane to the problem of time and the Kingdom. In fact, we can say that, without a position akin to the basic principles of time and eternity held by Berdyaev, the New Testament problem of the Kingdom's coming remains unresolved.

As James Moffatt pointed out [24] as far back as 1912, perhaps before many theologians were prepared to take sufficient account of it, and as Harold Roberts has helped vivify for contemporary theology,[25] we cannot do justice to New Testament theology without retaining *both* the present and the future aspects of the Kingdom. It is our contention that the basic principles we have received from Berdyaev and appraised comparatively lend themselves most provocatively to the resolution of this conflict in New Testament interpretation. The existential eschatological principles as set forth in the preceding chapters allow for an embracing of both the Kingdom as *come* and *to come*. The existential view of *kairos* and *eschaton* is to be seen basic to this. It allows us to relate the eternal Kingdom to the present and, by intensifying and qualifying *chronos* from above it, to relate the Kingdom to the future in the *eschaton*.

Schweitzer's idea of Jesus' anticipation of a future Kingdom tends to undermine or negate the meaning of its presence. It makes Jesus' teachings essentially an "interim ethics" on the grounds that the apocalyptic parables are thought to refer only to a future catastrophic coming of the Kingdom.[26] But Schweitzer seems to miss the supratemporal character of the Kingdom as eternal, though he sees the importance of the apocalyptic element in Jesus' teachings as something not to be dismissed, as it was by much nineteenth-century liberal theology geared to an empirical historical perspective.

At this point we see where Schweitzer becomes a pivotal liaison between "liberalism" and a subsequent "neo-orthodoxy." In general, the thinking of David Strauss, the Tübingen school and of Schleiermacher, Ritschl, Troeltsch, and Harnack would represent the former, while the thinking of Kähler, Barth, Brunner and, to some extent, Bultmann would represent the latter. But on a broader and more contemporary basis, we contend that Berdyaev becomes a stronger type of liaison, for he neither negates the historical factor with its respective tenses nor forsakes the transcendent dimension of "filled time" and its implications for the Kingdom. Schweitzer's emphasis upon the future coming of the Kingdom is overdone in the sense that it remains too horizontal and futuristic in terms of *chronos*. With reference to Matthew 10:23, for instance, he recognizes Jesus' Transfiguration as "the little Apocalypse" or as a miniature manifestation of the Kingdom. Luke's account makes it clear that there was a strong transcendental and supratemporal factor involved here, which centered in a great time of prayer. This has marked eschatological as well as Christological significance (Cf. II Peter 1:16-18). There is a breaking-in, an *ekstasis* here not to be ignored; it would imply the Kingdom's *presence*, something Schweitzer neglects.

As far back as 1906 Schweitzer helped abolish the modern nineteenth-century attempt to rely upon the objective historicity of Jesus,[27] an effort to be understood in view of the higher criticism of the Scriptures and the demand of the modern mind to be convinced about Christianity from a rational to empirical standpoint. The hardest blow to this rational effort of liberal thought actually came from Schweitzer's strong claim that Jesus' teachings and mission were consistently eschatological,[28] something obscured by the former objectified and idealized treatments of the historical Jesus and his teachings. Thus Schweitzer helped pave the way, indirectly at least, for the reactionary eschatological and transcendental emphases of men like Karl Barth and Rudolf Bultmann and their influence upon much contemporary theology. In 1918, in his *Römerbrief* Barth boldly enunciated the primacy of the transcendent Word and the independence of the Christ of faith from the historical Jesus as hitherto defined.[29]

Schweitzer's work had done much to keep the eschatological issue alive, whereas the idealistic interest in the Jesus of history represented by Adolf Harnack, for instance, was prone to negate or overlook the distinctiveness of the eschatological perspective.[30] Recognizing the problem, Schweitzer not only stressed the future of the Kingdom but, in view of its delay, went so far as to say, "The abiding and the eternal in Jesus is absolutely independent of historical knowledge and can only be understood by contact with His Spirit, which is still at work in the world." [31]

It would seem in this respect that theologians are reluctant to give Schweitzer the credit that he deserves for anticipating much in contemporary theology. While his final appraisal of Jesus becomes one of an immanental mysticism rather than something transcendental, Schweitzer saw the cruciality of this issue for Christianity. "History," he said, "will force it to find a way to transcend history. . . ." Meanwhile, his own position is inadequate, since it does not declare whether Jesus is a visionary prophet or the eternal Christ.[32] While Schweitzer sees that Jesus adapted the Judaistic apocalyptic idea to the hope of a Kingdom that would break into history in the future, he only restates the problem.

Even an unbeliever can settle for a Jesus who is a prophet, but a believer sees him as "more than a prophet." Furthermore, if Jesus stood for an imminent Kingdom which did not come, objectively speaking, he failed. How could a man of Jesus' insight and integrity be so self-deceived? The alternative here is still a live issue. Either Jesus was a mistaken man or he was the Christ of the Eternal Presence. It is noteworthy that David F. Strauss, in his revolutionary *Leben Jesu* back in 1835, the work that induced George Eliot to lose her faith upon translating it, sensed that even after objectifying the historical Jesus he had not dissolved the "Christ of dogma." [33] The Hegelian dialectic was first thought by Strauss to preserve it; however, later Strauss rejected the claim.

Substituting the transcendent Word for any immanental idea, including Schweitzer's mystical Jesus as the eternal "Spirit still at work," Karl Barth, though directly indebted to Martin Kähler, appears to have been influenced, at least indirectly, by Schweitzer's view that somehow Jesus cannot be limited to history. As the pivot man between modern theology and subsequent neo-orthodoxy Schweitzer, to a degree, helps anticipate the theology of encounter without clarifying what is involved. In his *Römerbrief* Barth stressed shrewdly the "nonhistorical" character of the revealed Word, thereby accentuating the "Christ of faith" and the post-resurrection *kerygma* as independent from the "Jesus of history." Not a new distinction, it was a new emphasis based upon the fact that the only Jesus we have is one given us by the post-Easter, apostolic faith portrait.

But there is an important distinction to be made here. Schweitzer conceded the need to come into "contact" with the eternal Spirit of Christ, but not out of relation to the historical conditions for knowing who he is in the contact. This is simply to indicate how, somewhat proleptic of Berdyaev, Schweitzer does more than either Barth or Bultmann to make sure that man's relation to the eternal is Christian and not Mohammedan or something religiously opaque.

Barth's earlier dichotomy of the transcendent Christ from the Jesus of history does not take into account the human conditions involved in this encounter. Nevertheless, Schweitzer's critical approach still dismisses the vital transcendental factor in the Jesus who is "more than a prophet" and who inaugurates the promised Kingdom. While he sees the claim to be present he even declares Jesus to be mistaken for thinking the Kingdom imminent, since influenced by contemporary Messianic beliefs. Schweitzer makes Jesus out to be an apocalyptic fanatic, but who sees eventually that he must die to condition the Kingdom's coming. This, we say, is a deficient answer to the problem.

Later C. H. Dodd stressed the present aspect of the Kingdom with its salvation and judgment operative in the time Jesus spoke of it. While he says that a destiny is also implied, it is obscured by the tendency to discount a goal related to time. The Kingdom's presence is such that it allows no significant interim between its presence and its fulfilment.[34] This, in a sense, anticipates something of the position taken today by Rudolf Bultmann, save that it is a more Platonic and temporal view of the Kingdom's presence, whereas Bultmann's view, as we shall elucidate, is an unbalanced supratemporal existential view, one "wholly supernatural" and alien to history.[35]

C. H. Dodd sees the Kingdom as already fulfilled historically in the New Testament realization of Israel's hope. But he sees no key to a reconciliation between the Kingdom's presence and history's ongoing. The Kingdom *is come*; but this tends to obscure its future coming in the sense that Schweitzer maintained. Here Dodd is, basically, too historical in his perspective and plays down the apocalyptic element in a way that Schweitzer's interim theory did not. Amos N. Wilder says in support of Dodd, "The conclusion is clear that not all of it can be viewed as interim ethics." [36] Granted, but that does not dissolve the temporal tension here. The New Testament speaks of the Kingdom both as *come* and *to come*.

Rudolf Otto has seen more shrewdly that we can abandon neither the future nor the present aspect of the Kingdom. He also asserts, that we may anticipate its "climax" in a fully actualized Apocalypse with an imminent end related to an ongoing history.[37] Noteworthy here is how this position more closely blends with the metahistorical eschatology of Berdyaev. Barring an unacceptable teleology, it is also tantamount to the position taken by Frederick C. Grant.[38] Here is a both/and tension or paradox which tones down the either/or antithesis we see posed between the views of Schweitzer and Dodd. Within an acknowledged discontinuity there remains a certain continuity as well. In keeping with what we see in the biblical eschatologies of Otto and Grant, Berdyaev's time-eternity relationship is, we believe, essential to the tenability of the Kingdom's tenses. It provides the needed metahistorical pattern for this adjustment in New Testament eschatology. While Berdyaev sees the transcendence of the Kingdom with Barth and Bultmann and the present aspect of it with Dodd and Bultmann, he, like Schweitzer, does not allow the historical future and the interim to be obtuscated. An existential *kairos* not alien to *chronos* while looking to the *eschaton* in terms of Apocalypse is the principle to be seen at work. "Existential time" is fundamental to this embracing of the tenses.

Despite his strong emphasis upon "realized eschatology," Dodd tries to make a place for a secular history lacking divine purpose. This is something we do not find in the position of either Barth or Bultmann. Not all recorded history belongs to God's purpose; it is simply the temporal scene in which it is being worked out. Dodd says, "It is only prophetic foresight of the Day of the Lord that makes it possible to see the whole of history as divinely governed." [39] In this respect, the rule of God is hidden; the hand of the Lord is on the past and the future, but evil obscures it in the present. Here Dodd begins to open up possibilities for an eschatology of relevance to the future. He says that "the radical difference between this age and the age to come implies a suprahistorical character of the Day of the Lord."

Dodd's qualifications bring him closer to Berdyaev, for he now strives to conserve a bifocal view of the *eschaton,* one side of which is historical, the other suprahistorical.[40] Dodd concedes here that the prophet sees the Kingdom's *eschaton* as imminent. Unlike Oscar Cullmann, Dodd comes to see that the prophet does not see himself standing in the middle of history; he sees history foreshortened. But here Dodd still tends to neglect the apocalyptic element which looks to a future transfiguration related to the historical time-stream. While Dodd is right in discounting the measurement of time, he makes appear quite fictitious what he calls a "teleology of history." [41] It is correct insofar as it does not make the end immanent to history, but Dodd does not show how the end belonging to the eternal is relevant to the end of history. Unless this is done there can be no justifiable theory of an eternal purpose for history. The supratemporal and the historical future are still not sufficiently interrelated by Dodd. This is because he lacks an existential basis for their interrelation without a total synthesis.

Dodd maintains that the New Testament, in using Old Testament apocalyptic imagery, differs from it. "The divine event is declared to have happened." [42] It has tasted of the powers of the Age to Come. The *eschaton* has entered history; hence, a "realized eschatology" with the apocalyptic idea of the Day of the Lord has been transferred to the historical plane in Christ's ministry and resurrection. "The time is fulfilled," as emphasized in Mark's Gospel and adapted to "the fullness of time" as seen by Paul. The New Testament miracle stories are said to parallel the apocalyptic symbols of the prophets, hence, a realized Apocalypse, an overthrow of evil through Christ and the judgment of the world as well as a condemnation of sin together with an eternal life now. This is good except that it depreciates the supratemporal distinctiveness of Apocalypse.

One thing which Dodd's emphasis does to support Berdyaev's claim that time and history are real is that the Event of Christ is hailed as a manifestation of divine power and purpose within history, not only beyond it. Also, it does not claim that nothing else can happen. Rather, history since the Christ Event is seen to be "qualitatively different!" The Christian Era is distinctive.[43] But we must ask: Is not this Era vitally related to the eternal Kingdom now and yet going somewhere? In his later works Dodd seems to concur and says there is a residue of eschatology yet to be realized, since sheer finality is not yet reached. Here is where the symbol of the Second Coming applies.[44]

But we must ask further: How can even this much be conceded, save as we recognize an existential relationship between an "eternal now" and the tenses of time such as held by Berdyaev? The Eucharist as an early eschatological symbol also bespeaks this problem. All three tenses are embraced by it, as Dodd himself sees it. Christ is present and by faith we are contemporary with him at his betrayal, crucifixion and rising, even as we are identified with his "coming and eternal glory." The suprahistorical and historical are related here without either being obscured.[45] Dodd tries to hold to this, but, we maintain, he cannot do so justifiably without a Berdyaev-like, balanced view of "existential time." It also suggests that Dodd's term "realized eschatology" is weak, for it is too temporal in connotation. In stressing the Kingdom's presence historically, one does not do justice to the future either historically or suprahistorically. Yet Dodd is right in rejecting any evolutionary teleology of history or any gospel of progress. Rather, there is a needed dying and rising. "The pattern of history is revealed less in evolution than in crisis," [46] he says.

210

Dodd gives us some important observations when, much in accord with Berdyaev, he says the following:

> The whole course of history, however, remains plastic to the will of God. This world of things, persons, and events can never forfeit, because of human sin, its title to reality—namely, its fitness to mediate the call of God to man. For it has once been the field upon which the great encounter was fought to a decision, and it bears the mark of that encounter forever. . . . The true prophet always foreshortens the future, because he, of all men, discerns in history the eternal issues which lie within *and yet beyond it.* The least inadequate myth of the goal of history . . . depicts its final issue in a form which brings time to an end and places man in eternity—the Second Coming of the Lord, the Last Judgment.[47]

But, again, we see where Dodd shies away from a realistic future involved in, or related to, the *eschaton.* Also, in referring to the Second Coming in a later work he says it is "not an event in history." It is "the point at which all history is taken up into the larger whole of God's eternal purpose." [48] While we are not literalistic here, this assertion tends to minimize the realistic future involved in what of the Kingdom remains unfulfilled for time. Dodd's "realized eschatology" tends to undercut what is, admittedly, futuristic about the *eschaton,* since he emphasizes the Kingdom as *come* in a way that minimizes the tension between *come* and *to come.* Dodd hesitates to say that what pertains to history's end must also to some extent belong to time. Berdyaev's view of the *eschaton* does not succumb to this.

In a somewhat Platonic setting, C. H. Dodd overstates himself in stressing a "realized" Kingdom of God at hand. True, God has acted in Christ, but this does not mean that God has fully actualized the final order. The decisive battle has been fought but the war is not over (Cf. Romans 8:23ff, 32; II Corinthians 1:22; 5:5; Ephesians 1:14). God has given us a basis for hope accompanied by precious promises which imply that there is more to come, more to be realized. Jesus spoke of the Kingdom's coming and the coming of the Son of Man, though he disclaimed any knowledge of its exact time (Cf. Mark 13:32). This, too, bespeaks a realistic and significant future to which the bifocal *eschaton* existentially relates itself through *kairos*.

The Scene of the Kingdom's Coming—Cullmann

Oscar Cullmann presents New Testament eschatology from the standpoint of what he deems the concept of time held by the Primitive Church. It is a strictly linear view, with Christ at the "midpoint" of history, as marked by the B.C.-A.D. division of the Christian calendar. Greek cyclic time is excluded.[49]

Since all history for Cullmann is judged by the "midpoint" as its seat of meaning, it is an upward sloping "time line" giving redemptive significance to all previous and succeeding events, even to the extent that history ceases to be secular. The New Testament witnesses to "the scene of redemptive history" in that sense. This view involves two principles: (1) Revelation and salvation are bound to an ascending time process and not to a transcendent realm. (2) All events of the time line are related to the unrepeatable, historic midpoint.[50] But Cullmann, we must note at once, fails to give account of the ascending factor of the time line, since, as we have seen, a mere temporal *telos* is inadequate to support the *eschaton*.

While neither Cullmann nor Berdyaev deny the role of linear time and history, and neither accepts cyclic time as meaningful, Cullmann fails to see any place at all for a deficient cosmic time. Does not the Bible itself speak of the seasons of the year as well as of the "seasons of the Lord"?[51] Berdyaev faces up to the evils of linear time and sees it cannot be redemptive in itself. But Cullmann fails us here, offering perhaps the most naive "temporalized" version of eschatology to appear in this century. The determinism which it implies is strangely medieval.

Cullmann, unlike Berdyaev, fails to see how the central Event of Christ is not only historical but also qualitatively eternal in a vertical sense. Cullmann is especially weak here, because his concept of eternity is essentially a temporal notion, its difference from time being merely a matter of degree. Eternity is infinite time, he says. The sterility of this view is seen in Cullmann's failure to show a vital relation between man's *limited* time and God's *unlimited* time. Brusquely dismissing an existential idea of an incursion of time by the eternal, he creates more problems than he solves, for the Christian norm is kept strictly within history.

Cullmann dreads the transcendent element in redemption. How can this jibe with anything but the most outmoded immanental Christology? Merely tipping his hat to the "inbreaking of these *kairoi*" [52] in I Thess. 5:1, Cullmann fails to note any real difference between secular and sacred history. Furthermore, an eternity deemed to be "endless time" is still sheer *time,* is it not? Does this do justice to God's transcendence and infinitude? In view of our foregoing examination of the basic problems, only a negative answer can be given. The closest Cullmann comes to defending his claim biblically is in his idea that the Greek *aion* or "age," when employed in the plural (*aiones*), refers to eternity. He deduces from this that eternity signifies neither a cessation of time nor a *timelessness.* [53]

While Berdyaev allows us to respect the latter point, he moves us beyond such a temporal notion of eternity and is more realistic as well as apocalyptic about the end of time. Cullmann has failed to learn from F. D. Maurice, deposed as a heretic a century ago for qualitatively distinguishing "eternal" from "everlasting." [54] He has failed to see how the plural *aiones* is a temporal word form pointing beyond itself. Cullmann's view has a legitimate tension between the tenses of time but too little conceptual tension between the eternal and the temporal to warrant respect for "the redeeming of the times." How can the "unlimited" redemptive factor give its meaning to history's time line when the very successiveness of time bespeaks what is "limited" and unredeemed? How can the "midpoint" be unique unless the eternal, which it involves, transcends or is qualitatively different from time? Cullmann leaves us at a total loss here, whereas Berdyaev's clue to a balanced existential time answers the problem without bypassing the historic time factor Cullmann wishes to preserve. Cullmann simply asserts that the acts of God are "so bound up with time that time is not felt to be a problem." [55] While the problem is not God's, we must reply that it is still ours, and we must not overly temporalize Him in interpreting His acts! Again, Cullmann merely tips his hat to an important thought, *viz.,* that God is "superior to time."

Cullmann stoutly maintains divine predestination as though God were temporally scheduled by the causal-Greek logistics bequeathed to Protestantism by John Calvin. Cullmann fails to ask the question of how God can *await* the future unless it *is*, a matter demanding existential consideration. He would do well to consider the graphic words of Edwin Lewis:

> Nor does God have a rigid time-table with which nothing can interfere. Heaven is not a railway dispatcher's office! Those unimaginative persons who identify a living moment with the necessary relation of an impeccable dialectic, and who therefore suppose fixed dates within the divine calendar which bind God in chains he cannot escape, understand neither the nature of existence with its element of irrationality, nor the nature of God nor the purpose of God nor the ways of God.[56]

So temporalistic is Cullmann's view of eternity and the Kingdom that not only is it an "endless time line" but something "measurable in time, although it is endless and therefore known to God."[57] Cullmann attacks Barth and others for asserting that Christ means that a timeless eternity "invades time."[58] This is not true of Barth whose view of eternity is far from timeless, as we have seen, though exclusively transcendent. The logical alternative offered by Cullmann is a peculiar monistic idea of the time-eternity relationship, its only strength being that time is not irrelevant to God and His Kingdom, for it is in history.

Referring to the future Cullmann says, "It is false to assert that Primitive Christianity had an eschatological orientation."[59] Here Cullmann, even more than Dodd, is averse to looking to the future as if that were still Judaistic. Jesus saw the norm only in the Kingdom *come*, not *to come*. But Cullmann asserts this without seriously considering the Lord's Prayer and the New Testament references to the unfulfilled Kingdom. The *telos* is in Christ, the end of the Law, Cullmann says. But is Christ limited to sheer *chronos?* Cullmann's eschatology seems to affirm it. Schweitzer's "consistent eschatology," with its mid-point in the future Kingdom, is attacked solely in favor of the past, crucified and risen Christ.[60] The "already fulfilled" and "not yet fulfilled" aspects of the Kingdom are implied in this "historic midpoint," Cullmann claims.[61] Primitive Christianity stressed the present because the present Lordship of Christ over his church was seen as his reign between his ascension and

Parousia. But this "present" is fully planted in history by Cullmann. This fails to do full justice to the eternality of Christ and the Sonship involved in the Incarnation. Needed is a balanced existential eschatology of God-manhood such as we have elucidated with the help of Berdyaev. The end is not only present to God and future to men of faith, but eternal to both. Cullmann falls far short of this, even as he fails to interrelate the beginning and the end.

Cullmann says the Christ Event "comprehends past, present and future." [62] But this is only through its significance in the time line, hence grossly deficient when both the Event and the significance are held to be intrinsically temporal. How is a past event consequential to the present of a man's faith, decision, death and destiny? Cullmann proffers us no real answer, yet dismisses Kierkegaard's provocative and helpful idea of "contemporaneity." [63] Redemption and the Kingdom are strictly on a temporal plane for Cullmann, a view which should leave time and history without possibility of transfiguration *now* and in the *eschaton,* though Cullmann asserts it. The failure to see the difference between *telos* and *eschaton* underlies this weakness. Since eternity is deemed an infinite temporality, men are still left unredeemed in the true sense, since they are still enslaved to time. Again, there is no real distinction between secular and sacred history on this basis. Yet Cullmann is right in asserting the interim of faith prior to the End, which is *to come* while real now in Christ.

In his treatment of the meaning of Christology in modern theology D. M. Baillie finds the central Christian revelation a vantage point essential to finding the meaning of history. In this regard he stands with Berdyaev and departs from Cullmann, for history is meaningless, he notes, without its points of eschatological significance making it a *Heilsgeschichte,*[64] which is more than so many events and more than human progress. But in emphasizing this historical center found in the Incarnation Baillie tends to slip into what I deem to be an overly linear and temporal view, similar to that of Oscar Cullmann. He asserts that ". . . faith could look backwards and forwards, and everything fall into its place in a sacred story. . . ." [65]

While opposed to a Tillich-like reduction of the God-man to a *mythos* which is not historically actualized and only a symbol of the true nature of history,[66] Baillie, quite like Cullmann, does too little to interpret the God-man as *more* than a once-for-all event in common history. It appears that he lacks the qualitative supratemporal, yet temporal, view of the Incarnation as preserved in Berdyaev's existentialism. In contrast, Berdyaev would have us recognize the God-man of eternity-in-time which demands a perspective of faith that sees not only a historical event but an existential communion with the Living God-man as well. Baillie improves the Christological implications of time and eternity, however, when he treats the doctrine of the atonement. He states in a manner quite congenial to our main eschatological argument that "God's reconciling work cannot be confined to any one moment of history." [67] But if so, does not the time-eternity relationship of the atonement reflect, or blend with, that of the Incarnation? If the atonement is "suprahistory," as Baillie contends, can the Incarnation be less so while every bit as historical? Cullmann needs to see what Baillie has at least tried seriously to reckon with here.

The Act of the Kingdom's Coming—Bultmann

Rudolf Bultmann is another New Testament scholar who has stressed the presence of the Kingdom, but in a manner much different from that of either Dodd or Cullmann. For him it belongs not to history but to the present moment of the faith encounter, a moment of transcendent intensity within existence. An attempt to retain the perspective of existence held by Heidegger, while Christianizing it with an echatological outlook, this has much in common with Karl Barth, since both thinkers have interpreted history as a relativistic phenomenon quite oblivious to the Divine Absolute. In his *Jesus and the Word* Bultmann asserts that the Kingdom is "wholly supernatural" and alien to history.[68] This is elaborated in his two-volume work *The Theology of the New Testament,* save that the transcendent factor which is emphasized is not deemed so supernatural in view of the open universe of a modern *Weltanschauung.*

In view of his *Formgeschichte* as a way of "demythologizing" the New Testament, Bultmann claims that the Kingdom must be seen solely from the standpoint of the post-Easter *kerygma* of redemption. This message pertains to "God's eschatological act of salvation," [69] which overarches the ethical teachings and ministry of Jesus. Jesus' central theme was eschatological announcing a present irruption of the Kingdom, something not to be understood as a Jewish futuristic hope but as an apocalyptic incursion of the reign of God. The Kingdom *is come* to efface the old one, and Satan's rule is about to be supplanted by the imminent coming of the Son of Man. The present is an hour of crisis, therefore, for the reign of God is dawning and a present decision is imperative. This reign is not historical or evolutionary but vertically eschatological.[70] We must note here the contrast to all horizontal views, including those of Schweitzer, Dodd and Cullmann, as well as the nineteenth-century historicisms of Schleiermacher, Ritschl and Harnack. Bultmann is Kierkegaardian in his stress upon the present.

Bultmann sees the Fourth Gospel as the high point of the New Testament, for it consistently declares the *presence* of the divine act of redemption, whereas the Synoptics and Pauline writings are largely futuristic. The Kingdom ethic is not one of a futuristic reform, nor is it of the past. It is one which stresses the individual in his present relation to God,[71] since the Kingdom is breaking in *now* with its new law and aeon of love. Harnack was wrong, Bultmann contends, in claiming that Jesus simply taught a superior ethics and the Church later put in his mouth the eschatological idea. Rather, the two are one. The Church saw the End as imminent.[72] Men must see the cruciality of this and see themselves in this light, much like Kierkegaard's Moment of encounter, for it spells both judgment and mercy *now*. Salvation is not of the past, Bultmann strongly asserts, but of the present. By it, profane history is ended and a new era opens up. Such a faith has neither rational nor historical foundation. The cross and the resurrection bespeak the present redemptive Act with existential relevance to the believer *hic et nunc*. If the resurrection is solely a supernatural event in the past, our salvation is past. Cullmann has overlooked this. A past event is not enough; the present relevance of the Word is the true Resurrection. At this point Bultmann and Tillich have much in common; Berdyaev's view is in accord save for his more temperate view of the time factors involved.

Bultmann's position is one of a fraidy-cat transcendence which almost dehistoricizes the divine Act upon deliteralizing the mythological elements in the faith-portrait's witness to the *kerygma.* His *Entmythologisierung* seeks to vivify what is central to the *kerygma;* however it treats the resurrection as an event God "causes to occur . . . in a mystical sphere outside the realm of human experience. . . . For the resurrection, of course, simply cannot be a visible fact in the realm of human history," says Bultmann. A believer is at the brink of the Kingdom-End, and there is positively no historical or group security in this. The dialectical paradox is that God meets each man "in his own little history." [73] Even if Jesus' Messianic consciousness could be proven, something Bultmann denies, it could yield no security, since it would be a mere historical matter. Seeing the relation of Christ to the *kerygma* is "a pure act of faith independent of the answer to the historical question." [74] The Messianic consciousness, Peter's confession and the Transfiguration are all post-Easter mythological embellishments of the Church's witness and not a part of an objective biography. Thus Christ *ends* history, i.e., negates it. Bultmann is much like Wilhelm Hermann, we note, in dropping all security geared to history's relativity.[75] Stressing the significance of the Christ Event, he depreciates the role of time or history related thereto. Meaning is practically severed from the events and persons who instrumentally convey the meaning.

Nevertheless, Bultmann is dialectically shrewd, creative and right in seeing the discontinuity of the Christ Event with Jewish eschatology, a matter which those who see the Resurrection as the exaltation of Jesus tend to obscure.[76] But Bultmann's one-sided dialectic tends to overlook the continuity of the Christ Event centering in the fact that Jesus adapted and corrected Judaistic apocalyptic and ethical ideas, which is enough to remind us that New Testament eschatology has a historical reference. Thus we need a combination of continuity and discontinuity, something which our balanced existential view of time supported by Berdyaev's main principles grants us, while retaining the strength of Bultmann's view and those of Dodd and Schweitzer accordingly. This is important if the eschatological act of God is to be seen centered in One who is more than a prophet while man among men. Without it the existential moment of encounter with the Word can hardly be identified as distinctively Christian.

Contrary to Cullmann, the primitive Church, as Bultmann understands it, saw itself as a congregation of the End, as attested by both Paul and the Synoptic tradition. The Church saw itself as the "vestibule" of the Kingdom. The *koinonia* had a present hope in an imminent Kingdom. The *kerygma* which it proclaimed meant that God had made Jesus the Messiah in a suprahistorical sense. Here the dehistoricizing factor of Bultmann's demythologizing and unbalanced existentialism is apparent. Retrospectively, the Church identified Jesus' appearance and his eschatological meaning, thus surmounting the scandal of the cross which was alien to a Jewish concept of the Messiah. Christ was viewed as the "salvation-bringer." But again we must question Bultmann's total depreciation of the historical element here.

Does faith function in an eternal vacuum as though one's existence were nonhistorical or nontemporal? Did the apostles leap completely out of time in their faith encounter? We think not. Their time-conditioned intelligence was not left behind upon meeting the Unconditioned as the Risen One. Bultmann has overstated his case in the interest of a Johannine, dehistoricized acceptance of the Word which has broken in as Light in the darkness. Faith means accepting a new "life that from the world's point of view cannot even be proved to exist."[77] It is one of an existential encounter with eternity now—a strong point, save for its alienation from time, almost as though man with his temporal consciousness were not in the least involved in that encounter. Not ascetic, this emphasis, nevertheless, shrewdly smashes all secular security and standards, including moralistic conversions and objectified historicisms. This is strong but overdone. It fails to reckon with the divine Absolute's condescension to employ what is human, temporal and relative upon redeeming them. This is untrue to the God-manhood of Christ.

Faith is a present divine *given* and it means eternal life now. For the author of the Fourth Gospel, the relationship of the disciples with the historical Jesus was not a vital faith relationship until the resurrection. Only then was Christ known in his true Sonship and Spirit from across the divide of time and eternity. He returns in the Spirit, the only way he shall return. Thus the Gospel of John is seen to abandon the futuristic view of the Parousia. The Risen One and Parousia are identified in His Presence, the Paraclete.[78] But eventually the Church in history is erroneously changed, says Bultmann, from a fellowship to an institution. The Spirit is deemed immanent to the institution through a sacerdotalism which restricts His breaking in with special gifts.[79] As the eschatological tension is relaxed the futuristic view of hope comes to dominate a "Christian-bourgeois piety." Thus, moral uprightness comes to supersede a present righteousness of divine salvation, there being certain New Testament precedents for this in Acts, Luke, I and II Timothy.

Also, Luke thinks more in terms of world history, which tends to make Christianity just another religion, thinks Bultmann, by playing into the hands of a temporal immanence at the expense of the eschatological transcendence to which John is true.[80] Unlike Paul, who refers to a history of salvation, John does not speak of the Church in temporally elective terms, but in the precious present. Here Bultmann is to be seen at the opposite pole from Cullmann's naive, temporalistic eschatology, while being himself an extremist. Bultmann is strong on the point of refuting any human criterion for the divine. It was here that the Jews missed the Christ; they wanted the other-worldly on a this-worldly basis.[81] That "the Word became flesh" is a revelation which transcends chronological criteria. This we can appreciate with Bultmann, but he presses it to the point where he neglects the fact that the Word uses the temporal media of that flesh. *Chronos* is involved in the eventful revelation and, subordinately, in the faith encounter as well. We find that both the appreciation and correction of Bultmann demand what we have contended for as a better balanced "existential time," allowing for a *kairos* and *eschaton* of bipolar connotation.

In his demythologizing of the *kerygma* in defense of a transcendent salvation relevant to a Heideggerian existence, Bultmann tends to reduce the Incarnation and Resurrection to mere symbols of the eternal, since they are not datable and are meaningful only to eyes of faith. This is an unnecessarily extreme reaction to all "historicisms" of Christ. Quite as for Tillich, the Resurrection becomes more of an event in the lives of the apostles than in the life of Christ. Minimizing the historical

220

medium, Bultmann fails to relate the eternal Word sufficiently to the Word-bearer and the salvation to the salvation-bringer. Likewise, he does not relate the end to the time of believing men of existence and the historical position of the Church. Both past events and future expectations are submerged under the primacy of the transcendent present. In Kierkegaardian fashion, this threatens to negate rather than redeem the times. Here, as we have seen, even Karl Barth has become sensitive and tries not to be so extreme in his later works. Bultmann severs the eternal Word from its historical forms of manifestation, those bridges which the divine builds to reveal and redeem. Barth has come to the point where he can write *Die Menschlichkeit Gottes*.

Bultmann relegates the future aspect of Apocalypse to sheer mythology. Here he radically departs from both Dodd and Schweitzer in his stress upon the disjunction between the temporal and the eternal. Yet this is far better than Cullmann's immanental fusion. We maintain that both extremes are in error in view of the meaning of *kairos* and *eschaton* as we have dealt with them in previous chapters. As Berdyaev has shown, both sheer immanence and sheer transcendence are wrong. Barth, then, is right in eventually taking issue with Bultmann at the point of the Resurrection as a history-related event.[82] Paul, may we suggest, saw this existential encounter related to the Incarnate Event. Bultmann thinks Paul began to secularize Christian faith with a historical security here. But what Bultmann is prone to do is to protect the source of salvation and the meaning of existence, without doing enough to show their *relation* to the time factors involved in their becoming *relevant* to men as men. He has the "treasure" but neglects its associations with the "earthen vessel" of events, which are remembered yet regarded in neither a realistic nor an idealistic sense.

Bultmann claims biblical history finds its unity in its goal, which is Christ; but in reaction from any analogy with nature and anything immanent to history, cosmic law and psychology, he refuses to concede that the meaning and goal are historically relevant.[83] The End ends the secular era of history now. There is no apocalyptic future transfiguration allowed for by Bultmann. Eternity negates fallen existence and history.[84] It fails to redeem other moments as though there were but one existential encounter. Sacred and secular histories have nothing in common,[85] which, we reply, may be questionable in view of the New Testament context in Israel's calling, experience, heritage and thought forms, not to overlook its Hellenistic backdrop and thought forms.

Bultmann refuses to see the scarlet strand of *Heilsgeschichte* running through the rope of biblical *Historie*; for him it is wrapped around or held above it, hence is vulnerable to severance and ambiguity. Citizenship in heaven is given no relation to citizenship in history. This has both eschatological and ethical weaknesses. Such total discontinuity tends to reduce Christianity to an escapism; it is really a new form of gnosticism. Yet, we must be careful here, for extreme reactions to Bultmann could slip into superficial moralisms and pseudo historicisms quite extraneous to the central *kerygma*, which points to an eternal Act.

Bultmann at least tries to let the eternal event of Christ and the subjective witness meet in the existential moment of the preached Word. Neither ideal universals nor moral propositions can displace this living encounter relevant to "my" existence where "I" am now. But what of the temporal aspects of "my" understanding of "my" existence to which the Word is addressed? Bultmann fails us here, quite like Barth. This is strange in view of Bultmann's debt to Heidegger, who does not depreciate time so intensely.[86] Is the past altogether dead and the future unreal? Not in view of our balanced existential time and end. Bultmann is unnecessarily as Docetic temporally as Barth, even more so. He neglects the fact that the *kerygma* was an announcement *in* history of something not *of* history but still associated with it. If the *kerygma* amounts only to a judgment which abnegates history, it offers culture and human destiny no hope of fulfillment. Only the individual has hope supratemporally. If so, is not God defeated in His struggle with an earthly evil related to His created order through men? Bultmann keeps the End solely in eternity and gives history to the devil! This is gnostic and almost Manichean as it depreciates the temporal media and redemptive efficacy of eternity-in-time via "the Word made flesh."

Bultmann stresses the apocalyptic presence of the Kingdom without future relevance.[87] Dodd stresses the historical presence.

Are the two views disparate? They need not be in the light of our claim to a dynamic, balanced existential time. Both thinkers are wrong while both are right! Both see Schweitzer's need to relate his futuristic view to Jesus' ethics and role as Word-bearer *now*. Dodd needs something of Bultmann's transcendence and Bultmann needs something of Dodd's history. Both need more of Schweitzer's future and Schweitzer needs more of their respective views of the present. How can there be an eternal meaning and goal for history without such an adjustment? Bultmann has a negative view of history's "breaking off," though he leaves the future "open." [88] Dodd has come to see the need of a fulfilled end of history. Both need a fresh point of view, one amenable to the eschatological dimension of existential time, whereby the Apocalyptic factor applies to the End through the present. This we shall seek to provide for more explicitly in the next chapter, in keeping with our discussion of the End in this and the previous chapter. Bultmann sees the Christian living by a promise, but he does not relate its significance to the unfulfilled aspects of that promise from the human standpoint. The ethical implications of this are marked. Victims of race prejudice among professing Christians, for example, would like to see more of the colony of heaven on earth. This is an eschatological matter that it might *be* an ethical matter!

Bultmann has submerged Jesus' Messianic consciousness and the teachings concerning the person of Christ. This seems illegitimate, for surely there was something about the historical Jesus, whoever he was, to cause the disciples to summon others to accept him. John Macquarrie thinks Bultmann is biased by existentialism.[89] It is our contention that this is not the issue so much as Bultmann's one-sided version of the existential present. Yet Macquarrie corroborates our judgment to some extent when he says the existential perspective is the most likely of any to be true to the thought of the biblical writers.[90] But Bultmann, we claim, seems to neglect the fact that the mythological thought forms of the New Testament writers were common historical parlance and correlative to a *kerygma* which involves a subsumed witness to an Incarnation relative to history and Jesus' role. Unless this is taken more seriously, the Incarnation is not just a Kierkegaardian "absurdity" but either an impossibility or something totally irrelevant to historic men. In that case

223

Bultmann should say that the *kerygma* itself is only a dramatic symbolism of the doctrine of Grace.

But we must ask: Has God in His unique revelation of the eternal Word scurried past all the scenes of history? The Incarnation should mean something quite to the contrary without which the risen, living Word is not an event relevant to a temporal existence. Even to say with Barth that Jesus was the Word *incognito* or *deus absconditus* is inadequate unless a dual relationship is implied eschatologically. Not a rational synthesis, neither is this an either/or so much as it is a tenable tension, a paradox of interrelated opposites. The Divine is surely "Other," but as the divine revealer and redeemer He is not *totaliter aliter* in every sense, for on His own kenotic terms (Philippians 2) He has accommodated men enough to unveil Himself to them. Bultmann fails to keep the eternal Kingdom and the announced Word associated closely enough with their unique agent and herald in history.[91] There is no real tension in such discontinuity. Alien elements know no tension! And without the tension there is hardly a mature doctrine of redemption.

Counterparting this injustice to the Incarnation is Bultmann's version of the eschatological position of the Church. Bultmann neglects to see that the Church's remembrance and account of the Risen Christ was part of her participation in his stunning eventfulness and was not a self-determined encounter.[92] The vertical dimension of the faith encounter in Bultmann's theology is so pronounced as to derogate the horizontal means and consequences of the encounter; hence, the interim between the revealed End of the Kingdom and its actualized fulfillment is totally neglected. Lost sight of is the New Israel as an instrument of God's purpose related to the future and a "new heaven and new earth." This obscures the tension between the *now* and the *then* in which the Church exists. Here Emil Brunner is more balanced with his "dualism of possession and anticipation," [93] whereas, unlike Berdyaev, Bultmann does not assure us of a future divine action, a new aeon related to the *eschaton*.[94] Thus Bultmann detracts from the full redemptiveness of the Word by keeping it utterly transcendent and hyperindividualistic.

What was stated above with reference to David Strauss as a Hegelian who detracted much from the historical Jesus as mythical can be reiterated here. What Strauss did to accentuate the Christ of dogma in an abstract Hegelian manner, Bultmann has done in a lopsided existential manner. The difference might be that Bultmann does not dispense with the mythical thought forms so much as he tries to reinterpret the *kerygma* behind them, though much to the jeopardy of the historical and the incarnate elements involved. In his later works Karl Barth tries to resist this weakness related to making the mythical element symbolic of the eternal irrespective of the historical, hence he prefers to speak of saga or legend, which is more akin to events and less vulnerable to either a gnostic outlook or Hegelian indifference to historical events.[95] Bultmann has overplayed his hand of insights in the interest of a consistently antinomian and nonempirical view of the Gospel to protect a desecularized view of the Kingdom and the eschatological Act of God.

Here Bultmann is given some support by the systematic theologian of Göttingen, Friedrich Gogarten, yet Dr. Gogarten once said to me in a discussion [96] that he was not certain to what extent Bultmann's view of the Risen Christ actually included the historical reference. This is understandable, yet in his *Kerygma and Myth* Bultmann begins to concede that the saving event is linked with a concrete historical person in whom God acts, though a historian could not deal with the latter point.[97] But in general while the cross is deemed historical, Bultmann hesitates to concede overtly that the Resurrection is historical. This debilitates the relevance of the gospel to the Church and her vocation in history.

What, basically, makes the Incarnation real to Bultmann? Nothing objective in history, only the "I-Thou" relation of faith to the present Word wherein God presents Himself to us in a way that transcends nature and history. What of the Kingdom, then? It is transcendentally present *now* with a profoundly existential relevance. It is the End *now* and not coming in the future, since it is not expressible in terms of worldly time. The fundamental problem here is that Bultmann has too strong an antithesis between the redemptive Event and End on the one hand, and their existential meaning and historical media on other. Again, what is needed is a balanced view of existential time and its end. This must relate *kairos* and *eschaton* to a balanced *Heilsgeschichte* whereby the redeeming and eternal are neither identical to, nor divorced from, *chronos* and *Historie*. True, an objective spectator's perspective of the great event is not existential faithwise; nevertheless, we must assert that the true existential perspective involves both the transcendent meaning and encounter together with the remembrance and "happenedness" of the meaning-giving event. Otherwise, we endanger the person-event of the Cross and the Resurrection together with the very *kerygma* itself. This is to slip into an extremely transcendental mysticism. P. T. Forsyth once showed that we must retain the sacramental function of history, its function as "vehicle" and not merely as fact.[98] This supports our claim that the divine Act was on the frontier of two worlds, though history is both "commerce" and "conflict" with the eternal Kingdom. It also corroborates our dialectic as focused on existential time and its eschatological dimension.

* * * *

In this chapter we have centered our attention upon the meaning, problem, scene and act of the Kingdom's coming as expressed from different points of view by New Testament scholars. In so doing we have made a dialectical comparison between them and Berdyaev. We have seen the merits and demerits of each scholar's position, even as we have seen how Berdyaev helps us embrace the strong points and correct or overcome the weaknesses of each.

With this close-range look at the royal mantle on Mount Eschaton, we can better examine her Apocalyptic apex. In so doing, her light is shed before us in the interim that belongs to faith's pilgrimage of ascent.

Notes

1 *Slavery and Freedom*, p. 89.
2 *Ibid., p.* 266.
3 *Freedom and the Spirit*, p. 308.
4 *Ibid.*, p. 324f.
5 *Ibid.*, p. 338f.

6 *Ibid.*, p. 339.

7 *Ibid.*, p. 353.

8 *Truth and Revelation*, p. 150f.

9 *The Divine and the Human*, p. 192.

10 *Ibid.*, pp. 201. Cf. p. 11, 80, 124, 126, 137, 165. Note double movement of *agape* and *eros*. Cf. Nels F. S. Ferre, *Christianity and Society*, pp. 4, 45ff, 90, 120. Tillich, *Systematic Theology* Vol. I, p. 281, may go too far in reaction to Nygren (Cf. *Agape and Eros*, pts. I, II, III) when he says, "If *eros* and *agape* cannot be united, *agape* toward God is impossible." More like Berdyaev and Ferre, it may be better to relate the two loves in *Caritas* or an "*agape*sized *eros*" lest we make them completely synonymous in reaction to Nygren's dichotomy of the two loves. The two loves must not be synthesized, nor left in absolute dichotomy, but interrelated so that the one is serviceable unto God when regenerated by the other.

11 Solovyov in *The Justification of the Good*, p. 172, does not sound altogether passive. He states, "Man is dear to God, not as a passive instrument of His will . . . but as a voluntary ally and participator in His work in the universe. This participation of man must necessarily be included in the very purpose of God's activity in the world."

12 *Spirit and Reality*, p. 197.

13 *Divine and Human*, p. 171.

14 *The Beginning and the End*, p. 165.

15 *Ibid.*, p. 166. Cf. pp. 174, 179, 188.

16 *Ibid.*, p. 222; *Solitude and Society*, p. 117.

17 *Divine and Human*, p. 191.

18 *Slavery and Freedom*, p. 265.

19 *Beginning and End*, p. 163. Cf. pp. 222, 254.

20 *Destiny of Man*, p. 290.

21 *Divine and Human*, p. 171. Cf. John Bright, *The Kingdom of God*, p. 215ff.

22 Schweitzer, *The Quest of the Historical Jesus*, Chaps. XV, XVI, XX.

23 Dodd, *The Bible Today*, Chap. VI; *The Parables of the Kingdom*, pp. 34ff, 49ff.

24 Moffatt, *The Theology of the Gospels*, Chap. II.

25 Roberts, *Jesus and the Kingdom of God*, Chap. I.

26 Schweitzer, *Out of My Life and Thought*, pp. 41ff, 46ff. Cf. Roberts, *op. cit.*, p. 15ff.

27 Cf. *The Quest of the Historical Jesus*, p. 401. Note, this refers to an objectively established Jesus, which is not to say Schweitzer denied a Jesus of history. Cf. *Out of My Life and Thought*, p. 50, also G. O. Griffith's essay on Schweitzer in *Interpreters of Man*.

28 *Ibid.*, p. 631. Ethically, it would appear that Schweitzer really fails to clarify how our present day ethics are to be viewed in relation to Jesus' teachings as an "interim ethic" in the face of the problem that the apocalyptic end, for Schweitzer, has not yet come. Do we still have an "interim ethic" or do we not? It would seem so, but it is dubious that Schweitzer makes it lucid.

29 This refers to the nonhistorical aspect of Barth's view of the revealed Word in relation to the Incarnation.

30 Cf. Harnack, *What Is Christianity?*, Lecture I.

31 *Quest of the Historical Jesus*, p. 401. In a sense, this anticipates Bultmann's nearly antihistorical view of Christ, his resurrection and Grace-wrought salvation, save that Bultmann is existential and transcendent in outlook. The kinship is strengthened, however, only to the extent that the latter

point is seen in mystical terms. Cf., p. 216ff.

32 *Ibid.*, Cf. Brunner, *Dogmatics*, Vol. II, p. 236, on the criticism.

33 Strauss, *The Life of Jesus*, Vol. I, p. 3f; Vol. II, pp. 867-899. Cf. Schweitzer, *The Quest . . .* , pp. 193-199, on Strauss. But Strauss later became skeptical of the Hegelian version of Christ.

34 Dodd, *op. cit.* Cf. Roberts, *op. cit.*, p. 18f. D. M. Baillie, *God Was in Christ*, p. 75.

35 Bultmann, *Jesus and the Word*, pp. 36, 38. Later works stress "transcendental" rather than "supernatural."

36 *Eschatology and Ethics in the Teaching of Jesus*, p. 41.

37 Roberts, *op. cit.*, p. 17f.

38 Grant, *The Earliest Gospel*, pp. 249, 147, 15f. Cf. Grant, *New Testament Thought*, p. 268f.

39 Dodd, *Apostolic Preaching*, p. 195.

40 *Ibid.*, p. 197.

41 *Ibid.*, p. 201ff.

42 *Ibid.*, p. 208.

43 *Ibid.*, pp. 210-216.

44 *Ibid.*, pp. 217-232.

45 *Ibid.*, p. 232ff.

46 *Ibid.*, p. 238.

47 *Ibid.*, p. 239f.

48 Dodd, *The Coming of Christ*, p. 24.

49 Cullmann, *Christ and Time*, pp. 17, 21, 32, 44, 54ff, 100.

50 *Ibid.*, pp. 19-25, 32f.

51 E.g., Genesis 1:14, Exodus 13:10, Acts 1:7. Cf. I Thess. 5:1.

52 *Op. cit.*, p. 45.

53 *Ibid.* pp. 456, 61.

54 Maurice, *Theological Essays*, p. 302ff. Cf. Edwin Lewis, *The Biblical Faith and Christian Freedom*, p. 34, and Neve, *A History of Christian Thought*, Vol. II, p. 219.

55 *Op. cit.*, p. 49.

56 *The Creator and the Adversary*, p. 162.

57 *Op. cit.*, p. 69. Cf. p. 53.

58 *Ibid.*, p. 93.

59 *Ibid.*, p. 138. Note the extremism of the this statement. It totally neglects the eschatology of the Synoptics and the early Pauline writings.

60 *Ibid.*, pp. 29, 60, 85.

61 *Ibid.*, p. 86. This tension is elaborated in his work, *Immortality of the Soul or Resurrection of the Dead?* esp. pp. 42f, 48.

62 *Ibid.*, p. 213.

63 *Ibid.*, pp. 234f, 168, 144f. Opposing Greek immortality, this book stresses a bodily resurrection at the End, with the dead also waiting since in imperfect state, though "with Christ."

64 D. M. Baillie, *God Was in Christ*, pp. 73-78.

65 *Ibid.*, p. 75.

66 *Ibid.*, p. 78.

67 *Ibid.*, p. 191.

68 *Jesus and the Word*, pp. 36, 38.

69 *The Theology of the New Testament*, Vol. I, p. 3.

70 *Ibid.*, pp. 4-8. Cf. *Jesus and the Word*, p. 131. Note how both Bultmann and Cullmann reject the element of the future in their respective ways, whereas their views of the Kingdom's "presence" are in opposition.

71 *Ibid.*, pp. 9-19.

72 *Ibid.*, p. 20.

73 *Ibid.*, pp. 295, 25. R. R. Niebuhr in *Resurrection and Historical Reason* pleads for a historical security just as extreme. See Appendix.

74 *Ibid.*, p. 26. Cf. Carl Michalson, *The Hinge of History*, Chap. 8, an adaptation of Bultmann's view.

75 *Ibid.*, pp. 25-32. Cf. Hermann, *Communion with God*, p. 66ff.

76 *Ibid.*, p. 36. Cf. Vol. II, p. 9f.

77 *The Theology of the N.T.*, Vol. II, p. 75.

78 *Ibid.*, p. 84ff. Note how in general Bultmann and Cullmann concur on the latter point.

79 *Ibid.*, pp. 112-114.

80 *Ibid.*, pp. 115. Cf. pp. 5-9, 27. Cullmann seems to have overlooked this.

81 *Ibid.*, p. 29.

82 *Die Kirchliche Dogmatik, III*, pp. 335-337. Cf. Archibald Hunter, *Myth in the N.T.*, p. 41 See above, pp. 140-146, and below, pp. 245-247, for our discussions on Barth's later concessions.

83 Bultmann, *The Presence of Eternity*, pp. 12ff, 21f.

84 *Ibid.*, p. 23ff, 37.

85 *Ibid.*, p. 38ff.

86 *Op. cit.*, Vol. II, p. 580f. Cf. Heidegger, *Existence and Being*, p. 110ff.

87 *Op. cit.*, Vol. I, p. 155 and Vol. II, p. 39.

88 The "dawning" Kingdom is imminent but qualitatively different in a transcendent sense, hence the "end" of common history.

89 *An Existentialist Theology*, p. 23.

90 *Ibid.*, p. 24.

91 Cf. *The Theology of the New Testament*, Vol. I, p. 303.

92 Cf. Robert E. Cushman, "Is the Incarnation a Symbol?" *Theology Today*, July, 1958, p. 181.

93 Brunner, *The Eternal Hope*, pp. 60, 118, 214.

94 *Op. cit.*, Vol. II, p. 39.

95 Cf. D. M. Baillie, *God Was in Christ*, p. 215.

96 At Temple University, April 21, 1958.

97 Cf. Baillie, *op. cit.*, p. 219, and Appendix.

98 Forsyth, *The Church and the Sacraments*, pp. 92, 87-93.

Chapter VIII

EXISTENTIAL TIME AND THE APOCALYPSE

We have seen from various points of view how time and eternity constitute a two-in-one relationship which is neither a synthesis nor a dichotomy, and how neither element need be obviated in acknowledging the other. The central indication of this lies in the Incarnate Event of Christ, the full meaning and mission of which are completed only in the End Event or "Second Advent," the eschatological complement of *kairos*.

As a form of *kairos,* the End as *eschaton* is a two-sided moment compounded of both time and eternity, with the latter transforming the former to the fullest extent. A sublime paradox, this lends pertinence to the New Testament symbol of Apocalypse adapted from the Old Testament. Representing the "fulfilling" aspect of the divine incursion, the Apocalypse also implies the redemptive factor, the divine disturbance which gives special endowment to the *eschaton* in a more-than-evolutionary or progressive sense. It is *kairos par excellence* in the sense that the eternal not only qualifies the temporal but ends it by elevating and transfiguring it. It is this transcendent endowment which adorns Mount Eschaton with her crystalline cap. One senses her majestic magnificence only as he stands on Kairos and with the right perspective by eyes of faith detects a depth dimension allowing her vertical and horizontal extremities to meet as one.

Apocalypse and Existential Eschatology

Berdyaev is one thinker who conceded an unresolved antinomy in the idea of the end of time. Logically, the end of time suggests a "timelessness" which should be extrinsic to history and man's *chronos* in concrete existence.[1] But a dynamic, redemptive eternity disallows this, as we have come to see. The Apocalypse signifies the divine act of redemption not only within or by means of time but at the end of time and history. Whereas the Second Coming and fulfillment of the Kingdom of God symbolizes the End-event as relevant to time spiritually and culturally, the Apocalypse, while akin to these symbols, is a reminder of the transcendent and eternal source of such a fulfillment and the revealing and transforming Act involved. Apocalypse means that eternity must do for time as destiny what time cannot do for itself. It must meet time that time may enter eternity—at the End. This links men of faith with the Alpha and Omega identified with time's beginning and end, while only because they are identified faithwise with eternity. As eternity invests itself in time, time is given a dividend in eternity.

Another eschatological symbol from the New Testament is the so-called "millennium." Berdyaev sees that this is neither to be literalized as in "fundamentalism" nor effaced as in last century "liberalism." Rather, like the Apocalypse and Second Coming, it must be reinterpreted. The millennium signifies the cosmic and terrestrial side of the End, that aspect of the Second Coming or Kingdom's fulfillment which implies great relevance for both human life and the cosmic program on this side of a perfect eternity of transcendence. To employ a figure, it signifies the historic or temporal narthex to the perfect sanctuary of the end-in-eternity. It is a form of *kairos* within the interim and lived in view of the *eschaton* in a manner which does not lift the believer and *koinonia* altogether out of time and the worlds of nature and social culture, but makes the supratemporal end highly significant to these temporal areas. The millennium pertains, then, to the end from the human standpoint of both the cyclic and horizontal *telos*. "It is the hope that the positive result of the cosmic process will be revealed in some intermediary sphere between time and eternity," says Berdyaev "This is the essential difficulty in interpreting the Apocalypse. The language of eternity must be translated into the language of time." [2] This paradoxical translation has been kept ambiguous by Karl Barth, as we shall see more clearly in the next section of our present discussion. For Berdyaev the idea of Apocalypse allows for a temporal (millennial) translation, as it were, keeping the end-in-eternity highly significant to the end *of* time. The millennium represents that intermediary point of transition which is the difference between the end as mere *telos* and the end *in* eternity. It is the element of *chronos* within the *eschaton,* which implies that the latter is on the border of time and eternity, i.e., not completely taken up into eternity itself but on the brink of it. This gives additional meaning to the petition: "thy Kingdom come . . . on earth as it is in heaven."

Berdyaev remains sensitive to the tendency in much modern theology to leave to a sheer futuristic view or chronological future those redemptive factors which belong to eternity and the transcendent prerogative of God. The liberal nineteenth-century practice of tossing out the idea of Apocalypse reflects this, while it is a symbol which should be retained with respect for the transcendent. Berdyaev sees the Apocalypse as that which paradoxically links the future *telos* of time with its qualitative dimension and end in the eternal present.[3] It is the eternal aspect of the End, of which the millennium symbolizes a temporal relevance. Together these symbols provide for an *eschaton* which is "the eschatological consummation of the existential dialectic of the divine and the human," the fulfilled dialectic of the eternal and the temporal.[4] Thus the eternal Now sheds light not only upon the existential present but upon an eternal destiny that qualifies man's future destiny as well. Eternity redeems not only in the present but what we might call the future present of faith and hope, both of which are significant to the existentially situated man of faith.

With some modification, Berdyaev would approve of the statement by F. H. Brabant: "It is true that in the later Apocalyptic the hope of the Messianic Kingdom on this earth recedes, but still the day of the Lord is a historical intervention of God and all history is a preparation for it." [5] While to Berdyaev not "all" history is a preparation for the Day of the Lord, history is such a preparation only to the extent that the Apocalyptic dimension has affected it through the existential encounter with God in moments of *kairos* as men of faith look also to the *eschaton.* To the apocalyptists this is related to the future while preeminently a matter of divine eruption, the Spirit's work of transfiguration.

As an Active Eschatology

Eschatology involves both God and man. Ethically speaking,

the Apocalypse does not provide a passive escape into a private heaven; rather, it includes a calling for men under God to help transfigure the stricken and fallen world of sinful existence as instruments in His hand. In other words, there is a co-creative eschatological role for the man of faith to play both *now* and *then*, i.e., in the Kingdom as *come* and the Kingdom *to come* into fulfillment at the end. However, the latter is not an evolutionary notion or a mere utopian dream let alone a man-made institution projected into a strictly horizontal future. Only an existentially oriented faith and ethic with an eschatological outlook can prove valid, for only from beyond sheer history can there be a solution to man's temporal frustrations caused by his betrayal of the eternal.[6]

This view helps to correct the extreme views in theology, we believe. It demands that we challenge the old liberal notion that man builds the Kingdom by emulating Jesus and the Sermon on the Mount on the one hand, and the overly conservative idea of the futility of any creative endeavor to cooperate with God unto the transfiguration of temporal existence on the other. Both views are weak. The one overaccommodates sinful man; the other shortens the saving arm of God. Apocalypticism, then, is not a passive retreat but a present, creative responsibility for the future from the standpoint of a present faith and hope.[7] It implies that a radically new epoch may be realized when men in their time take seriously now the power of God in His eternity. It comes about only as something divinely cataclysmic happens from *above* man and his time while vitally efficacious within it.

In stressing the importance of a rejuvenated eschatological *Weltanschauung* for today, Berdyaev repudiates any idea of a historical theocracy not geared to the existential and eschatological interpretation of life. Here is where another Russian thinker Solovyov, for instance, is weaker as an eschatologist. He is not truly Apocalyptic, despite the fact that his religious background was more eschatological than that of most Western Christians.[8] Berdyaev is aware of this and he sees, too, where Roman Catholicism withdraws from a genuine eschatology, since the Apocalyptic motif is "incompatible with the academic, socially organized character of Roman Catholicism." [9] That is, the direction of men's souls by the institutional Church jeopardizes a truly eschatological consciousness. Anticipating subsequent discussion, may we assert that the precedent was set by Augustine in this respect. His *City of God* looks to a fairly temporal victory.

Here the "Russian idea" opposes the "Roman idea," as Dostoevsky also asserted. The Russian people in general have held to a more free, prophetic type of Christian spirit, despite the obvious objectifications within the Orthodox Church.[10] This is true even to the extent that the Russian Christians have felt that theirs is a positive, though not exclusive, role in the fulfillment of the Kingdom and that the Apocalypse is functioning *now*. This attitude reflects their strong eschatological consciousness allied with the spirit of *Sobornost* ("togetherness"; note kinship to the New Testament *koinonia*), something in marked contrast to Western ideas of Utopia and evolutionary optimism, as well as individualism, both in and outside the Church.

Berdyaev states with considerable justification,

> Eastern orthodoxy is the most eschatological form of Christianity, the least submitted to the influence of processes which are unfolded in the world. This eschatology possesses a meaning different from that of Protestant movements like Barthianism. Western Christianity—Catholic and Protestant alike— have always been more social.[11]

While this may be true in principle, it remains open to serious questioning whether Eastern Orthodoxy has been consistent with what Berdyaev describes as the active, creative and expressive aspects of the eschatological outlook. Hardly any religious body has been more obeisant to tyrannical political leaders than the Eastern Church, a matter to be taken seriously, especially in terms of the modern era. Furthermore, the more astute Russian prophets of the past two centuries have not been the official leaders of the Church but laymen of a strong eschatological and ethical consciousness, men like Khomiakov, Solovyov, Dostoevsky and Berdyaev himself.[12]

Nineteenth-century Russian thought for the most part had an undercurrent of man's search for the Kingdom of God with a more meaningful life and a concomitant social justice based upon Christian charity and communion. It attacked the bourgeois spirit associated with a Western "love of 'this world' in the New Testament sense of the word." [13] Somewhat akin to the Messianic consciousness of Israel, social justice to the Russian people always has been linked with an eschatological hope, not a mere utopian dream of human progress. It was an Apocalyptic, God-conscious disposition rather than an evolutionary-to-revolutionary confidence in common history. It seems understandable that this consciousness or outlook should be exploited by Bolshevism and a Marxian materialism linked with a revolutionary proletariat. While not compatible in principle, the one is a secularized version of the other in socialistic terms, while parallel to Western secularization in terms of "progressive education," technology and industry.

But it must be understood that the outlook of Russian Christianity has known two basic types of Apocalyptic consciousness: [14] first, the ascetic type of passive, monastic reaction from a social and cultural point of view, one which sees the Antichrist in certain social movements; and second, the creative active type with a vision of Christian justice in society based upon brotherhood in Christ, yet a view which passes judgment on the smugness of the bourgeois society and calls men to a common cause of reform in view of the End. Berdyaev belongs to the more prophetic Apocalyptic consciousness of the latter type. Both a passive millennialism and a superficial progressivism are held to be immature. Hence, Berdyaev can say firmly, "The Apocalypse is not only the revelation of the end of the world and the last judgment. It is also an interior judgment upon history, for the end is always near." [15] Thus we see how the Apocalypse signifies the relevance of eternity to history's true consummation, its *eschaton*, even as Apocalypse offsets what makes for the eschatological failure of history and the Church that chooses to accommodate itself to a temporal culture.

As a New Spirituality

The Apocalypse is eternal truth symbolically addressed to the spirit of men; therefore, it is not to be identified with any particular political, social or ecclesiastical system. Even so, it inspires a "spiritual and social revolution" within historic time. Only persons of faith can understand and help instrument the outpouring of the Spirit of God which transforms men and their world. An eschatologically minded minority in this respect can outweigh a materialistically minded majority. But this cannot be rationalized. It belongs to the mysteries of the eternal kingdom. No time schedule can be imposed upon the Apocalypse. At the same time, any passive view of its meaning lends itself to religious and ethical decadence. Berdyaev declares, "To regard apocalyptic prophecies with passive resignation means to interpret them in a naturalistic sense, to rationalize them and deny the mysterious combination of Divine Providence and human freedom." [16] Such a position is sound and corrects both the literalistic premillennialists and the ultratranscendental Barthians as well as the one-sided existential position of Rudolf Bultmann. Neither does justice to the place of faith's related decisions, let alone all forms of consecrated creativity looking to the coming of the End. They keep the end utterly God's business and in no sense man's, not even for the redeemed man whose faith, life and vocation are held to have nothing to do with the realization of the end. To Berdyaev this is an enervating outlook both religiously and culturally.

The social crisis of today is of profound concern to Berdyaev, yet he regards Tillich's speculations in religious socialism to be utterly "historiosophic" rather than eschatological in character.[17] A more basic need today is a "new spirituality," a new existence based upon the existential perspective of human destiny as treated in the preceding chapters. Sociology *per se* cannot do justice to this; it can only deal with the symptons which accompany it. Needed is a new spirituality with respect for the End, a culture based upon the New Testament *kairos* to foster from within historical existence an eschatological perspective on all things under the inspiration of an apocalyptic transfiguration which yearns to be realized among men. While triumphing over time even as it regenerates it, such an End can be anticipated only because of what has been revealed, *viz.*, that the Eternal Spirit makes himself known *through* time and history that this new spirituality might be possible.[18] Just as this is basic to the meaning of history, so, too, it might be described as the activization of the end of history; it is the overture to the Kingdom's eternal symphony.

Khomiakov's strong emphasis upon *Sobornost* applies well here,[19] for personal and social acts are indistinguishable in the Spirit. Individualistic ethics and salvation are incomplete, for a person's life always involves others. The "new spirituality" of Apocalyptic consciousness is not altogether elective,[20] then, or partial, since it leads men to share each other's pain, peace and destiny. Personal salvation now includes a spirit of *agape* with its concern for others. This entails an interest in social betterment, since both the person and his society are products of spirit.[21]

As substantial as this observation is, Berdyaev reflects an unnecessary aversion to the elective factor related to the biblical idea of Grace. Berdyaev himself recognizes that the true freedom enjoyed by man can only be in and of the Spirit. But at times he sounds a bit Pelagian in his aversion to Protestant theology; however, it would be more shrewd of him to couch his statements of this kind in modified Arminian to semi-Pelagian terms which keep man dependent upon a saving Grace while "respons-ible" to the movements of the Spirit. Actually, this would be more in accord with his own paradoxical dialectic of unity-within-duality.

While Berdyaev does not equate the Church with the Kingdom as did Augustine and subsequent Roman churchmen, the Church is meant to be a colony of persons looking to the Kingdom in the End. This agrees with Vladimir Lossky who speaks of "a living tradition, the incessant revelation of the Holy Spirit in the Church, in the life of which each of its members can participate according to his measure." Also, her "doctrine and experience are mutually conditional." [22] Berdyaev concurs that the Church has an eschatological place to fill unto the *theosis* of mankind and the coming of the new aeon of the Spirit. Founded upon the incarnate Christ, the Church is both in time and eternity, and her eschatological vocation must express how the two are related. As early Church Fathers like Irenaeus, Athanasius, Gregory Nazianzus and Gregory of Nyssa were known to have said, "God made Himself man, that man might become God." [23]

While probably overstated in mystical terms, this is something which Berdyaev can appreciate. It is a double movement belonging to the principle of God-manhood and blending with *kairos* and *eschaton*. It means, too, that the divine *kenosis* (Philippians 2:6-11) was essential to mankind's eschatological *theosis*, and that both the Incarnation and Apocalypse make eternity relevant to human existence and destiny within and beyond history.

While Berdyaev's doctrine of *theosis* epitomizes his mysticism and blends with his idea of an eschatological transfiguration of which Apocalypse is an important symbol, it threatens to dissolve the identity of the individual within the mystical body of a redeemed mankind. While it need not do so, and in other contexts Berdyaev guards his mystical insights from doing quite that, it tends to do so as it stands alone. It also tends to blur the distinction between man's finitude in relation to divine infinitude. While this need not be the case when seen in the light of Berdyaev's own doctrine of "celestial history" and a symmetrical doctrine of immortality, it tends to do so. *Theosis*, then, is a doctrine which plays down the temporal fallenness of man together with his sinful wretchedness. While we need not be overly preoccupied with this problem, neither can we sell it short.

Neither a glorious past nor a utopian future can be equated with the Kingdom of God. Historical forms of the divine revelation are not sufficient in themselves as custodians or portrayals of the full truth. Historical and nationalistic settings are apt to be too provincial and thus restrict the meaning of what is eternal and universal. Even the contemporary ecumenical movement is insincere until every denomination senses that it is incomplete. The Church is not "heaven on earth" [24] and her ecclesiastical, sacerdotal, legalistic and individualistic doctrines must be modified by a prophetic eschatology. Most needed is a fresh messianic consciousness to prepare for the Kingdom's coming comparable to that of the first Coming of the Messiah.[25] Christianity must be prophetically concerned about the future, but in a more-than-temporal sense, i.e., the future in the End, the "transcendent" Kingdom of God made "immanent" only in the existential sense. Clarence Tucker Craig, manifesting an ecumenical spirit similar to that of Berdyaev, states that the very nature of the Church is eschatological. "Its true character," he says, "is never found within the compromise of history but in the Beloved Community which lies beyond history." Craig then suggests that the unity of the Church is actually centered in "the end of time," and a theology which provides for that unity sets the *kerygma* in the center of things.[26] This is congenial to Berdyaev's position.

The transition to an eschatological outlook must be one that moves from ecclesiastical authoritarianism to spiritual creativeness; from a preoccupation with an empty and dead time to a concentration upon the living End. An apocalyptic awareness of a dynamic eternality in vital relationship to the present must displace the bad temporality and objectified temporal infinity of a bourgeois consciousness. "The search for the Kingdom of God on earth is a search for a way out of every adaptation to natural necessity; it is a thirst for the liberation from the burdens of this world." [27] As a new social life it is communion not with the horizontal but with the vertical in relation to the horizontal. Based on the spiritual rebirth of personality and not on the evolution of an old society, it is the New Jerusalem of a transformed life, a theocracy not of the state but of the Spirit. Man prospers in this Kingdom solely in proportion to his spiritual growth. And as Berdyaev says, "There must be pushed aside all rationalistic debate over the chiliasm, over the millennial reign of Christ." [28] While such a Kingdom is not born of elements of the fallen world, this is not to say the Kingdom will not come on earth. The earth is more than physical, and it belongs to eternity as well as to time. When the Kingdom comes in the End, it will be experienced in the glorified spiritual bodies of men, not the physical. In that sense it will be cataclysmic rather than evolutionary as the fullness of God-manhood prevails in all relationships. The conquest of evil, enslaving time through the displacement of a spurious infinity by a dynamic eternity, will be seen in true existential time, in man's true *Existenz* and Destiny.

Berdyaev does well in stressing man's creativeness and possible co-creativeness under God and admits that while man longs for eternity in much of his creativity, the products of his creativeness are always culturally temporal. Still, the Fall of man and "original sin" need not be regarded as an egocentric "iron curtain" between man's eyes of faith and his vocational goal under God.[29] This challenges the extreme emphasis upon the depravity of man, even redeemed man, by such contemporary theologians as Karl Barth and Reinhold Niebuhr. Unlike Barth, Berdyaev still sees fallen man as a spiritual being with great possibilities of self-transcendence in Christ. Barth leaves the redeemed man about as dead in the sin of the "flesh" as he was before meeting Christ. Here the doctrine of the Holy Spirit is important. Barth sees the Spirit working upon man only from without. Berdyaev sees the Spirit also working from within, as Subject with subject, Spirit with spirit. Without this the redeeming work of Christ remains unfulfilled, says Berdyaev. Just as the "redeeming work of the Son" concerns the nature of man, Berdyaev rather extremely says, the "deifying work of the Holy Spirit" concerns the person of man.[30]

Here we see the danger in *theosis,* as mentioned above, Berdyaev is inclined to see man as almost deified rather than redeemed in eternity. This is a serious weakness borrowed from Eastern mystical thought. It is not necessary to the acceptance of his basic eschatology, however. His adaptation of *theosis* should not move beyond his doctrines of ultimate transfiguration and "celestial history." The latter especially retains time in eternity and allows for a certain individuality and humanity within immortality. Yet even this confirms Berdyaev's intention to see man as "an interior moment" in the mystery of eternity. This is acceptable but not in terms of an apotheosis of man. Man must remain man throughout eternity. Here Karl Barth's idea that even Christ retains his manhood at the right hand of God the Father is apropos. The parallel is to be seen in the immortality of every redeemed child of God. Just as eternity does not negate time in redeeming it neither does it dissolve human individuality or threaten to do so.

Berdyaev tries to resolve this problem in the following distinction: "It is inexact to say that man is spirit; but it can be said that he has spirit. The distinction between *being* and *having* is only resolved in God."[31] This is an important observation, yet it must be said that even as man returns to eternity to be spirit and not just *have* spirit, he is still individual man and not mystically obscured or lost in an infinite eternity. The strength of the idea lies in its stressing that man is meant to *become* and to participate fully in the divine life of the Eternal Spirit. Even so, the tendency to lay himself open to a mysticism of union befalls Berdyaev, though he does not quite succumb. In his maturest thought Berdyaev does not slip into this, for he is sensitive to the duality of man as a being involved in the antithesis of spirit versus flesh.[32] The transfigured man, then, requires a transfigured flesh. (Compare this to the changed "spiritual body" of the Risen Lord and to St. Paul's observa-

240

tions on immortality in I Corinthians 15.) Man is meant to experience not the loss of his identity in the end but the fulfillment of himself, the true destiny of the existential subject.[33] This comes about in the perfect freedom, the life of the spirit upon being transfigured into the *pure existence* [34] of eternity. This is the true destiny of man with which the Apocalypse is concerned in principle.

Amos N. Wilder also gives support to the idea of an active Apocalypticism, but he plays down the distinctive side of the Apocalypse accepted by Berdyaev, *viz.*, the place for "divine intervention." [35] Wilder, however, concurs that the Apocalypse entails both an eternal destiny and a socio-historical future.[36] Either extreme is held to be wrong. But Wilder leaves the Parousia "imaginative" for fear of the otherworldly element being necessarily an "imminent catastrophe." [37] He sees the meaning of history dependent upon God's "historical activity," but is reluctant to apply this principle of dynamic activity to the anticipated end. Unlike Berdyaev, Wilder thinks apocalyptic eschatology dissolves history by transcending the distinction between time and eternity. This reflects a rationalistic failure to see the time-eternity relationship from the existential perspective.

Though Wilder's anxiety seems feasible in the face of a passive eschatology of total transcendence, it is not the last word, as Berdyaev shows us, for history can be "transfigured" at the end of time. The Kingdom belongs to the "eternal now" while being more than symbolic for men in history because it entails a future fulfillment in an *eschaton* which is both temporal and eternal.[38] Wilder misses all this in failing to preserve the existentiality of eternity's redemptive time-embracing character. Therefore, he resorts to a mysticism somewhat similar to that of Schweitzer.[39] While Berdyaev's position is mystical, it reconciles both the eternal and historical aspects of the end together with the same in Christ's God-manhood and doctrine of the kingdom, something which Schweitzer does not do in his mystical eschatology, nor Barth and Bultmann in their transcendent dualisms. Here, again, we see the practicability of Berdyaev's better balanced existential eschatology. He brings the time elements of the Kingdom into relationship with the eternal now in such a way as to keep *both* vital and real to the scriptural problem of eschatology and its resolution.

Having crystallized the basic insights of Berdyaev pertaining to the place of the Apocalypse, we will further compare it with those of neo-Reformed thinkers of our day like Barth and Brunner.

The Position of Barth

As seen in Chapter IV, Karl Barth shifts to a more dynamic view of eternity than orthodox theology since Augustine has dared to entertain. Not merely a transcendent immutability, eternity is at least seen to embrace its own kind of time consisting of both duration and succession.

Faith includes a "new time" impregnated with eternity in every moment (*Jetzt*), Barth maintains.[40] This is the seat of eschatological intensity inasmuch as it belongs to God's time, not man's. Thus faith, for Barth, is a kind of Kierkegaardian leap out of ordinary historic time. Faith yields hope because God has revealed the fulfillment in eternity of that which for men has yet to be fulfilled. This appears to imply an interim of transition, since it is expressed as a future consummation.[41]

But the question arises: Is it man's time in any sense? It is not. Barth fails to wrestle with an eschatological interim involving man's time and faith-conditioned expectation. Eschatological time, as it were, is not attributable to history and human existence, only to God's transcendent time within eternity. Barth neglects the *eschaton*, in the true sense, because for him whatever belongs to time, including the future, belongs strictly to eternity's "fulfillment and execution." [42] This, we maintain, is not the *kairos* which spells out a regenerated *chronos* as previously discussed. Barth neglects the relation between the redeemed man's existence in *chronos* and his faith in eternity. A stringent duplicity prevails. Thus common time is something in which God has no investment. It will be given no divine dividend in the End.

Barth once catered to a Platonic concept of a timeless eternity overshadowing the present[43] together with a nonhistorical revelation. But his shift to a dynamic view still keeps eternity protected; it does not relate a dynamic eternity to historic time as men know it. The time-eternity dialectic is retained within eternity *per se*, an extremely transcendental position. Thus a future end as conceded by Barth seems eschatologically promising but remains sterile. The interim for faith is still irrelevant to the *chronos* and *Historie* of men. Time ends while God still *is*, Barth stresses, and man shall return to God from Whom he came. "Eternity is both the limit and end, behind and above which another cannot stand, because it is the substance [*Inbegriff*] of everything." [44] Barth adds, "And so God is the absolute, the unsurpassed future of all time and all things in time." [45] Thus the equivalent to the *eschaton* is for Barth utterly transcendent of history. This gives the man in time no eschatological responsibility or role pertaining to his end and that of history. Barth's view of eternity's sovereignty still keeps it incapable of fully redeeming time and history. This rigid dualism allows no *Anknüpfungspunkt*. Thus it lacks a balanced existential time such as we have contended for, a time amenable to eschatological meaning and its instrumentation.

Barth speaks of a "general resurrection" in a moment, but he debilitates the symbol, since it pertains to the future strictly within eternity and not in a form of transfigured time comparable to Berdyaev's *eschaton*. There is a present joy in "the eternal future," in God's time only.[46] For God is now. True, we say, but this obviates the tension between man's time and God's as if they were mutually alien, even for the faithful. Thus Barth fails to keep the end as existential as the Incarnation should imply. Using the language of eschatology, Barth strips its temporal form of all temporal relevance. The interim to which he refers is within eternity's "predestined time." [47] This actually pushes Augustine's scheme into heaven. One wonders how Barth could gain such a celestial perspective! The apocalyptic element of eternity relating itself to *chronos* in the *eschaton* is neatly obviated. God does not redeem what is deemed unreal by Barth. Here Augustine was better balanced in regarding time as created by God, hence something to be reckoned with. Thus the "miracle" [48] Barth speaks of is not a miracle. He fails to see eternity entering temporal Becoming even to the extent that Kierkegaard allowed for it. For Barth, God does not stoop to save. Revelation and redemption are solely within eternity. The end has no reference to man's future, only the

Jetzt of faith. We must ask: Are not man's existence and history redeemable? Is God too short-armed to save the products and by-products of creation centered about the created and redeemed minds and souls of men? Instead of regenerating what is lost, God, according to Barth, only negates them. Is this the true picture and full meaning of a redemptive destiny? We think not.

The Second Coming for Barth is "the goal of time that is coming to an end." [49] This appears better balanced but does not prove to be. The Christian lives faithwise in the end.[50] But his future is held to be "at the end of time." [51] This, again, is in "eternal time" [52] and severed altogether from *chronos.* The goal is really beyond this time which comes to an end, giving the latter no consequence or meaning. Barth's ultimate "eschatological monism," mentioned above, is legitimate in principle but not in its dialectical operation within the prevalent dualism. Thus, hope is not anticipation for him. The monistic victory supersedes but is not involved in the dualistic controversy. This is artificial. Barth epitomizes the matter thus:

> Christian monism is not a knowledge which is presently possible, but a *coming* knowledge . . . it must only be comprehended now as a Christian dualism, as the tension between promise and fulfillment, between 'not yet' and 'one day,' and it may *not* be anticipated.[53]

Thus, it should be illegitimate for Barth to use futuristic terms, because they are inconsistent with his meaning. For him the eschatological hope is strictly supratemporal and has nothing to do with man's ideas of time. It would be fairer of him to brusquely assert this and drop all biblical thought forms and language pertaining to the end. For him the man of existence is totally irrelevant to the time-eternity dialectic that remains solely within eternity itself. But a redemption completely within God's time and foreign to "our time" is too transcendent to be fully redemptive. It were better suited to unfallen angels than to redeemed men!

Redemption to Barth means "God's time for us." It is "fulfilled time." To the Old Testament it was an expectation; to the New Testament, a recollection of a special "encounter." It is a given time which God alone possesses and in no way a

244

product of human existence. The Fall of man is the basic differ-ence between God's time and man's. "God-created time remains a time hidden and withdrawn from us." [54] It is "eternal time." But Barth, while very realistic about Christ's involvement in man's flesh and fallen time, is Christologically inconsistent here because he asserts that Christ's return to the Father includes his flesh.[55] If this is the case, Barth should also include common or fallen time in Christ's eternal Sonship, in which case time cannot be so alien to eternity and the divine purpose as Barth claims. Basically, if Christ were fully man and retains his man-hood in his Sonship, then the common time of said manhood is not overlooked by the Godhead. Barth has failed us here.

In his *Dogmatik* Barth says, "Time, by becoming the time of Jesus Christ became a different, a new time." It belongs to "the Lord of time" and is "mastered time;" it is a "real and fulfilled time." It pertains to the man of faith in the present and is of the eternal Word, which undergoes no change.[56] Aside from the inconsistency of the latter with Barth's dynamic eter-nity, this is in error, because what he really attributes to the transcendent Word and Son Barth ascribes to Jesus Christ. This is no less than cumbersome, for Barth has argued that Jesus participated in man's "fallen time." The basic problem is Barth's Nestorian Christology. It is not a genuine doctrine of the Incar-nation, because of the lack of ample interrelation between the two kinds of time involved, "fallen time" and "eternal, new or fulfilled time." Yet Barth comes to the point where he says the Word elevates the time into which it is spoken, i.e., raises fallen time up to "His own time," thus giving it a "part in the existence of God." [57]

This is a remarkable concession for Barth. But, again, a defect in the picture is to be seen. As it stands, Barth, in essence, plants an impediment within eternity, *viz.*, the Son's implied involvement and retention of a fleshly, meaningless, finite time. How can this concession be settled for in any sense whatever unless eternity and man's common, fallen time have something in common through divine involvement in the created and exis-tential orders? How can this be accepted unless Barth is willing to concede that man's time and its end are not unknown to God and His time and that the *eschaton* is more than a symbol of what transcends time, since it is an Event involving both *chronos* and eternity's redemptive Act? Even to make this adjustment in his thinking Barth should have to modify his earlier claim: "Revelation becomes history, but history does not become revelation." [58] This is because we cannot alienate revelation from the divine concern and relation to the end, an end which is both divine and human.

In his later works, Barth, as we have begun to see, sometimes tones down his extreme position as though the "act of God" and the message of "God with us" involved something of "worldly time," [59] thus allowing *Heilsgeschichte* to be related to general *Historie,* something for which we are contending in this discourse. He even begins to concede that Christ is the "true time" Who entered man's "fallen time" without ceasing to be eternal. In this context Barth refers to Christ as "Eternal in time." But this is not handled consistently by Barth. Salvation is given by God prior to creation and means, too, that the "*eschaton* is given by God." God is in the present but is still not sufficiently related to man's future. The future is already present for God, and Christ *is* that future for the man of faith, not as the means to it but the very content thereof. This affords a type of Kierkegaardian depth dimension by which all is in God, and Christ is the one who "comes as the end of time." [60] Thus the Christian's hope amounts to an upward look but without any real forward look. It implies an "eternal future" but is not related to a temporal one. The divine promise allows no realistic division between today and tomorrow.[61] Yet closer to Augustine, Barth tries to retain a "teleological direction" to a person's life in time, strange to say, one with relative and provisional ends, but he fails to link it with the eschatological direction. Berdyaev succeeds where Barth fails.

The Parousia is the living Presence of Christ beginning at the Ascension, for Barth, but it is not involved in an actual consummation. In "our time" there is only an "imperfect coming." [62] Eternal life is "hidden" in the temporal present. Barth says,

If God in Jesus Christ has reconciled the world with Himself this also means that in Him he had made an end, a radical end, of the world which contradicts and opposes Him, that an old aeon, our world time . . . with all that counts and is great in it, has been brought to an end.[63]

246

Barth writes as though the second coming included Christ's "final coming in His resurrection as the Judge of the quick and the dead," [64] but this is the end-time, the goal of the *koinonia* which holds the Easter faith. This faith means that eternal life became an event, thus implying a final revelation and judgment —save that it was of a "penultimate character." It means a new time had begun [65] because the old time was abolished. But we say Barth keeps this new time too aloof from the old time with which even men of faith are still involved as men of the world, though their "citizenship is in heaven" (Cf. Ephesians 2:19).

Barth is an evangelical universalist who believes all men are elected of God's Grace *now* to share His eternal life; thus all are restored in the End. But to claim this, Barth must obscure the competition of man's time (*chronos*), and this is hardly true to the total biblical picture. Easter is the clue, for it is the dawning of the Last Day.[66] True, we say, but some temporal darkness still surrounds us as the dawn breaks in to vanquish it. High noon is still before us, though a great promise. A promise is a present assurance about a real trusted future—trusted because it belongs to God not just man.

"The love of God," Barth says, "is . . . the unobservable place where the consummation of all things has already been completed." [67] Granted, we say, with the utmost respect for the dynamic eternal now, but why such a claim if the consummation is a transcendent unity completely alien to the historical and anthropological side of the absolute *Gegensatz* which it is meant to heal? The only thing resolved is eternity's time. While it may be possible to have a faith related to that kind of heavenly time, as it were, it keeps the Christian hope irrelevant to the man of existence and his mundane affairs, let alone the created cosmos. If there is no realistic time side to the hope it is hardly a hope, we deduce, for we should be in heaven now—which we are not! In this respect, Oscar Cullmann is perfectly right in saying that what is future in Barth's system is not what is "future for us." [68] It is future only for God. *Berdyaev, on the contrary, preserves both sides of the Christian hope.* While a fulfillment for God, it is a faith-conditioned anticipation for men and is still related to the historic interim. Emil Brunner also sees the end in eternity, but he can say, "Hope means the presence of the future. . . . Hope is the positive, as anxiety is the negative mode of awaiting the future." [69] This implies a realistic time related to the hope that is from eternity.

Barth is misleading, if not unfair, in employing the language of the New Testament *Parousia* while keeping its meaning unhinged from history. Even speaking like a millennialist he can say, "Since He [Christ] is present as God is present, it already admits of being said that He shall come again as the person He once was." [70] This is obscure, for, as we have seen, Barth keeps both the Eternal Son and the End insufficiently related to history. This is not the case with Berdyaev, who sees the Incarnate Event redeeming man not just in the eternal now, potentially, but in the eternal now, actually, i.e., both now and at the transfigured end of history. Berdyaev sees men of faith having an eschatological role in the interim between the revealed and fulfilled end (s), a part to play in the spiritual conditioning of "the age to come," as St. Paul speaks of it. The closest Barth seems to come to this is in regarding a deed of Christian service as "prophetic." He says,

> It rests upon the Kingdom of God as *come* and *to come*. . . . It represents what to God has happened and will. . . . It signifies the death and resurrection of Jesus Christ as the beginning, his return as the end of all things, and even his present Lordship, being, life and work as the Savior of the World. [71]

While the interim is suggested here it is not defended as actual. *"Heil* is created being," says Barth, yet "more than being," for it is "fulfilled being," and only in the latter sense is it *eschaton*. [72] It is kept out of relation with the *chronos* of men in existence; it is in heaven, not on earth! Why, then, should Barth wish to make eschatology basic to preaching and theology so as to provide "a realization of the vocation of man" and even to color his culture? Do not these functions pertain to what he calls the "aeon of flesh and sin"? [73] Should not his eschatology be such that it *can* effect this temporal age? How on his terms can there be anything but a pessimism for history and civilization? [74] And what need is there to preach a determined salvation and end? What need Christ and his cross? Barth's monistic eschatology bypasses what his stringent dualism entails. This serves to demonstrate that Berdyaev is right in

248

denouncing transcendent dualisms as well as overly simple monisms. *Like Kierkegaard, Barth jeopardizes the reality of historic time to gain eternity. Berdyaev, on the contrary, relates them while keeping them both real with eternity victorious over time.*

For Barth, history is utterly hopeless, meaningless and despicable. Not even a means to God's redemptive purpose, it is scorned by what is eternal. This is because it is seen totally vitiated by man's Adamic pride and depravity. God can only say "No!" to whatever pertains to history, for it is corrupt, even though Barth acknowledges Christ to be its center and goal. Historical development is an impossibility, even if given eschatological orientation.[75] The one hope lies beyond death, and this is not in a changed life with an unending future but in the "eternalizing" of an ending life.[76] The basic idea of a life being "eternalized" is parallel to Berdyaev's spiritual transfiguration in the *eschaton,* save that for Barth it is strictly individualistic and irrelevant to the Kingdom's fulfillment at the end of time. For Barth it is the resurrection of the dead. It connotes that God is in every sense beyond, so that the "eternalized life" is alien to any temporal continuation. While not challenging the latter idea *per se,* we must take note here of how it does not blend with Barth's ideas of a Christ who returns to the Father via a fallen time, nor with his more mature ideas of an eternal time which includes duration and succession. Why should Barth be averse to the one while not the others? Is it only a theological expediency?

While Barth, with Berdyaev, has come to acknowledge a dynamic eternity, he does not allow it to step existentially and genuinely into history to redeem history. The "bolt from the blue" is extraneous to time as men know it. By keeping time within eternity, both Barth's doctrines of Christology and eschatology suffer from a debilitating Docetism. Man and his mundane history are left irrelevant to God's eternal program. Thus Barth's eschatological gangplank does not really bridge the great abyss, for there is nothing on man's side to buttress it, not even a minimal addressability. The "vibrations" of eternity and time are not synchronized or, better, "synkaironized" so as to make for a meaningful span. Barth's harsh dualism constrains his ultimate monism to be an apologetic device, an escape from the very dualistic problem of time and its end via a plank that totters with temporal irrelevance. Barth has failed to see how a bridge of eternal timber once assumed the shape of a cross that was dug into the mundane mucks of time and history. He leaves the eternal, transcendent God too small, since His sovereign Love (*agape*) is not truly *emptied* in the temporal settings of man, who is His "other."

The Perspective of Brunner

The balanced existential eschatology of Berdyaev has much in common with the adjusted dialectical eschatology of Emil Brunner. It appears that, directly or indirectly, Brunner has been influenced by Berdyaev's thought. Like Berdyaev, he sees the basic principle of the time-eternity relationship to be a dynamic "theanthropomorphism" [77] which echoes Berdyaev's similar claim for "God-manhood." While Brunner is not as shrewd in clarifying existential time and a dynamic eternity [78] even as he erroneously addresses the problem of the *eschaton* much in terms of *telos,* his over-all perspective is almost parallel to that of Berdyaev.

Brunner, like Berdyaev, accepts historic time as a reality to be seriously reckoned with. Yet there is a "fullness of time" only as God releases it from Himself. Biblical time is distinctive since the "historic event" is of "eternal decree." [79] In principle, this is much like Berdyaev's view of *kairos* and is much more balanced than the position taken by Karl Barth. Yet Brunner has much in common with Barth with respect to time as "preformed and posited as a reality in God's supra-temporal nature and will." [80] While closer to a naive "scheduled" predeterminism here, Brunner sees eternity using time and history more positively than either Barth or Bultmann. Proleptically, not only the Old Testament but all of world history is deemed Messianic by Brunner. [81] This is from the divine standpoint, however. Like Berdyaev, Brunner embraces both continuity and discontinuity between time and eternity without restricting the theological content to a binding ontology. This is sound.

Instead of totally negating Bultmann's thesis Brunner helps correct, broaden and develop it so that, biblically, eschatology is an eternal hope which also vitalizes the future. Quite as for Berdyaev, the basis is a more balanced existential orientation of time. The future involves an element of Apocalypse but, somewhat as for Bultmann, the mythical Judaistic and gnostic forms thereof are seen to be uncongenial to a modern *Weltanschauung* as well as the present assurance proffered men by the *kerygma*.[82] History is more than a cosmic process, and Brunner stands with Berdyaev in seeking to rise above all rational objectification on the one hand, and all empirical or immanental subjectification on the other.[83] Brunner appreciates Bultmann's idea of a dawning Kingdom or New Age in contrast to the emphases of Dodd and Cullmann upon an imminent Parousia. But, much in accord with our arguments in the previous chapter, Brunner says,

> The tension between the time of the End which had already dawned and the Hope of its fulfillment exists; it is an integral element—not only of Primitive Christianity, but also of all genuine Christian faith.[84]

Required for systematic correlation, we contend, is a balanced existential perspective lest time and eternity be confused in either a mythological or cosmological interpretation. In clarifying this problem, Bultmann goes too far in depreciating the tension and historical element of the New Testament revelation, what Brunner calls "The Fact of Christ as an Event in the continuum of history." [85] Noteworthy is the fact that Brunner has moved beyond a position taken by him several years ago when, closer to Bultmann, he denied that the divine element of Christ entered into history.[86] Brunner's more mature view is that the Incarnate Word is linked with a "Jesus of history" with a fleshly temporal existence even subject to critical research.[87] Jesus not only declared but represented and inaugurated the Kingdom in his person. "He is the Kingdom's dawn; it comes with him." [88]

For Brunner, the biblical revelation is positively related to history. Like the Kingdom it is *in* history while not of history.[89] But this being in history is still something to be reckoned with. The Evangelists point us to more than a "Jesus of history" who is a mere man; they give us the one who is Christ through the work God did in and through him.[90] This blends with our above-stated claim for a "Jesus of history" related but subordinate to the "Christ of faith." Here is a both/and paradox similar to the basic perspective of Berdyaev. It is the basic "scandal" and "offense" of the Gospel not amenable to a naked human reason. Thus, Brunner acknowledges that the saving *kerygma,* while distinguishable from its mythical forms, cannot be separated from them entirely lest it be too pantheistic, impersonal or deanthropomorphic to be relevant to men.[91] Mythical thought forms at least suggest that God intervened in time even making for a "history of salvation" not altogether alien to it. As we have contended in previous chapters, this can be denied only by those who insist that the Gospel either is based upon a timeless metaphysics or involves an unrealistic view of time and history.

Brunner's "dualism of possession and anticipation" underlines our claim that Christianity is robbed of much of its redemptive meaning, if hope in a future consummation is defaced. Even more brusquely than Berdyaev, he says, "A church which has nothing to teach concerning the future and the life of the world to come is bankrupt." [92] A meaningful interim in an eschatological outlook upon life and culture is needed. Does this debilitate the strength and distinctiveness of the existential Moment of encounter? Supporting our rejection of the extremes in Kierkegaard, Barth and Bultmann, this strengthens its relevance to a concrete existence steeped in temporal frustration while raising life to a new level of meaning and hope. As for Berdyaev, faith looks up but also ahead to an event presently hidden. "This 'now' and 'then' is essentially one thing," says Brunner, "but in the order of dispensation constitutes the difference between the phase of faith and that of sight." [93] Both matter to the believer, who is still human and involved in time's passing.

Faith in the risen Lord implies more than the significance of his death. Rather, his death has atoning significance because he is the Risen One.[94] The resurrection is the nexus between time and eternity, sin and redemption, death and life. Time mediates the work of the Eternal even as it is redeemed by it. Thus the existential immediacy of our faith encounter is not alien to the mediacy of its setting and the revelatory event to which it looks. Paradoxically, the new life is the "first installment" of eternal life. Though temporalistic in expression, this is Brunner's equivalent to Berdyaev's combination of *kairos* and *eschaton*. Also, Christ's conquest of death has cosmic significance implying subordination of the cosmic powers to Christ in the End. [95] Here we see how the resurrection of Christ anticipates the Apocalypse, much as it does for Berdyaev.

Fundamentalists literalize apocalyptic imagery so that the end amounts to a Judaic, cosmic cataclysm identified with historic time. This is unacceptable. On the other hand, Rudolf Bultmann relegates the apocalyptic element to sheer myth, leaving the future open but without a goal, since all is fulfilled for God. Both extremes are wrong. The End must imply an end for history. The great doctrines of Grace and justification need not mutilate this. Christ is a dual Event in history as well as in the cosmos, Brunner maintains. It not only affects our present and past but future, too. It implies "His future advent." [96]

Thus, like Berdyaev, Brunner sees the end as the goal of history neither lost in cosmic process nor denied by eternity. Within history are "radically apocalyptic traits," says Brunner. This prevents history and culture from being subject to an optimistic view of progress. Even more than modern astronomy, atomic science today reminds us of how sudden the end of history may be. While viewing the end more negatively and realistically than Berdyaev at this point, Brunner has much in common with Berdyaev's two-sided *eschaton* when he asserts, "It might very well be that the end of history were the this-worldly aspect of the coming of the Lord." [97] Can Brunner's realistic time side and Berdyaev's creative time side of the end be conjoined? Neither thinker seems to have done full justice to the other's emphasis in this respect. It appears possible, however, to accept both views. The one side may represent a final judgment upon secular history and culture, the other a final vindication of a redeemed, sacred history centered qualitatively in a *koinonia* with a positive mission both ethically and spiritually. In other words, a sheer meaningless *chronos* will spell death, hell and oblivion, while a meaningful *kairos* will spell life, the eternal Kingdom and creation's *true* fulfillment—though the latter is realized only through the redeemed, for whom creation and history are scenes of learning and growth amidst a profound struggle of moral and spiritual forces. Does not the *pro* and *con* imagery of the Apocalypse substantiate this paradox as it combines judgment upon man's temporal idolatry with the vindication of an eternal source of hope?

Brunner sees the end as a paradoxical mystery which closes history as eternity's dawn becomes as day. It is in error either to reduce the eternal to prolonged time or to make it appear timeless. It is suggestive in itself that the Fourth Gospel and Book of Revelation may have been written by the same author. This points to a dialectic sometimes overlooked in theology, one amenable to Berdyaev's eschatological tension. Brunner states,

> Whoever takes seriously the term (s) eternal life . . . cannot but feel the inadequacy of apocalyptic dramatization as a symbol of the wholly other. And whoever takes seriously the words, advent, Parousia, realization of the Kingdom of God, despite their inadequacy, will not be able to disallow the apocalyptic symbols . . . [98]

Thus a one-sided, transcendent view as held by Bultmann is as inadequate in its way as a temporalized eschatology of the literalists is in its way.[99] "The promise of the future advent of Christ implies a fulfillment of meaning both for the individual and for the history of humanity as a whole, even for the cosmos." [100] The future is real to a faith which includes hope, for hope implies an expectation. The life *in* Christ is to be fulfilled *with* Christ (Cf. I John 3:2). As Christ completes his work, history regains the ultimate meaning which was lost through man's sinfulness. The cosmos, which God loves (John 3:16), will find its goal and fulfill its divine purpose as revealed in Christ (Eph. 1:9).

The Christian hope is Emmanuel. He who has come as a servant will come in glory. The equivalent of this glory is Apocalypse, the future unveiling in fullness of what remains hidden—the Parousia or presence. To de-mythologize this should not be to lose the meaning of it. The apocalyptic day of the Parousia is as real but as mysterious as the day of creation. It ends history as sheer history, because eternity cannot be completely identified with it. The Kingdom of *Agape* will hold sway in this End. Its spirit of victory is to suffer wrong rather than do wrong; hence, paradoxically the double symbolism of the lion and the lamb, the crucified King of glory. Now the truly human is seen to be the truly divine.

Is this Kingdom of the end inherent in the cultural interim? Only to the extent that human creativity is of the Kingdom and stems from "communion with the Creator," says Brunner. This blends with Berdyaev's creative ethics and eschatology while it is perhaps more explicit respecting the Grace-wrought communion basic thereto. The genius of a cultural Babel must be distinguished from "the minstrel of God," lest culture become "a surrogate for the Kingdom of God." [101] For Brunner as for Berdyaev, true cultural maturity is of the Kingdom. Even religious institutionalism must be overcome and consummated by the Kingdom.[102] Here Brunner surpasses the weakness of Augustine and the Roman tradition. All consummation lies in a transcendent rather than an immanent fulfillment. Thus, the end is to be seen in terms of a "time shot through with eternity." [103] It is the perfect present symbolized by a marriage, a festive meal and "the vision of God face to face." Not common time, this is *kairos* brought to *eschaton*. It is transformed time, existential time in the perfect moment just on the brink of eternity itself.

* * * *

In this chapter we have enunciated Berdyaev's principle of the Apocalypse as the eternal factor which operates at the end of time, transfiguring rather than negating it. In sharp contrast to the view of Barth, and much more in common with Brunner, we have seen how the meaningful end is a transcendent mystery truly relevant rather than irrelevant to time. It is that which gives *Mount* Eschaton a steaming apex which dazzles finite eyes steeped in finitude and existence but which is both above and ahead for one who stands by faith on Kairos, stunned into the realization that only crystalline showers from above can mitigate the molten rumblings from below.

1 *Solitude and Society*, p. 114f. H. R. Mackintosh in his *Types of Modern Theology*, p. 210, shrewdly discerns that "timelessness" could not imply a spiritual existence.

2 *Destiny of Man*, p. 289. This should clarify to some degree the uncertainty of P. Bernhard Schultz as to whether Berdyaev's theocracy is an eschatology "beginning with the second advent of Christ or as chiliastic, preparing in meaning for a millennium." Cf. his *Die Schau der Kirche bei N. Berdiajew*, p. 178. Schultz himself recognizes that the Kingdom for N. B. is not a purely historical theocracy, nor the same as the historical Church being a product of the eschatological idea of the Kingdom (cf. pp. 183f, 122, 241, 240).

8 *Ibid.*, p. 290. Cf. *Essai de Métaphysique Eschatologique*, p. 207; *Slavery and Freedom*, p. 128.

4 *The Divine and the Human*, p. 197. Here is the heart of this work by Berdyaev.

5 F. H. Brabant, *Time and Eternity in Christian Thought*, p. 35, n.Z.

6 *Dream and Reality*, pp. 200f, 297, 326.

7 *The Russian Idea*, p. 243.

8 *Ibid.*, Cf. p. 195. Cf. Solovyov, *The Justification of the Good*.

9 *Ibid*, p. 194.

10 *Ibid.*, *p.* 154; Cf. Dostoevsky, "The Grand Inquisitor," *The Brothers Karamazov*, V, v.

11 "Le Christianisme Russe et le monde bourgeois," *De l'esprit Bourgeois*, p. 61, also in *Esprit*, 1st Mars, 1933, no. 6, p. 933.

12 See: Nicholas Zernov, *Three Russian Prophets*, for good sketches of the first three.

13 N. Berdyaev, "The Truth of Orthodoxy," *The Student World*, July 1928, pp. 249-263. Cf. footnote 11, p. 64 of ref. cited.

14 *Op. cit.*, p. 66.

15 *Ibid.*, 65. But at times it appears that Berdyaev tones down the transcendental, eternal or "cataclysmic" factor belonging to his doctrine of the Apocalypse.

16 *Destiny of Man*, p. 264. Cf. *Slavery and Freedom*, p. 264f. *The Divine and the Human*, p. 200. Cf. Chapter 14. But it can be said of Berdyaev's cosmic theory of "meonic freedom" that where motivated by his strong interest in keeping man and the universe morally free it jeopardizes the relation of freedom to divine creation and redemption. This is done by identifying freedom as the *mé on*, a kind of basic *hula* outside of God comparable to Jacob Boehme's *Ungrund*; it is called "nothingness" out of which God creates, but proves itself a "something," a freedom outside both God and man upon which the freedom of either depends, necessarily, conditionally. Cf. Berdyaev, "Deux Études sur J. Boehme," *Mysterium Magnum*, Tome I, p. 8ff. Cf. Lampert, *Modern Christian Revolutionaries*, p. 346.

17 *Christianity and Class War*, p. 63.

18 *Spirit and Reality*, p. 163.

19 Khomiakov, *The Church Is One*. Cf. Nicholas Zernov, *op. cit.*, Chap. II.

20 *Spirit and Reality*, p. 167. Cf. God is "no respecter of persons" (Acts 10:34).

21 *Ibid.*, p. 175. There seems to be a defect in Berdyaev's idea of spiritual creativeness, however. It is his failure to distinguish clearly between the "natural and redeemed" man's role as co-creator in existential time (*Métaphysique Eschatologique*, p. 236) and how this relates *kairos* to

eschaton. While allowing for the interim this is intensified, it would seem, by his assertion in *The Destiny of Man*, p. 136, "All the products of man's genius may be temporal and corruptible, but the creative fire itself is eternal. . . . It is the tragedy of creativeness that it wants eternity and the eternal, but produces he temporal and builds up culture which is in time and a part of history." This points to the problem of objectification. But does it not logically intimate that true creativeness is to be subsumed completely under the redemptive factor? Berdyaev's outline in the latter work suggests it in principle, while his treatment does not sufficiently clarify the distinction spoken of here.

22 V. Lossky, *Essai sur une Théologie Mystique de l'église d'orient*, p. 235.
23 Cf. V. Lossky, "Redemption and Deification" *Sobornost*, Autumn, 1947, p. 47. There is a touch of neo-Platonism here. It tends to lend support to a mysticism of union or a kind of apotheosis of man to which Berdyaev does not really subscribe, though he, too, appreciates the quoted words.
24 "The Unity of Christendom in the Strife Between East and West," *The Ecumenical Review*, Vol. I, Autumn, 1948, p. 11, Cf. *Dream and Reality*, p. 190.
25 *The Divine and the Human*, pp. 168-174.
26 Craig, *The One Church*, pp. 23, 138. Italics mine.
27 Berdyaev, *Der Sinn des Schaffens*, p. 305.
28 *Ibid.*, p. 315. Cf. pp. 210ff.
29 Cf. *Spirit and Reality*, pp. 180f, 193 Cf. *The Divine and the Human*, p. 133.
30 *Ibid*, p. 149 Cf. *Freedom and the Spirit*, p. 317f, 349f, 176-179, 222; *Truth and Revelation*, p. 151
31 *Spirit and Reality*, p. 171.
32 Lossky, *op cit*, p. 48. The idea of *gnosis* at the heart of Berdyaev's type of theosophy tends to be substituted for pistis. Cf. Brunner, *Man in Revolt*, p. 287.
33 *Freedom and Spirit*, p. 171. Cf. p. 298.
34 *Ibid.*, p. 180.
35 Wilder, *op. cit.*, pp. 30, 36f.
36 *Ibid.*, p. 47.
37 *Ibid.*, Chap. XI.
38 *Ibid.*, p. 211f, Berdyaev, *The Divine and the Human*, Chap. 14.
39 *Ibid.*, pp. 193-195.
40 *Die Kirchliche Dogmatik*, Band II, halbband I, p. 705.
41 *Ibid.*, Band III, halbband 2, 47:5 and 3:51. H. R. Mackintosh in *Types of Modern Theology*, p. 312, sees this problem, also. K. J. Foreman in "Eschatology," *Twentieth Century Encyclopedia of Religious Knowledge*, p. 392f.
42 Cf. H. R. Mackintosh, *op. cit.* p. 312.
43 *Op cit.*, p. 286. Cf. Cullmann's criticism of Barth cited above, though, we maintain, Cullmann missed Barth's later qualification of eternity as including time.
44 *Die Kirchliche Dogmatik*, Band III, halbband 2, p. 709.
45 *Ibid.*, p. 710.
46 Barth, *The Resurrection of the Dead*, pp. 218f, 221.
47 See *Die Kirchliche Dogmatik*, Band II, halbband 1, p. 689.
48 Barth, *The Knowledge of God and the Service of God*, p. 71.
49 *Dogmatics in Outline*, Chap. 20.
50 *Die Kirchliche Dogmatik*, Band I halbband I, p. 62ff.
51 *Ibid.*, Band III, halbband 2, 47s, p. 722.
52 *Ibid.*, Band III, halbband 4, 55:3, p. 584.

53 *The Resurrection of the Dead*, p. 179.
54 *Die Kirchliche Dogmatik*, Band I, 2, p. 47.
55 *Ibid.*, pp. 50, 80.
56 *Ibid.*, p. 51f.
57 *Ibid.*, p. 52f.
58 *Ibid.*, p. 58. Cf. *Epistle to Romans*, p. 145f.
59 *Die Kirchliche Dogmatik*, Vol. IV, i, pp. 8ff, 160.
60 *Ibid.*, pp. 112, 116f. Cf. pp. 296, 324, 573, 594, 604.
61 *Ibid.*, pp. 119f, 318.
62 *Ibid.*, pp. 324-326.
63 *Ibid.*, p. 294.
64 *Ibid.*, p. 725.
65 *Ibid.*, p. 334.
66 *Ibid.*, p. 661f.
67 *The Epistle to Romans*, p. 320f.
68 *Christ and Time*, p. 66.
69 *The Eternal Hope*, p. 7.
70 Barth, *Dogmatics in Outline*, p. 129.
71 *Die Kirchliche Dogmatik*, Band III, halbband 4:55, 3, 584.
72 *Ibid.*, Band IV, halbband 1:57, 1, p. 7. "*Heil*" means salvation or "wholeness."
73 R. Birch Hoyle, *The Teaching of Karl Barth*, pp. 221, 219.
74 *Ibid.*, 221-223.
75 Cf. Wilhelm Pauck's Introduction to Barth's *Christ and Adam*, pp. 14-16 for a similar appraisal. Cf. *Die Kirchliche Dogmatik*, Band IV, halbband I, pp. 505-510.
76 Berkouwer, *The Triumph of Grace in the Theology of Karl Barth*, pp. 158-165.
77 *Eternal Hope*, p. 206. Cf. pp. 219, 208ff.
78 *Ibid.*, p. 50. Cf. pp. 197, 204. Eternity is still held to be "timeless" by Brunner, a notion not congenial to his over-all view of redemptive eschatology.
79 *Dogmatics*, Vol. II, p. 237.
80 *Ibid.*
81 *Ibid.*
82 *Ibid.*, p. 260.
83 Cf. *Eternal Hope*, p. 211ff.
84 *Dogmatics*, Vol. II, p. 262, Cf. 60, 265.
85 *Ibid.*, pp. 268.
86 *The Mediator*, 1947 edition, p. 343n.
87 *Dogmatics*, Vol. II, p. 224. Cf. Gunther Bornkamm, *Jesus of Nazareth*.
88 *Ibid.*, pp. 279f, 299f, 335.
89 *Ibid.*, 193, 196f.
90 *Ibid.*, pp. 252f, 273, 308.
91 *The Mediator*, p. 377ff.
92 *Eternal Hope*, p. 219. Cf. pp. 60, 118, 224.
93 *Ibid.*, p. 112.
94 *Ibid.*, p. 110.
95 *Dogmatics*, Vol. II, p. 375.
96 *Ibid.*, pp. 113, 186, 190. *Eternal Hope*, pp. 122, 124.
97 *Eternal Hope*, p. 127.
98 *Ibid.*, p. 132.
99 *Ibid.*, p. 214, 218ff.
100 *Ibid.*, p. 84. Cf. pp. 85-89.

101 *Ibid.*, p. 164.
102 *Ibid.*, p. 115.
103 *Ibid.*, pp. 204-209.

CHAPTER IX

EXISTENTIAL TIME AND THE INTERIM

Why consider and especially lead up to the problem of the interim? The answer is that it tells us where we are right now—in what for men of faith is a history being redeemed. The idea of the interim intensifies in a practical manner the kinship yet difference between *kairos* and *eschaton,* the meaningful time to eyes of faith which look up and glance ahead at the same time.

This closing chapter presupposes the distinctiveness of existential time and its eschatological dimension as it concentrates on contemporary theological contributions to the understanding of the interim. But first a digest of Berdyaev's interpretation is again in order for comparative and corrective purposes.

The Interim and Sacramental Eschatology

For Berdyaev the interim bespeaks a sacramental history. It is secular history regenerated unto sacred history. Faithwise, common time and history are made uncommon, affording a "new look" at human existence from within. History gains a higher meaning from the Light which the End sheds upon it both *now* and *then.* Men can live both *from* and *to* that end. For this reason all of life and culture take on a fresh orientation. The chief agency of this is the Church with its eschatological mission and purpose. Not simply by divine law, but by the divine Act is the new outlook born. This not only puts demands upon men but inspires obedience and a creativity [1] amenable to the Kingdom of Christ as it seeks to redeem the Kingdom of Caesar.[2] Thus, as God redeems time and history, he uses it both in redeeming it and upon redeeming it. History is made meaningful and fulfilled as otherwise not. Its *chronos* is reborn or *redirected* through moments of *kairos.* In this respect the Christian interim is that history which lies between the revealed meaning of human existence and its ultimate fulfillment. Christ-centered, it is pregnant with significance and possibility. Things are not the same once the Light has penetrated the darkness and by faith men still see the Light—even if "through a glass darkly."

Such a view of the interim gives special significance to the spiritual and ethical vocations of men in this world. Among other things it means that Christians need not disrelate their faith and salvation from the course of this world. They can combat the sinful enslavements of men and the cultural barbarisms which threaten to undo their witness and work.[3] Such a balanced eschatological perspective gives new direction and fresh incentive to be "in the world but not of it," while not neglecting what being *in* it involves both as a human problem and a divine-human possibility.[4] Thus the interim becomes a venturesome time of faith as the "eschatological community" of the *koinonia* seeks to manifest all that the Incarnate Event discloses then, now and at the End.

As we have suggested, a new and balanced view of history is needed today. This is needed in theological circles, both to understand Christ and the new perspective of time and its end which his revelation proffers men. A part of this is the meaning of the interim, for just as Christians now share a lively hope, they are now in the *interim* of that hope. The *eschaton* is before them yet meaningful *to* them, even as by possession and promise they know life eternal. As men of both faith and hope, time and eternity, the present and the future, they now know a new dimension of life, both in view of eternity and the end of transition, a transition which, individually, is the end in the form of death and, collectively, as the *eschaton* of Life.

Much in keeping with the spirit and outlook of Nicholas Berdyaev is the interpretation of Evgueny Lampert, lecturer at Oxford. Both thinkers hold to an existential eschatology. With a similar background in Russian thought, religion and culture, Lampert also takes seriously the apocalyptic factor affecting the perspective of the interim of time as sacramental. For him, too, the proper view of history "is to be aware of its End, to know the 'ends of Time.' "[5] A dual perspective, it looks to a dynamic *eschaton* of eternity-in-time, a fulfilling *kairos*. Lampert concurs that the End is "full of eternal, transcendent meaning, it is Apocalypse."[6] This gives special significance to a faith-qualified existence and interim. "Man's existence is existence in Time and Time is that material into which the apocalyptic sparks must and do fall in order to reveal its meaning." [7] The central clue is revealed in Christ's God-manhood. By it history can be transcended both from beyond and within. This gives it destiny through men who live in awareness of the apocalyptic consciousness which both transcends and transfigures time. [8]

In view of this Berdyaev-like perspective, Lampert constructs a theology of sacramental existence whereby the extremes of ontological monism and dualism are overcome, as in Berdyaev's eschatology. The interim of Christian history is "a progressivism," says Lampert, "which gains meaning from an End while its center and end are linked in the Incarnate Christ." [9] Yet Lampert may be even more emphatic than Berdyaev in asserting that history itself is apocalyptic, not only its End, the *eschaton*. While beyond, the End is also seen from within the interim of history, since it is coming while already come. As for Berdyaev, this demands of the Christian that he neither find his security in history nor forsake his sacred trust as a steward of the Word, the Spirit and the ethical implications thereof, whereby God may spread and instrument His eternal leaven in the midst of time. This makes the eschatological interim profoundly sacramental.

In view of this dynamic and balanced existential view of the interim, how do other theologians think of it today? Comparative summaries and appraisals follow, but preceded by the backdrop of Augustine's progressive eschatology.

The Interim and Theological Adjustments

A Progressive View—Augustine

Augustine failed to blend his eschatology with his basic existential view of time. His scheme was a progressive view of the Kingdom that paved the way for much in both medieval and modern versions of eschatology. It is for this reason that we turn here to Augustine, especially that we may take note of his remarkably "modern" deficiencies.

Augustine's Platonic concept of an immutable eternity really conflicted with his latently dynamic idea of "an ever-present eternity." For this reason his *City of God* departs from his *Con-*

fessions. Emulating its ideal identified with ultimate Being, the temporal city of Rome was seen moving progressively toward the eternal City of God. In this context time is regarded as "created being," hence belonging to a Platonic realm of Becoming. As such, God in no way adjusts or alters "His eternal resolution" in creating it.[10] Here we see how Augustine loses the existential perspective of time reflected in his *Confessions* and inconsistently allows determinism to hold sway in the name of divine immutability, thus setting many a precedent for Western theology.

On this basis, Augustine's idealistic eschatology is a progressive movement of Rome, the institutional Church, ascending to the perfect Kingdom. Christian history for Augustine is an interim in which the immanent unfolds the transcendent. Thus the apocalyptic factor of redemption's relation to the end is obscured. The spiritual events within history are not incursions of a dynamic "eternal present" which disturbs and re-orientates history's continuity; they are only historical. Neglecting the existential encounter that he sees in his way, and the apocalyptic qualification which should counterpart it, Augustine sees the Church not living *from* the eternal end so much as *to* it from a temporal standpoint. The end is an idealistic *telos*, not a transfiguring existential *eschaton*. Platonically, then, Augustine identifies the Church with the Kingdom of God through its potentiality; the Church militant is implicitly the Church triumphant. On this basis her instrumentality readily becomes a sacerdotal institutionalism, and the prophetic, apocalyptic dimension of eschatology is lost in a secular form of thought and structure.

Augustine is hailed as the first thinker to acknowledge the progress of history.[11] This is reflected in his futuristic view of *The City of God*. But his Platonic version becomes, quite unwittingly, a secularized eschatology. While Berdyaev sees how the modern idea of progress was a perversion of biblical eschatology, he does not seem to acknowledge that Augustine was an accomplice to this Western secularization. Had Augustine consistently retained the pre-existential to existential ideas of time and eternity seen in his *Confessions* and applied them to much of his other thought, he might have saved historical theology from much of its accommodation to ontological concepts derived from the Greeks. Also, he would have helped prevent the biblical doctrine of eschatology from being put in the background by much Scholastic and empirical theology, both Roman and Protestant.

We cannot quite agree with Roger Hazelton's assertion that both Augustine and Plato held to an eternity which "may and does become temporal" though time does not become eternal.[12] Rather, God is changeless and, as indicated in his *Confessions,* Augustine sees God outside of time altogether.[13] Eternity is as removed from time to Augustine as Being is from Becoming to Plato. Even in his *Confessions,* as we have seen above, Augustine keeps the "ever-present eternal" disrelated from a real linear time. In *The City of God* he strongly asserts that Plato stood for divine immutability, and he appeals to this repeatedly.[14] "All the world's frailty is opposite an immutable eternity," says Augustine.[15] Eternity implies an unchangeable will, he declares.[16] Thus, it involves a predestined scheduling of the times,[17] together with divine foreknowledge, election and providence.[18] Providence is such that God's judgment even permits enemies to exercise their lust upon the bodies of Christians.[19] And of God's immutable nature Augustine says, "He moves all things through time, but time moves not Him, nor knows future effects otherwise than present." [20]

What does this mean for the two cities? It means that the sole significance of the earthly city of time lies in its looking for and moving toward its heavenly translation into eternity proper. The end implied here is relevant only to the faithful, and is consequential only beyond death. The temporal and earthly have no opportunity but to be in contempt of God, whereas the heavenly is the reward of faith.[21] "For what other thing is our end," says Augustine, "but to come to that Kingdom of which there is no end." [22] Thus the future hope is not integrated with a present faith involved in a terrestrial existence and common history and time. Faith, then, becomes a futuristic looking beyond the world of time entirely. The eternal does not leaven the temporal interim with an apocalyptic factor from beyond. There is an intrinsic progression toward the temporal *telos,* which is then superseded by the eternal. This view provides no hope in an *eschaton* of supratemporal dimension that follows through on a *kairos* that regenerates the temporal. It preserves the immutable sovereignty of God so as to make the end a predetermined fulfillment in an eternity beyond all time.

A Teleological View—D. D. Williams

Much in contrast to both existential eschatology and dialectical neo-orthodox theology the position taken by D. D. Williams is a teleological approach to the end and the interim. Williams sees a better world based on a synergistic relation between man and God from within history, yet he tries to modify the optimistic anthropology of the liberal theology of the past century even as he tones down the pessimistic anthropology of thinkers like Barth.[23]

Much concerned about the modern problem of progress from an eschatological perspective, the precedent for which goes back to Augustine, Williams thinks in terms of "the history of the work of redemption." [24] Liberal thought has been too confident in man's change of outlook and environment, Williams contends, whereas neo-orthodoxy is insufficiently assured of "redemption as transformation of our human existence." The spirit of this concern has much in common with Berdyaev's active eschatology and creative ethics, while it is not as far removed from Brunner as from Barth and Bultmann, In relation to the interim of time Williams says, "What we need is a theology which will hold together the fact of the creation of the good world, the fact that evil invades that goodness, and the fact of a redemption which brings hope in the midst of tragic failure and loss." [25] True progress is redemptive, thinks Williams. Redeemed life is not only meaningful but consequential in time and history despite the tragic course of the latter.

Though Williams, like Berdyaev, opposes the notion of a static ontology, he endeavors to base his eschatology on a *process* teleology quite in opposition to Berdyaev's dynamic existential eschatology. This must call to mind the philosophical debate which we carried on in Chapter VI between process philosophy and a balanced existential eschatology. Williams becomes much too naturalistic in his framework for human progress, while conceding the need of what Berdyaev calls a "transvaluation of values." [26] Williams neither means to equate the Kingdom of God with those of the world nor to alienate it altogether. He desires to relate the sacred to the secular under divine grace.

265

A good creation corrupted by sin can be redeemed, he thinks, as God works through history. "Can we believe in the progress of the reign of God in history," asks Williams, "or is the ultimate conflict between His Kingdom and the Kingdoms of this world unresolved to the end of time?" [27]

Berdyaev would appreciate this question but would not find the answer so ready-made as Williams does in his teleological metaphysics. The central weak point in Williams' scheme is that for him the eschatological resolution is basically immanental unto the debilitation of the uniqueness of the transcendent redemptive factor of the God who is not limited to His creation. A liberal view of progress and a neo-realistic view of divine judgment on human existence are conjoined by Williams. The biblical symbol, he thinks, is the "embattled reign of Christ" of I Cor. 15: 25, 26. This is meant to allow for a more realistic theology than that expressed by an optimistic "building the Kingdom" in history.[28] An activated ethics within a spiritual regeneration is basic to Williams' position, but the tension between time and eternity demanding an existential irruption in *kairos* and *eschaton* is lost sight of in favor of a gradual, temporal victory of good over evil.

Here both Berdyaev and Brunner are superior to Williams, who claims that the future resolution and interim of history is based on an eschatology of evolutionary process. Such a scheme fails to relate the future and *telos* to the present. The end and the Kingdom's fulfillment are beyond the embattled reign of Christ. Berdyaev more shrewdly sees the end in the existential present while also in the future. Williams sees the Kingdom symbolizing "an ultimate victory which we can know only as promise and share in hope." [29] This fails to relate men existentially to "the eternal now" of the Kingdom whereby meaning, promise and hope can be conjoined in the present.

In general, Williams tries to support a dynamic view of God somewhat like Berdyaev's, but on an immanental basis. Concerned about the futurity of God much in accord with Edwin Lewis,[30] who also rejects a static simultaneity, Williams says,

> . . . God's life itself must be conceived as having an element of adventure and movement into an open future, else we cannot conceive that He enters sympathetically into our human experience.[31]

But Williams does not satisfactorily relate the time factor to eternity. The cosmic teleology of process philosophy is hardly adequate. The dynamism of Spirit, Grace and "the eternal Now" cannot be synthesized with an evolutionary process. Needed is a Berdyaev-like doctrine of "celestial history." The *ek-stasis* of the Incarnation and its apocalyptic counterpart are not allowed for by Williams, even as *kairos* is not seen different from *chronos*. Williams fails to see that redemption and evolutionary teleology are not correlative ideas. The one is of the free will and Grace of God, the other of a necessitative process, one really demanding a transfiguration of the *telos* into *eschaton,* as Berdyaev has seen it.

Nor can a "redemptive progress" be evolutionary. In attacking Berdyaev, Williams fails to see that Berdyaev does not deny all meaning to moral progress the way Kierkegaard is inclined to do. On the other hand, Williams may fail to see where lies genuine progress. For Berdyaev it demands a supratemporal orientation of life and thought while related to history and culture. Basically, Williams remains bogged down by one of the very problems which keep men from fulfilling their eschatological role, *viz.*, their enslavement to time and a necessitative cosmic process. On this basis both the end and the interim are more philosophical than eschatological. Furthermore, Williams needs to see with Edwin Lewis that God "broke into human history." "Eternity" says Lewis, "accommodates itself to time; time opens to receive eternity." [32] This moves beyond an evolutionary teleology which Lewis himself once leaned toward.[33]

A Bipolar View—Paul Tillich

Basically, the eschatology of Paul Tillich is much like that of Berdyaev. Neither eternity nor time is the exclusive locus of time's full meaning. Both of these philosophers of religion see how God-manhood related to *kairos* implies not only the eternal God who disturbs man in his time but who involves himself in time. Seeking to correct the extremes in both nineteenth-century liberalism and twentieth-century neo-orthodoxy, Tillich holds to a bipolar view interrelating transcendence and immanence.

Quite as for Berdyaev, time is basic to a sinful finitude, thinks

Tillich, while qualified by eternity through the existential faith perspective. Time and history may be taken much more seriously than Barth would concede. Faithwise, the vertical qualification of horizontal time gives it "eternal meaning," quite as for Berdyaev, hence a sacramental potentiality is ascribed to an otherwise empty time.[34] The Christian *interim* now may be characterized by the angle between the strictly vertical and horizontal, implying a dynamic tension between the actual and the possible, the present and the future. As for Berdyaev, the *eschaton* is seen by Tillich to involve both elements. This too helps challenge any static idea of the eternal Kingdom as seen in orthodoxy.[35] Eternity, to Tillich, is the "dynamic unity of the temporal modes and moments which are separated in empirical time." [36] This blends with the view of Berdyaev to a great extent.

Again quite like Berdyaev, Tillich sees the ultimate philosophical questions given theological answers via a more balanced existential perspective and eschatology. While Christ is the present End of history, he is also the goal of history as it moves ahead. The end is revealed in qualitative significance while pertaining to a quantitative estrangement from the absolute Being.[37] Thus there is paradoxically a vital relation and yet a tension between the "already" and the "not yet" as symbolized in the first and second Advents. The *eschaton* is both above and within history making the interim of profound significance to both God and men. On this side of that end, divine and demonic forces clash. The Kingdom of God, however, also symbolizes a "purified history" in which the demonic element is being overcome.[38] The Church is the agent of the Kingdom in this respect that the latent Kingdom may be instrumented into the actual through the regenerated life of New Being in Christ [39] whereby estrangement from true eternal Being, "the ground of all being," is overcome.

This, in principle, is much like the paradoxical dualism of Berdyaev, save that Tillich has ontologized it by projecting the "is" of "existence" seen by Heidegger into the realm of the Absolute so as to represent the pure Being of God, who is Essence while not existence, the latter representing what has fallen from the former. Whereas Martin Heidegger sees a fallen existence, he does not show from whence it has "fallen." [40]

Tillich has an answer. But is Tillich's answer a dangerous philosophical objectification? Berdyaev would likely answer affirmatively, since only a God of *both* Being and existence could or would be dynamic and knowable in any sense. Tillich has no basis for limiting God to pure Essence, we claim, since not even *via negationis* can the philosophical theologian take the perspective of such perfection. He must see more consistently what Berdyaev calls the "philosopher's tragic situation," [41] that of being steeped in his own refracted existence. Tillich almost forgets this. Unless God is known by revelation in terms of an existence to which He is not immune He remains a philosophical inference. Thus, Pure Essence without existence and "God was in Christ" are not compatible ideas. The one is a grandiose "It-Idea," the other a Person-Spirit Event. In the attempt to communicate his theology in philosophical form, Tillich over-accommodates a secular ontology. The philosopher Richard Kroner supports this observation and says Tillich is still "a disciple of Schelling." [42]

Tillich's Christology makes the Incarnation a mere symbol, yet he asserts that a symbol *participates* in the divine Being.[43] But this seems incompatible to a *kairos* which conjoins eternity with a realistic *chronos* and history. Tillich asserts, "If Jesus as the Christ were seen as a God walking on earth, he would be neither finite nor involved in tragedy." [44] Our reply is that it depends upon what you mean by the Incarnate Christ. Tillich is thinking quite rationally here at the expense of any basic mystery. We must see Jesus Christ as personifying God-manhood: very human with the Divine Plus while very divine with the human minus. Unless Christ is an actual person-event in history while more than event in history the Incarnation is meaningless and cannot give occasion to a redemptive *kairos* let alone *eschaton*. These are God-invested moments making common time and history uncommon. This cannot be so if God-manhood remains but symbol. It is Event—but on the frontier of faith, in both time and eternity. Tillich needs to see more consistently a dynamic, personal, pneumatic eternity which is not immune to its own form of existence and even the existence and time of men. An eternity of Pure Being remains impersonal, immune and oblivious thereto; it can even invent no symbol! But Christ, we say, is an eternally invented Event. Apart from his involvement in both eternity and time he yields neither the meaning nor end of history. Tillich treats the incarnation and resurrection of Christ too analogously. "Factual element is basic to symbol," he claims, "but historical research can never give more than a probable answer." [46] This may be true, but what of the apostolic memory? Whom did the Apostles remember and trust themselves to? Surely to more than a symbol, though also more than a historic man. A symbol based upon a "factual element" or event involves history more than a symbol of the eternal *per se*. If not, *kairos* is not the clue to the *eschaton* in the light of a once-for-all God-manhood.

Tillich sees the Second Coming as symbolic, quite like Berdyaev, while it is not deemed a superior manifestation of New Being.[46] It stands for the new aeon which surpasses the old and substantiates Christ as the Messiah; therefore, it also implies the existential tension of the *interim* for the Christian and the perfect *kairos* in the End to which he looks. In this respect the New Testament deliteralizes eschatology without demythologizing it, thinks Tillich. The sacramental perspective of history is thus allowed for as the *eschaton* is anticipated when eternity meets time in full redemptiveness. Thus the meaning of history and the interim of the faith community springs from beyond history while purposefully related to it. This is wholesomely removed from any process teleology or any immanental determinism, quite as for Berdyaev.

An Ethical View—Reinhold Niebuhr

The position taken by Reinhold Niebuhr may be considered an interim ethic within an eschatological view of existence. History has meaning, says Niebuhr, only as man relates himself to the "second Adam," the Messianic "synthesis" of the temporal and the eternal in Christ.[47] This also parallels Berdyaev's principle of God-manhood. Similarly, history's significance is reflected in the "interim" between the disclosure of its meaning and its ultimate fulfillment in Christ.[48] It gains meaning paradoxically only from a more-than-temporal end in the Kingdom that is *to come*, though it *is come*. Niebuhr declares, "Historical religions are therefore by their very nature prophetic-Messianic. They look forward towards an *eschaton* [end] which is also the end of history, where full meaning of life and history will be disclosed and fulfilled." [49] This is based upon the apocalyptic intervention of the "transcendent" into the "historical" quite as for Berdyaev's view of the *eschaton*.

While Niebuhr seems to see an existential relation of time and eternity here, his dualism provides a defective view of eternity, one which actually should disallow this "intervention." Rejecting the ideas of the "infinity of time" and the "undifferentiated unity of being" Niebuhr, nevertheless, says eternity is "the changeless source of man's changing being." [50] In view of our discussions in previous chapters, this concept is too static to allow for either *kairos* or *eschaton*. Niebuhr sees temporal events swallowed up in a divine "simultaneity" [51] that reminds us of the *omnitempus* concept of Nicolas of Cusa. But to both Barth and Berdyaev this is too congenial to the Augustinian notion of an immutable eternity.

While Niebuhr retains the Christian historical interim he, like Berdyaev, soundly rejects any view which sees eschatology strictly from within history. He states of this tendency,

The *eschata* which represent the fulfillment and the end of time in eternity are conceived literally and thereby made a point in time. The sense that the final fulfillment impinges on the present moment . . . becomes transmuted into a "proximate futurism," into the feeling that the fulfillment of history is chronologically imminent.

This is the grave error of both millennial and teleological theories of the end, the latter including Augustine's progressive scheme. On the other hand, Niebuhr is aware of the importance of history as the scene of God's encounter with man. He says, ". . . whenever the complexities of history's relation to eternity are not known to be characteristic of history on every level of its development, the Christian claim that God has been revealed in Christ cannot be taken seriously." [52] Here lies the importance, we believe, of the two basic issues of *kairos* and *eschaton* made compatible by Berdyaev's existential eschatology, while jeopardized by Karl Barth and Rudolf Bultmann with their extreme emphases upon the transcendent Word and End.

For Niebuhr it is not man's finitude which is the cause of

temporal frustration and the meaninglessness of existence for modern man as much as it is man's false pride and self-sufficiency. With Berdyaev he sees man projecting his pseudo-eternities. Thus the chief locus of cultural crisis is man's will to power and the usurpation of divine prerogatives. Such proud rebellion has fostered decadence through the superficial optimism of eighteenth-century rationalism and nineteenth-century evolutionism. While Niebuhr retains the *imago dei,* he sees man's perversion in this light. Berdyaev sees it mainly to be a false and limited orientation of the human spirit, the loss of true freedom through the discreative objectification of finite ideas in contrast to the revealed infinite. This difference in anthropology accounts, in part, for Niebuhr's seeing less possibility for a new birth of human culture within the interim of history. If Berdyaev is a bit too hopeful of man's creativeness at times, Niebuhr is a bit too pessimistic of man's situation and possibilities.

Niebuhr sees, however, that the Christian lives in an interim which is a new kind of history, one in which both the judgment and the transfiguration have begun. But, while prompted to see man's creativity, Niebuhr is less inclined than Berdyaev to see its relation to the eschatological End making a positive impact upon the interim now, so that the new era might be actualized and thus dispel the Spenglerian hopelessness, which Niebuhr dislikes as much as Berdyaev does. Yet this resurgence is latent in Niebuhr's ethics. He concedes, "The finite world is not, because of its finiteness, incapable of entertaining comprehensible revelations of the incomprehensible God." [54] Man's finitude is only a symptom of a cantankerous pride, the basic problem. Niebuhr says that nothing contributes to the nemesis of culture quite like man's irresponsible *hubris,* (pride), which is the existential core of original sin. Consequently, nemesis is the vengeful disease which decays society as "mortal men contend against God."[55] Unlike D. D. Williams, Niebuhr says, "The real problem is . . . that all history is involved in a perennial defiance of the law of God." [56] Of this Niebuhr says,

The issue of Biblical religion is not the finiteness of man, but his sin, not his involvement in the flux of nature but his abortive efforts to escape that flux. The issue is not primarily the problem of how finite man can know God but

272

how sinful man is reconciled to God and how history is to overcome the tragic consequences of its "false eternals," its proud and premature efforts to escape finiteness.[57]

From Berdyaev's perspective, pride is not so much a first cause as the second, i.e., when man gets lost in the illusoriness of his temporality he erects his false eternities through his mental objectifications. It is when he accepts the temporal for the eternal that he becomes proud in the superficial sense. Man, to Berdyaev, is not simply a rebelliously depraved and sardonically proud being by nature so much as by his temporal self-enslavement. It is his fall into finitude and idolatrous confidence in common time which causes him to become inflated by his falsely oriented achievements and accruements of power.

If Niebuhr were perfectly correct in his position here, he should leave his anthropology thoroughly rotten to the core, which he almost does in his treatment though not in his *theory*, for he retains the core of *imago dei*. The criticism of H. D. Lewis is not without foundation, especially with regard to Niebuhr's most influential works as a neo-Realist in ethics:

The conclusion that is forced upon us is a double one. On the one hand, it seems evident that Niebuhr is dissatisfied with the extreme and uncompromising kind of Protestantism which deprives human activity of all significance and worth. He wants to make some concession to the more liberal and "Modern" views which emphasize "growth" and achievement in history, and he wants religion not to seem an escape from present reality but the transformation of it by infusion into it of spiritual forces. He deplores the tendency of certain Protestant versions of the Christian faith "to betray a defeatist attitude towards the social existence of mankind," and he condemns Luther for placing "The Gospel in Heaven and the law upon earth." But, on the other hand Neibuhr is not able to provide an effective alternative to these gloomy views, and he has nothing to offer us in the way of a new understanding of the nature of revelation as the impact of the divine upon finite experience. All that we have, therefore, is a very desperate attempt to subject the traditional Protestant view to modifications, of which it does not really admit, and which compel Niebuhr . . . to remain, for all practical purposes, no less trustful of human action than any of his precursors.[58]

As for human life and history, Niebuhr still sees that all is moving toward the *eschaton*. The "rational freedom" of man, which to Niebuhr preserves his guilt but little else, is essential to the end as an eschatological *telos* rather than a temporal *finis*, which it would be were man completely subsumed under nature. This *telos*, though better rendered *eschaton*, is for both Niebuhr and Berdyaev a "fulfillment and dissolution," the coming of the Kingdom together with the cessation of history in sheer *chronos*. But Berdyaev sees a terrestrial counterpart to the Kingdom's fulfillment in eternity, which, when realized under the Spirit, will slip into eternity. This represents the fulfilled work of God among men in the interim as a new spiritual epoch. Including an "ethics of creativity" implicit within the "ethics of redemption," Berdyaev's view helps overcome total pessimism for the *interim*.

For Niebuhr the *Parousia* is a New Testament symbol of the end and the redemption of history by eternity. It points to the eternal ultimate from within the conditions of history. "If the symbol is taken literally," says Niebuhr, "the dialectical conception of time and eternity is falsified and the ultimate vindication of God over history is reduced to a point in history."[59] Yet Niebuhr agrees with Berdyaev that to dismiss the symbol of Apocalypse is to presuppose an idea of eternity which annuls rather than fulfills the historical process. The Second Coming is the full realization of the Kingdom, the vindication of Christ and the repudiation of all forms of utopianism on the one hand, and consistent otherworldliness on the other. The *Parousia* consummates and fulfills the process of human history rather than negates it.[60] This is parallel to Berdyaev's position even as it supports our above criticisms of the eschatologies of Barth and Bultmann.

The symbol of the *last judgment*, Niebuhr shows, expresses the refutation of all people and nations which make history its own redemption or self-made emancipation. Not only at the end of history, the judgment *is come*; revealed truth judges every act of man even within the historical interim. The last judgment is the final vindication of eternal verities in time. It is also eternity's acknowledgment of man as a free, responsible and creative being who, being able to see his situation in time, stands faithwise in relation to eternity as he transcends history from within it. This, too, parallels Berdyaev's view as it sees the various tenses of time existentially in the light of eternity.

The symbol of the general *resurrection* to Niebuhr, quite as for Berdyaev, means that ". . . eternity will fulfill and not annul the richness and variety which the temporal process has elaborated." [61] It stands in contrast to all linear philosophies of progress, which assume an ultimate consummation strictly from within the finitude of time, nature and man. The fulfillment of the end, while not simply chronological but eschatological, links time and eternity.

Niebuhr's recognition of man's relation to eternity allows him to accept inspiration from Berdyaev's doctrine of the "transfiguration" of history. But for Niebuhr it is realized in a "timeless order," [62] a concept of eternity which to Berdyaev is most restrictive, existentially and redemptively. While both thinkers see the tragic abuse of human freedom relative to a contemporary cultural crisis, they also see the spiritual antidote, Berdyaev more provocatively than Niebuhr in relation to man's creative freedom while Niebuhr more realistically in relation to man's necessitated freedom. Both men acknowledge the possibility of a rise in culture [63] as well as a fall, though Niebuhr does little theologically to account for a possible rise.

Though Niebuhr, influenced by Brunner, stresses original sin as both an act and a state of existence rather than as a mere inheritance,[64] he seems to be too obsessed with the dividedness of man despite his place for man's responsible freedom. In contrast, Berdyaev, while maintaining a premundane cosmic fall affecting man's temporal fall in history, preserves man's spiritual freedom and creativeness to the extent that man as a co-creator of history redemptively helps to bring about the transfiguration. In view of this end the future is more hopeful in the interim. Berdyaev sees more possibilities for man within the spiritual interim of history as a conditional aspect of the *eschaton*. It is questionable whether Niebuhr's preoccupation with man's state of sin really allows the eschatological redemption of man to materialize. It takes more than a doctrine of eschatology; it takes a man who can commune with the Eternal responsibly, when the Eternal chooses to commune with him.

Niebuhr directly attacks Berdyaev's position set forth in his book *The Russian Idea* as a pretentious, heretical nationalistic Messianism.[65] This is something of a misunderstanding. True, Berdyaev asserts that Russian thought in history has had an underlying Messianic motif. Soviet Communism, however, is shown by Berdyaev to be a grave distortion of the Russian apocalyptic hope due to a materialistic and futuristic philosophy and imperialistic will to power. Berdyaev is not asserting a nationalistic Messianism so much as he is declaring that the long-standing Messianic consciousness of the Russian people, influenced but not limited to Orthodoxy, has accompanied their strong religious sense of vocation. The basic Russian idea has been eschatological, a looking to the end.[66] The tenor of this has not been one of nationalistic pride, such as Niebuhr avers in his criticism of Berdyaev's interpretation, but a unique spirit of camaraderie in Christian love or what the people call *Sobornost* (togetherness). It should not be overlooked that this is Christ-inspired and universal in scope, not implying that Russia will save the world but that the Christian spirit of unity and ecumenicity is intrinsic to its salvation. A materialistic Communism cannot eradicate this spirit any more than it can create it. Such a spirit puts love before any power, hierarchy or imperialism. Love is the very spirit of Apocalypse, says Berdyaev.

Niebuhr also holds to a "transfiguration" but disparages the outlook of a people contributing to its realization, because their spirit is more congenial to it. Their end, after all, is not of their nation but their Christ! We of the West must capture more of this spirit from the Christians of the East so that the transfiguration may be less theory and more fact. The West is not seen by Berdyaev to be totally corrupt but in need of an apocalyptic spirit of *Sobornost* seen more positively in the East. "This outlook is as different from the older one [of Russian nationalism] as that of a man who gently awakens a late sleeper [is different] from that of another who drives him from his bed with a whip." [67] Then, too, Berdyaev never shared Dostoevsky's idea "that Russia was a Messianic nation with something to give to the West but nothing to receive from it." [68] Berdyaev belonged to the East and adopted the West while fully embracing neither; he saw the whole world steeped in sin, yet he felt the spirit of Antichrist was given more fertile soil in the West due to its greater secularism and religious individualism, an individualism for which Protestant theology must take a major responsibility, *extreme* contemporary versions notwithstanding.

The East and West must stand together, thinks Berdyaev, in combating cultural barbarism under the eschatological perspective of a new spiritual epoch of universal significance. In ecumenical spirit, Berdyaev declares, "Against nationalism must be set up universalism which does not deny national individualizations, but unites them in a concrete one-ness. . . . All great peoples, with their own ideas and their special calling in the world, have attained universal significance through the high achievements of their cultures." [69] This universalism is to Berdyaev an eschatological matter of the interim for which the Church universal must be the spiritual basis in a new era of the Spirit.[70] Only from this can eventuate a federation of peoples. In this eschatological hope Berdyaev is far more specific and daring than Niebuhr and most of his contemporaries. Berdyaev lets the Apocalypse speak to "our time," allowing it to breathe with relevance upon the interim of time and the world of today.

The Interim and Our Existential Conspectus

As we draw to a close our comparative approach to time and its end from an existential point of view, a few conclusive observations are in order. This amounts to our conspectus of the study even as it relates itself to the very interim of time in which we find ourselves, faithwise and existentially, both in thought and life.

Upon clarifying the basic existential perspective of time and declaring our problem, purpose and dialectical thesis in Chapter I, we proceeded to elucidate, demonstrate and defend our view of the matter in terms of various views of time, eternity and the end found in historical philosophy and theology. On a comparative basis, keeping existential and pre-existential views paramount, we saw how Nicholas Berdyaev, more consistently than the other existential thinkers discussed, helps us to retain the important combination of a dynamic eternity and a realistic, yet existential time. The strength of this is that we neither risk the reality nor mitigate the significance of either time or eternity and the respective aspects of the End. This was shown characteristic of the existential Moment of *kairos* and its eschatological complement of *eschaton*. The paradoxical unity-in-duality which this entails, without implying a rational synthesis, was seen to be disclosed in the incarnate *ekstasis* of the Eternal Christ into time even as its purpose is fulfilled through Apocalypse as a matter not to be dissolved on the one hand, nor overly temporalized on the other. These two revealed truths are basic to the necessary interrelation of *eschaton* to *chronos* via *kairos*. The dialectical issue and locus of the Christian clue to the meaning of time and the redeeming of the times is neither history *per se* nor eternity, but their meeting on the faith "frontier of time and eternity."

Upon summarizing existential and pre-existential insights into the problems of time and the knower, especially in Plato, Plotinus and Augustine, we saw them enhanced and crystallized by Soren Kierkegaard. We noted, however, that Berdyaev improved upon his precursors by keeping both cosmic and historic time real while brought into vital relationship with an eternity that includes "celestial history." The Incarnate Event was the basic key to understanding existential time as the seat of a meaningful existence and destiny. This called for a defense of the temporal actuality of Christ along with his eternality in relation to the New Testament *kerygma*. Karl Barth was shown to be defective in his Christology at this point in keeping with his overly transcendent view of eternity and the end.

The eschatological dimension of existential time was brought to the forefront of our thinking in Part II, based on an examination of the existential and pre-existential views of the nature of eternity and its attributes. Here Berdyaev was seen to improve upon Plato and Augustine as well as on Kierkegaard. With a somewhat neo-Platonic dynamism related to the nature of eternity, Berdyaev was shown to displace the static ideas of eternity in favor of a more vigorous, personable and time-embracing view. Here Barth was shown to have drawn closer to Berdyaev than to S. K. but at the expense of keeping time in eternity, rather than in the realm of man's existence and history. Barth's dualism was seen too rigid to impart eschatological fulfillment and significance to the world of time and history. It implied an eschatological monism insufficiently related to the dualistic problem and biblical setting of time.

Since Berdyaev retains the seriousness of cosmic time that it, too, might be seen to be a part of eternity's program of redemption, he was shown to provide a more meaningful solution to the inadequate teleologies of modern process philosophies. This lay in his pointing to the supratemporal element of the *telos* which some, admittedly, seek but cannot find on a strictly immanental basis. Seeing what the end is *not*, Berdyaev, maintaining discourse with both the theologian and the philosopher, was shown to point us to what the end *is* in the eschatological sense. Upon delineating Berdyaev's view of existential time's end, we saw more clearly the spiritual meaning of destiny, history, cultural progress and eschatology. With some kinship to Paul Tillich's basic view of time, Berdyaev was shown to challenge the extremely otherworldly eschatology of Karl Barth. We saw how Barth's view of the end was completely retained in eternity, an extremism which skirts around and leaves unresolved, since unrelated to, the basic problems of his own dualism. Such a one-sided transcendentalism must be appraised as of minimal redemptive meaning.

Thereupon, it was shown that Berdyaev's existentialism renders the Kingdom, Apocalypse and Parousia more intelligible and relevant to history and the cosmos, and to man's time as he knows them. It keeps the *eschaton* both in eternity and at at the end of history, while making the Christian interim a period of genuine hope both for "this world and the next." Existential time or *kairos* was seen to be highly significant for man's existence, especially because it means not only a potential destiny in eternity but an actual one through an *eschaton* which belongs to both eternity and redeemed time. The meaning of the fundamental tension of eschatology was seen to be neither an ontological monism nor ontological dualism, neither extreme transcendence nor total immanence, lest the normal tension be obscured. It is rather an existential paradox expressed and symbolized by the Incarnation and Apocalypse, which are not only symbols, but events. This accounts for the dynamic two-in-one relation of time and eternity, which jeopardizes the reality of neither element while allowing for eternity's vigorous "redeeming of the times"—all times.

Berdyaev's version of existential time has enabled us to challenge all views which either pronounce time an unreality, leave it meaningless or keep it unrelated to the end. At the same time it must derive its meaning from beyond itself quite like man himself, who is at the center of time and existence. Neither self-contained views of time nor temporalized interpretations of eternity are adequate. Thus all pseudoprogressive theories based upon cosmic teleology, all evolutionary notions of Hegelian or Spencerian types, and all fatalistic views of history based upon Greek cyclical time are grossly deficient. Eschatologies limited either to immanental ontology or overly transcendental theology are unbalanced, while a pneumatic-ethical dualism of time and eternity, unity and multiplicity, freedom and necessity is very much needed. This can be provided for only by a *balanced* existential perspective of the present, one which embraces all the tenses while recognizing their meaningful interrelationship only in a revealed eternal endowment of marked significance to the concrete subject and the Christian interpretation of human existence and destiny.

While giving intensity, quality and depth of meaning to an otherwise dull, lifeless, quantitative time and history, Berdyaev was seen to yield a more realistic existential basis for interpreting the time-eternity relationship than most existential thinkers provide. This is based upon biblical concepts even as it helps clarify the problematic issues of biblical eschatology without either scuttling biblical symbols or distorting them through imposed temporal and secular thought forms. Christian eschatology and Christology were seen to blend in terms of a dynamic view of eternity redemptive of time as men know it. This is of marked significance for contemporary theology, even as it provides for the theological answers to many of the ultimate questions which philosophy must raise, especially a philosophy of existence. It also measures up to what theologian Harris Franklin Rall once enunciated as a basic theological problem and responsibility:

> The task of faith in relation to history . . . must show how time and the Eternal belong together, and how the Eternal enters into time. If time without the Eternal is meaningless, there is equal danger in the effort to posit the Eternal as

something apart from time. Then we come to the static conception of God.[71]

While we have seen Kierkegaard's and Barth's sensitivity to the problem of a static conception of God we have also seen the deficiency of their own creative but excessively transcendental adjustments. Berdyaev gives basically sound answers to the questions S. K. and Barth leave unanswered or unreckoned with.

Berdyaev's existential eschatology is seen comparatively as one which keeps eternity and time in vital relation through a dynamic eternity not remote from human existence and time but the very source and end of their meaning, fulfillment and conquest. Among other things, this gives a special dimension to the Christian view of the *interim*. As the theological answer to a philosophical problem, this also provides itself the key to what philosopher **Alfred North Whitehead sought to imply** culturally when he said: "That religion will conquer which can render clear to popular understanding some eternal greatness incarnate in the passage of temporal fact." Such an observation demands an eschatological perspective. It cannot be removed from the eternity which belongs to the transcendent element in theology, as philosopher Immanuel Kant also conceded, yet it must be related to what is immanent.

But the cosmic process is engulfed in meaninglessness when men settle for either an infinite time or an eternity of timelessness. Berdyaev sees man's relation to cosmic time, but he also sees the danger of history being engulfed in a cosmic nihilism. Needed is the eschatological dimension of existential time related to history to save it from either absorption or negation. In contrast to Bultmann, neither the look back nor the look ahead need be sacrificed entirely for the primacy of the existential present, as basic as the present is. More like Brunner, Berdyaev has seen that to assimilate history in the cosmos is heathen and Greek; to negate either is an absolute idealism or remote transcendentalism; to recognize both factors through a balanced existential view which retains both subjectivity and objectivity is soundly Christian. The beginning and end of creation qualified by the meaning and purpose of redemption provide the balance in a "theanthropocentric" view of things.

The freedom that has been forfeited everywhere to false dialectics must be recovered by the Spirit, which alone can break down the antithesis of subjectivity and objectivity. For this reason the traditional doctrines of Providence and Grace require revision, thinks Berdyaev. Ulrich Simon has expressed himself with appreciation for Berdyaev's stand here.

> The act of God is not strictly causal in the sense that it is primary and human response is secondary. The act of God is simultaneous with the act of spiritual freedom in man. Grace and Freedom are no contradictions, but Grace and determination, slavery and coercion are quite incompatible. We can be bold enough to advance on the Fathers in this matter of freedom because we *are no longer chained to a conception of time which is deterministic* through and through. Existential time and the eternal act of God are outside the closed system of a succession of historical events. It is therefore no longer necessary to stint theology of freedom in favor of some orthodox acrobatics which have ceased to be orthodox.[72]

Thus, the experience or realization of destiny is also a profound matter of freedom in relation to time's meaning.

In this regard, Berdyaev stressed the existential subjectivity of the spirit [73] and opposed any objectivized view of the end being strictly within history rather than in eternity as well as time. He saw that only existential time and a correlative subjectivity can yield a vital eschatology. What does this mean for today but that Christianity has come upon a crisis. Historical Christianity as founded on either the sheer past or future is being superseded. A recrudescence of genuine Christian life and interpretation is to be found in a religion of the Holy Spirit, which includes a needed transition to a strong eschatological outlook, a higher balanced view of time and its end.

* * * *

In short, the dialectic of time and eternity has been shown amenable to an existential perspective and resolution and given the best-balanced treatment in Berdyaev's eschatology. Significant to a thoroughgoing Christian view of life, this interpretation of existence and destiny has been shown to be a down-to-earth philosophy of time and its end. The Isle of Kairos with its eschatological focal point in Mount Eschaton is to be remembered as the enchanting center of our nautical journey. With this in mind we may return to our mundane tasks knowing more clearly that as Christ lived not in vain we need not have lived in vain, and as certain men wrote their observations of him, in a subordinate sense we, too, fill our logs with testimony and reflection with hopes that they may have a place in the interim as we look by faith to the tremendous End in the "Kingdom that fadeth not away."

NOTES

1 *The Destiny of Man*, pp. 126-153.
2 *Slavery and Freedom*, pp. 154ff, 128, 221, 226.
3 *Slavery and Freedom*, pp. 139ff, 247ff.
4 *The Realm of Spirit and the Realm of Caesar*, pp. 62, 159.
5 Lampert, *The Apocalypse of History*, p. 14.
6 *Ibid.*, p. 66.
7 *Ibid.*, p. 14.
8. *Ibid.*, pp. 50f, 45, 57, 18, 29, 156.
9 Lampert, *The Divine Realm*, pp. 146, 6, 177. Cf. Chap. IV. Cf. Berdyaev, *The Realm of the Spirit and Realm of Caesar*, p. 160.
10 *Confessions*, Bk. XI, par. 40, and *The City of God*, Bk. XI, Chap. 4 end. Cf. Chap. 5.
11 McLaughlin, *The Spiritual Interpretation of History*, pp. 67, 78.
12 *God's Way With Man*, p. 122.
13 *Confessions*, Bk. XI, x, xi, xiii.
14 *The City of God*, Vol. I, Bk. VIII, XI, p. 236.
15 *Ibid.*, Bk. XII, II p. 345.
16 *Ibid.*, Vol. II Bk. XXII II, p. 360.
17 *Ibid.*, Vol. I, Bk. IV, XXXIII, pp. 141, 286.
18 *Ibid.*, Vol. I, Bk. V, IX, pp. 151-156.
19 *Ibid.*, Vol. I, Bk. I, XXVII, pp. 32-33.
20 *Ibid.*, Vol. I, Bk. X, XII, p. 286.
21 *Ibid.*, Vol. I, Bk. XIV, XXVIII, p. 58.
22 *Ibid.*, Vol. II, Bk. XXII, XX, p. 408.
23 *God's Grace and Man's Hope*, pp. 17, 32.
24 *Ibid.*, p. 19.
25 *Ibid.*, p. 33.
26 Cf. Williams, *op. cit.*, p. 80. The quoted term here is adapted by Berdyaev from Nietzsche, though not applied in the same way.
27 *Ibid.*, p. 107.

28 *Ibid.,* pp. 129ff.
29 *Ibid.,* p. 134f.
30 *The Creator and the Adversary,* p. 161f.
31 *Op. cit.,* p. 116.
32 *The Biblical Faith and Christian Freedom,* p. 61. Cf. pp. 44, 154, 119.
33 Cf. Lewis, *Great Christian Teachings* and *A New Heaven and a New Earth.*
34 *The Protestant Era,* p. 187.
35 *Systematic Theology,* Vol. I, p. 82ff. Vol. II, pp. 336, 348.
36 *Ibid.,* Vol. II, p. 340.
37 *Ibid.,* p. 119f.
38 "Reading History as Christians," *The New Christian Advocate,* Oct. 1956, p. 44f.
39 *Ibid.,* p. 45f.
40 Cf. Heidegger, *Sein und Zeit,* pp. 42f, 117, 133, 298, 314, 336 and *Existence and Being,* 319ff, 334-346. His theory of *Dasein* is basic here, while man yearns for his true *Existenz.*
41 Cf. *Solitude and Society,* p. 3ff. Cf. "the egocentric predicament" stressed by Ralph Barton Perry.
42 From a conversation with Dr. Kroner.
43 *Systematic Theology,* Vol. I, p. 240.
44 *Systematic Theology,* Vol. II, p. 133.
45 *Ibid.,* p. 155
46 *Ibid.,* p. 162ff.
47 Niebuhr, *The Nature and Destiny of Man,* Vol. II, p. 76.
48 *Ibid.,* p. 47ff, p. 287f.
49 *Ibid.,* p. 4. Cf. pp. 16, 20-22.
50 Niebuhr, *The Nature and Destiny of Man,* Vol. I, p. 124.
51 *Op cit.,* Vol. II, p. 229. Niebuhr senses a problem here (Cf. p. 297), but leaves it unsolved.
52 *Ibid.,* p. 50, Cf. p. 47ff.
53 *Ibid.,* p. 54 Cf. *Faith and History,* p. 147.
54 *Op. cit.,* Vol. I, p. 126.
55 Niebuhr, *Discerning the Signs of the Times,* p. 61—Noteworthy here is the stress which Arnold Toynbee puts on *hubris* as preliminary to *atē* or the fall of civilizations. Cf. *A Study of History,* pp. 308f, 337, 403, 455.
56 *The Nature and Destiny of Man,* Vol. I, p. 28f.
57 *Ibid.,* p. 147.
58 H. D. Lewis, "The Theology of Reinhold Niebuhr," a printed discourse delivered before the Victoria Institute, Monday, May 1, 1950, at the Caxton Hall, Westminster, London. p. 12f.
59 *Op cit,* Vol. II, p. 289. Cf. pp. 287-290, 299f. Cf. Niebuhr, *An Interpretation of Christian Ethics,* pp. 24, 35ff, 82, 94.
60 *Ibid.,* p, 290. Cf. Niebuhr, *An Interpretation of Christian Ethics,* p. 68f.
61 *Ibid.,* p. 295.
62 *Ibid.,* Cf. Niebuhr, *Faith and History,* p. 147. Cf. p. 157.
63 *The Nature and Destiny of Man,* Vol. II, pp. 302-313.
64 *An Interpretation of Christian Ethics,* p. 100f. *Op cit.,* *Nature and Destiny,* Vol. I, pp. 266-270.
65 Cf. Niebuhr's review of Berdyaev's book, *The Russian Idea* in *Religion in Life,* 1949, Vol. VXIII, no. 2, pp. 239-242.
66 *The Russian Idea,* pp. 248-255. Cf. Berdiaeff, "Christianity, Nationalism and the State," *World's Youth,* Vol. X, no. 3, October, 1934, pp. 223-226.
67 Translated from Otto Freiherrn von Taube, "The Purification of Russian Nationalism," *Preussische Jahrbücher,* Vol. 210, 1927, p. 199.

[68] J. M. Cameron, "Nicolas Berdyaev and the West," *The Dublin Review*, 1948, 2nd quarter, p. 21. See Berdyaev's provocative work *L'Orient et l'Occident*, pp. 20-25. Cf. *Russian Idea*, p. 69, 71, 87f, 129, 140, 192, 245; also *Dream and Reality*, pp. 283. 252, 43f, 87, 110, 128, 130, 197. Even in discussing Dostoevsky's view of Russian Messianic consciousness Berdyaev asserts to the contrary that it is universal and not nationalistic. *Dostoevsky*, p. 177ff.

[69] Berdyaev, *The Realm of Spirit and the Realm of Caesar*, p. 152.

[70] *Ibid.*, p. 159f.

[71] *Christianity*, p. 312, Cf. p. 89f.

[72] Ulrich Simon, *Theology of Crisis*, p. 199f.

[73] *Dream and Reality*, p. 292. It is noteworthy that *The Descent of the Dove* by Charles Williams would be just another summary of the developments of the historical Church were it not for his underlying and penetrating thought motif of the coinherence of the eternal spirit in the historical Church. Williams appears to have been inspired by a Berdyaev-like view of existential time.

APPENDIX

ESCHATOLOGY AND RESURRECTION

Related to the centrality of the *kerygma*, the preached message of the Apostles, and the relevance of the eschatological outlook of the *koinonia* or faith community, two of the live issues in contemporary theology, is the problem of history and Christ's resurrection.

The German scholar Rudolf Bultmann in his two-volume work *The Theology of the New Testament* asserts that the resurrection of Christ occurred "in a mystical sphere outside the realm of human experience," for it "cannot be a visible fact in the realm of human history." While we cannot settle for this neither can we concede to moralistic substitutes in the pulpit or to pseudohistoricisms based on a rational equation or synthesis of the transcendent and historical aspects of the Event. Contending that only a balanced existential perspective can do justice to this problem, it is chiefly to the latter type of reaction that we shall address ourselves.

Richard R. Niebuhr in his book *Resurrection and the Historical Reason* attempts to vanquish the hypertranscendentalism of Bultmann. This is done by appeal to an "historical reason" deemed essential to the New Testament witness. Faith in Christ is said to involve "participation in the same kind of historicity that we attribute to him." The resurrection and historical reason are said to blend. This is supported by a refutation of Kant's skepticism of pure reason in favor of the claim that the practical and theoretical reasons are homogeneous.

But R. R. Niebuhr's reaction proves to be as extreme in its way as Bultmann's is in his. The dialectical issue here is one of empirical historicity versus mystical transcendence, an identification versus a disrelation of history and the Word. While we agree that Bultmann almost severs the Word from the historical Word-bearer, we find Niebuhr's reaction grossly deficient in failing to show how the eternal and the temporal can be "forged" without negating or obscuring either factor. In synthesising "external" and "internal" history (events and their subjective relevance, respectively) R. R. Niebuhr fails to do justice to the existential and supratemporal elements of the resurrection, that which enables the Risen Lord to confront Paul, for instance, irrespective of a historic memory.

While condoning his appeal to the Church's memory, we cannot condone Niebuhr's refusal to clarify the difference, along with whatever similarity prevails, between the encountered Christ and the remembered Jesus. Too trustful of a supposedly objective reason based on historic memory, he fails to retain the primacy of the faith-subsumed reason as essential to this association. Bypassing the epistemological tension within the existential perspective of the subject-believer, Niebuhr reacts to Bultmann in an extreme way so as to fall overboard into the brine of a naive kind of orthodoxy. For him to help reopen the question of history's role is perfectly legitimate, but his rational fusion of the transcendent mystery with objective history is illegitimate. The problems of *Formgeschichte* and higher criticism are still with us to a marked degree.

Minimized by Niebuhr is the fact that only via the encountered Christ is the historical Jesus given place in the New Testament. The Gospels are kerygmatic faith portraits, not biographical camera shots. Niebuhr identifies the Gospel with common history, which becomes the very locus and foundation of the Church instead of its setting and medium. The gospel spark is confused with its temporal wire! This becomes an eschatological correlate to the Roman Catholic doctrine of transubstantiation. Substance and form, the absolute and relative are rationally blended into one.

While Bultmann does too little with the apostolic memory, Niebuhr does too much. The polarity between them can be handled adequately, we maintain, only by a balanced existential perspective, one which sees the primacy of the Moment of encounter while being neither above historical memory nor identified with it. Though memory instrumentally contributed to the Apostles' understanding of the Risen Christ, it took far more than memory for them to recognize him and call him Lord. The Jesus to whom Stephen prayed transcended his memory, but not completely. Memory played a lesser and indirect role when Paul at his conversion heard the Living Lord say, "I am

Jesus of Nazareth. . . ." Most scholars concur that Paul likely never met Jesus around Jerusalem. But that Paul's memory had no function here is questionable, because he learned much about Jesus from others. True, memory is an agent of historical knowledge, as R. R. Niebuhr stresses, but the real issue is whether or not it is an "agent of eternal truth," as posed by Berdyaev. Christ is the eternal Word central to the *kerygma's* electrifying truth. The proclamation assumes the Jesus of history but colors him in shades and hues of the faith perspective of the writing evangelists. Theirs is not an objective "historical reason" but a faith-qualified reason. "A neutral reason is fiction," says Berdyaev. Both the objective and subjective poles of inward and outward history and knowledge must be retained, but without negating or suffusing the respective elements. There is association here, but not an identification. Only a faith-subsumed reason can accept this interrelation, which is an intellectual tension or paradox.

The main dialectical issue here is not an either/or with Bultmann nor a pseudorational synthesis with Niebuhr but a both/and tension of interrelated opposites. The eternal and transcendent are primary, but the historical is mediational. Thus the vertically existential Present is not completely alien to the horizontally historical past. Yet this does not allow us to treat the resurrection like any other remembered event. To do so with Niebuhr is to seek a historical security for something which cannot be proven. This is a form of secularization in theology.

Fusion of a historical reason and the central Event of the Gospel makes the Gospel dependent upon the historical Jesus in a way that makes the eternal Word completely immanental to history. This identifies secular and sacred history, a dangerous equation. While we say Jesus and the Word are not disassociated, they are not to be rationally "forged" or synthesized lest the basic mystery and faith factor be bypassed. Niebuhr's "historical reason" places a claim on objectivity and human authority in such a way as to make *ratio* dictate the terms of *pistis*. But reason, including memory, is a tool, not a tribunal. Only a balanced existential view prevents us from going to the extreme of either Rudolf Bultmann or R. R. Niebuhr. The eternal and historical are to be seen interrelated without being either synthesized or divorced. Sacred and secular histories are related, not identified. Eyes of faith must see what the eyes of reason cannot and memory can even miss. Where faith is essential to the grasp of a Truth Event, there is both continuity and discontinuity with reason and history. If not, pagans and critics should be easy to convert!

Yet, Niebuhr at times concedes the tension between the objective and the subjective. He sees, for example, the unity and separation between the Resurrection and historical Church. In general, however, he overarches this, neglecting the fact that both reason and memory are enmeshed with the believer's existential situation. Knowledge of the risen Lord is made dependent upon the remembered Jesus. "The genesis of the Church's faith and hope is in history, and it must not seek another ground of assurance," says Niebuhr, much like Oscar Cullmann. This is precarious, for the true ground is an eternal God who chooses to *manifest* Himself in history, and this He did even before Jesus appeared on the historical scene. History is instrumental, but not the locus of revelation. Rather, the locus lies on the frontier between time and eternity. If the Resurrection is the "key to our history"—which it is—there is both continuity and discontinuity between it and a historical reason. One might liken it to the key and the lock. Jesus would have been forgotten had it not been for the resurrection. The *kerygma* gives us Jesus through faith-colored portraits and faith-qualified memories. True, no Jesus—no Risen Lord. But knowledge and witness to the latter is what yields our knowledge of the former. Contrary to Niebuhr, Jesus is in our memory and in our past only indirectly, i.e., via the *kerygma* of the cross and resurrection as preached in our past and present. The Word-Event is primary, as Bultmann asserts, but the person-event is still instrumentally important, and not to be discounted, as Niebuhr avers.

Whereas Bultmann submerges the role of the historical Jesus, R. R. Niebuhr tends to submerge the primacy of the eternal Word, not intentionally but by giving priority to a temporal understanding of the Event. It is significant that throughout his book Niebuhr says little or nothing about eternity. Dialectically this, too, is lopsided. The forging of the sacred and secular in a "historical reason" becomes a dangerous invitation to the critics to smash the eternal substance of the gospel along with its temporal thought forms. It demands objective proof of an event that cannot be proved. Niebuhr's argument presumes to dissolve the basic polarity and mystery which a Kantian skepticism of reason maintains. While Bultmann tries to rise above the tension, Niebuhr obfuscates it, when we should stay right with it. Faith should neither shelve the Risen Christ in Gnostic fashion nor stuff him in an intellectual pocketbook of memories.

Confronted by the Risen Christ, the Apostles understood who he was in terms of their remembrance of Jesus. But was this solely an empirico-historical cognition? Hardly. It was extra-historical also, perhaps more so. The words "Touch me not . . ." warn us against empirically "cornering" Christ just where we want him. That kind of "rational faith" is reserved for doubting Thomases. The Risen One does not commend it but says, "Blessed are they that have not seen, and yet have believed" (John 20:29). Contrary to Niebuhr, the historical memory of the disciples was really inadequate for recognizing the Risen One. When the men on the Emmaus Road were joined by him they failed to recognize him, though they remembered Jesus. Their memory was instrumental but not authoritative. It took a suprarational "plus" even to instrument their memories in the moment of recognition. The Lord even left them about the time they began to reminisce and keep him in their past—a perennial temptation.

In conclusion, the appeal to a historical reason which fuses the Risen Christ with the remembered Jesus is as extreme as an appeal to a transcendental mystery immune to history. It cramps him in our mental mould. Only a balanced existential perspective can express the faith-conditioned association of Jesus and Christ in terms of the eternal Word's instrumentation of history and memory. This it does without either identifying the Living Word with the remembered Word-bearer in rational cocksureness on the one hand, or dichotomizing them in mystical obscurity on the other.

SUBJECT INDEX

NAME INDEX